Ireland's Generals in the Second World War

Ireland's Generals
in the Second World War

RICHARD DOHERTY

FOUR COURTS PRESS

This book was set in 9 on 12.5pt Sabon
by Mark Heslington, Northallerton, North Yorkshire for
FOUR COURTS PRESS LTD
7 Malpas Street, Dublin 8, Ireland
Email: info@four-courts-press.ie
and in the United States for
FOUR COURTS PRESS
c/o ISBS, 920 N.E. 58th Avenue, Suite 300, Portland, OR 97213.

A catalogue record for this title is available from the British Library.

ISBN 1–85182–865–6

Printed in Great Britain by
MPG Books Ltd, Bodmin, Cornwall

To the memory of

Colonel Kendal George Fleming Chavasse DSO and Bar
Commanding Officer, 56th Reconnaissance Regiment 1942–5
Commanding Officer, 2nd Bn The Royal Irish Fusiliers (Princess Victoria's) 1946–7
A friend, an inspiring leader and a true Christian gentleman
Faugh A Ballagh!

Contents

Illustrations

Between pages 160 and 161

Credits

12, 35, 36 author's collection; 40 Gurkha Museum; 1, 13, 25, 32, 49 Irish Guards; 3, 4, 5, 6, 7, 9, 10, 11, 14, 15, 17, 18, 20, 21, 23, 24, 26, 27, 28, 29, 30, 31, 33, 34, 38, 39, 51 Imperial War Museum; 41 Inniskillings' Museum; 46 King's Royal Hussars' Museum; 16 Lisburn Museum/Robert McKelvey; 2, 37, 45 McCreery family; 22 National Archives of Canada; 19 Royal Green Jackets Museum; 44, 48 Royal Irish Fusiliers' Museum; 47 SHAPE; 8, 41, 43 US National Archives

Foreword

Major-General The O'Morchoe CB MBE
(President, The Irish Regiments Historical Society)

Richard Doherty continues, in this book, to inform us about Irishmen at war. It follows his publications *Clear the Way* (the story of the 38th Irish Brigade in the Second World War) *Irish Winners of the Victoria Cross* (with David Truesdale) and *Irish men and Women in the Second World War*. In doing so he adds significantly to our knowledge and understanding of the Irish Military Heritage, an interest in which is steadily developing throughout the Ireland of today and hopefully is gaining interest elsewhere.

The author has given us a formidable line-up of generals in this book, all of whom had some connection with Ireland, some by domicile and education, others by background or through their ancestry. All served in the British Army, were born at a time when all of Ireland was part of the United Kingdom but most were at the end of their active careers by the time Ireland left the Commonwealth in 1947. Although the author mentions the effect their Irishness might have had on their military prowess he wisely leaves that to another day to explore further! Few set out to reach the top but all rose to the occasion in Britain's hours of need and filled critical positions as players in the winning of the war.

Of the military success of those in his book there is no argument, though some are at lower levels than others. Some were formidable figures during the course of the Second World War: Dill, subsequently Britain's key link with the United States Chiefs of Staff, and Brooke both served as Chiefs of the Imperial General Staff, and were involved in the conduct of the war at the highest level. Montgomery, Auchinleck, and Alexander were major figures on the battlefield. Pile, in a different role, not widely publicised, was Commander in Chief of Anti-Aircraft Command in the United Kingdom throughout the Battle of Britain and for the rest of the war. His story is fascinating in that it is completely different from the challenges of those on the battlefield but was nonetheless just as demanding.

Others included were highly successful as senior commanders in battle, or as staff officers, with experience ranging from North Africa and Europe to the Far East.

Some were commissioned into Irish Regiments: Dill into the Leinster Regiment; Templer, Scott and Russell into the Royal Irish Fusiliers; and Alexander and Vandeleur into the Irish Guards. Dawnay, a cavalryman, had a distinguished period in North Africa in command of the North Irish Horse, equipped with Churchill tanks, and later in Italy when he had them in his Brigade. These were therefore unique amongst those in the book in that they had experience of serving with and leading Irish soldiers. Templer, after the war, went on to become Chief of the Imperial General Staff having immediately beforehand held the appointment of High Commissioner in Malaya where he was responsible for the defeat of the communist uprising there between 1952 and 1955.

Having known some of those included, having been a Royal Irish Fusilier myself, and its last commanding officer before amalgamation, and having retired to the land of my birth and upbringing, I am very proud to have been asked to write the fore-word to this book. It tells the story, however briefly, of major military figures of whom, we who live on the Island of Ireland can be justifiably proud and have no difficulty in claiming kinship through their Irish connections. Their stories are often interlinked and cover action in most if not all of the theatres in which British soldiers were involved in the Second World War. The author does not dodge the interrelation-ships between those who served together, nor the controversial aspects of their views of one another nor of their opinions of each other's place in history. The book makes for interesting and thought provoking reading and contains a fund of historical knowledge and research. I hope and believe that many others, as I have done, will enjoy the read.

Major-General D.N.C. O'Morchoe CB MBE
President, The Irish Regiments Historical Society
June 2004

Prologue

One of the most famous dates in British military history is 23 October 1942. On that evening the artillery of Lieutenant-General Sir Bernard Montgomery's Eighth Army opened fire along the El Alamein line in Egypt in the greatest bombardment since the First World War. Shortly afterwards, Eighth Army's infantry advanced through minefields against the positions of the Italo-German Panzer Armee Afrika. The final battle of El Alamein had begun. It was to end with victory for Eighth Army and the beginning of a retreat by Axis forces that would end in surrender in Tunisia in May 1943 and the capture of over 200,000 prisoners.

El Alamein has since become one of those mythical names in history, ranking alongside Agincourt and Waterloo in Britain, and the victor, Bernard Montgomery, was acclaimed as one of Britain's greatest ever generals. But the battle of El Alamein has been fought over and over again in print and on radio and TV discussions and programmes. The reputation of Montgomery has been savaged and defended many times, to the extent that it has become almost an industry. To admirers of Montgomery, he was the victor of El Alamein, the saviour of British arms, the man who led Eighth Army to victory, having restored its morale after a series of defeats; his was the plan that won the battle – and he predicted and won the battle at Alam El Halfa, the second battle on the El Alamein line. Above all, Monty was the man who decided that there would be no further retreating for Eighth Army, that it would fight or die on the El Alamein line. To those who are not admirers of Montgomery, he was a man who refused to give credit to his predecessors who had made the preparations and developed the sinews of war that would win the battle for Egypt; he was a petty and vindictive man who claimed that all went according to plan, that he made all the correct decisions and knew exactly how the battle should be fought; in the words of one non-admirer, 'Monty was a bounder'.

One of Montgomery's most severe critics has been the historian Correlli Barnett whose first major work, *The Desert Generals*, published in 1960, challenged the orthodox version of the history of the desert campaign. That orthodox version owed much to Field Marshal the Viscount Montgomery of Alamein, but Barnett sought to broaden the screen of history to allow other generals to take their places. They included men who had been criticized, if not demeaned, by Montgomery in his *Memoirs* and elsewhere, as well as others who had simply been written out of

Monty's version of history. And among those were some of Montgomery's fellow Irishmen. These included Richard O'Connor, who had gained Britain's first victory in the desert war, Claude Auchinleck, who had fought Rommel to a standstill and created much of the basis for Montgomery's later success, and Eric Dorman-Smith, who had been a trusted aide to Auchinleck but was sacked with him and remained bitter for the rest of his days.

Montgomery was also less than fair to his own commander-in-chief in North Africa – Sir Harold Alexander – who, he suggested, merely did as Monty indicated. Alexander, too, was an Irishman, and one of the elite group of British field marshals of the Second World War, most of whom were Irish by birth or family. One of Alexander's best staff officers, and an authority on armoured warfare, was Richard McCreery, who would later command Eighth Army in Italy. McCreery was the man who made the critical suggestion that led to the final breakthrough at El Alamein; he also was of Irish descent.

With General Sir Alan Brooke at the head of the Army in Whitehall and Brooke's immediate predecessor, Sir John Dill, heading the British military mission in Washington DC, there was a very strong Irish influence in the upper echelons of the Army at the time of El Alamein. That makes El Alamein, and the men who fought in the desert, a suitable starting point for this study of Irish leaders of Britain's armies during the Second World War but it is worth remembering the tradition from which those men came. Irishmen had served in Britain's forces for generations, providing the bulk of the Army in the early part of the nineteenth century. Long before there was a British Army, Irishmen were soldiering for England; Shakespeare's 'English dead' at Harfleur omitted the Irishmen of Henry V's army but, even before then, Irish soldiers had served under English kings in the Crusades and the Blarney Stone is even said to be a souvenir brought back from the Holy Land by an Irish crusader who believed it to be the stone used by Jacob as his pillow.

This tradition continued down through the centuries with Irishmen serving in the armies of English and then British sovereigns, including Elizabeth I, James I, Charles I, Charles II and James II. In the reign of the last-named monarch, they fought also for his rival William III. Thereafter, Irish folklore would have us believe that Catholic Irishmen fought against Britain in the armies of France and Spain and that no Irish fought for Britain. The truth is very different: more Catholic Irishmen have fought for Britain than have ever fought against her. And Catholic Irishmen even managed to wear the red coat of Britain's army when no Irishman – Catholic, Protestant or Dissenter – was supposed to be under arms.

But the high point of Irish involvement in the British Army began at the end of the eighteenth century and lasted throughout most of the nineteenth. In the wars against revolutionary and Napoleonic France Ireland proved a rich recruiting ground for soldiers. Not only were many new regiments raised in Ireland, but Irishmen were also to be found in the ranks of regiments that were nominally English, Welsh or Scottish. During the Peninsular campaign Wellington's army was largely Irish and his infantry was almost two-thirds Irish while one Irish regiment, the 88th Foot or Connaught

Rangers, achieved a reputation second to none that, today, would have it classed as an elite unit. Wellington acknowledged the Army's debt to the Irish Roman Catholic soldier when, as prime minister, he spoke in parliament in favour of Catholic emancipation and stated that Britain owed her military supremacy to such men.

Even after the devastation of the Famine in the 1840s, Ireland continued to contribute large numbers of soldiers to the British Army – and to the East India Company's army in India. In his study of the Crimean war,* David Murphy shows that at least a third of the British force in the Crimea was Irish, with some regiments (presumably non-Irish units) having almost half their soldiers – 40–45 per cent – from Ireland. He also quotes an estimate of 35,416 Irishmen in the British Army in 1854, a figure that had risen to 59,635 by the end of the war. This was the war in which the Victoria Cross was instituted and the very first soldier to earn that decoration was an Irishman, Sergeant Luke O'Connor of the 23rd Royal Welch Fusiliers at the battle of the Alma; O'Connor was commissioned and retired from the Army as a major-general. The very first Victoria Cross also went to an Irishman, a Royal Navy midshipman, Charles Davis Lucas, and a total of thirty-one of his fellow countrymen earned the award during the war in which 112 Victoria Crosses were awarded to soldiers or seamen.

In the following decades the number of Irish in the British Army decreased but in 1873 at the outbreak of the Ashanti war there were 42,284 Irish soldiers while, five years later, the number was 39,121. By the time of the South African, or Boer, war in 1899 the proportion of Irish in the Army had reduced to equate with Ireland's population as a proportion of the United Kingdom; this was about nine per cent. Even so, the courage of her Irish soldiers so inspired Queen Victoria that she ordered the formation of a regiment of Irish Guards and also proclaimed that Irish soldiers should wear shamrock on St Patrick's Day. The First World War brought a surge in the number of Irish soldiers and, although the overall total is disputed, it would appear that about 270,000 Irishmen served, of whom about one in ten lost their lives.

And it was from the many Irish officers of the First World War that most of the men who feature in this book first came to prominence. For those who led Britain's Army at the highest levels in the Second World War had been blooded in the earlier war. They included the three wartime Chiefs of the Imperial General Staff, two of whom were Irish and reached the highest rank in the Army – field marshal. Thus they continued in the tradition of Wellington who was probably the first Irish field marshal, and certainly the first of that rank to carry the field marshal's baton. But it seemed as if the Irish had some special attribute that enabled them to reach that exalted rank, for every other field marshal of the war was an Irishman.

In addition to the two Irish Chiefs of the Imperial General Staff, Sir John Dill and Sir Alan Brooke, Sir Claude Auchinleck, Sir Harold Alexander and Sir Bernard Montgomery were also promoted to field marshal while Sir Gerald Templer achieved that rank in the post-war era. With the exception of Templer, all were involved in some way or other with the battle of El Alamein, and Templer served in Tunisia in

---

* *Ireland and the Crimean War* (Four Courts Press, Dublin, 2002).

the aftermath of that battle. At the very beginning of the North African campaign, Sir Richard O'Connor had given Britain its first land victory of the war when he defeated and destroyed Tenth Italian Army in Operation COMPASS, in December 1940, and the subsequent pursuit that ended with the battle of Beda Fomm in Cyrenaica. As the campaign drew to an end in Tunisia, Templer arrived as commander of 1st Division in First Army while an Irish Brigade also served, commanded by Brigadier Nelson Russell, an Irishman, who had been commissioned into the same regiment as Templer, the Royal Irish Fusiliers. That regiment also provided the Irish Brigade with its next commander, Brigadier Pat Scott, who was also Irish (and Sir Richard O'Connor's father had been an Irish Fusilier).

At brigade level a number of Irishmen distinguished themselves. Some may argue that a brigadier is not a general but it should be remembered that, in the Great War, the rank was brigadier general, as it is in several armies today, including the Canadian and Irish forces; it should also be noted that, in NATO, a brigadier is denoted by a single star and, in modern parlance, is, therefore, a one-star general. In addition to Russell and Scott, the Irish brigadiers of the war included Adrian Gore, J.O.E. Vandeleur, and David Dawnay. Divisional commanders include the names of Frederick Loftus Tottenham, Allan Adair and Templer while the sole British commander-in-chief to remain in post throughout the war was the Dubliner Sir Frederick 'Tim' Pile, who was responsible for Britain's anti-aircraft defences. Others did not get the opportunities to distinguish themselves as they might have done: Corkonian Sir Harold Franklyn, having commanded 5th Division in the BEF in France in 1940, had no opportunity for an active command during the rest of the war; for part of that time he appears to have been Britain's liaison with the Irish Defence Forces. Nor did all those who saw action distinguish themselves: Joe Lentaigne commanded a brigade in Wingate's Chindits but was an unremarkable brigade commander, and certainly did not share the vision of his chief, and an even more unremarkable successor to Wingate after the latter's death in a plane crash. He did, however, make such a success of establishing the Indian Joint-Services Command College that he was asked to stay on in the post. Noel Beresford-Peirse commanded a corps in the North African campaign but is chiefly remembered for the defeat inflicted on his corps by Rommel in the summer of 1941. Eric Dorman-Smith was so disenchanted with his treatment by the Army establishment – he was sacked from a brigade command in Italy after his commanding officers allegedly complained about him – that he subsequently changed his name to Dorman-O'Gowan and is said to have advised the IRA during its 1956–62 campaign against Northern Ireland.

Although not usually regarded as Irishmen, Generals McCreery and Horrocks had Irish blood and some of the characteristics that are said to come with that blood may well have shaped their style of command. There is a danger here of straying into stereotyping and it must be emphasized that there is no template into which all the men considered in these pages can be fitted. What they had in common was the profession of arms and the fact that they were Irish. Whether one led to the other or influenced the other in any way is something that we may try to discover but which would require a much more detailed study of each than is possible in this book.

~ I ~

Montgomery

He is probably the best-known British general of the Second World War and, to his many admirers, the best of those generals. After Eighth Army's victory at El Alamein in October/November 1942, Montgomery's became a household name in Britain and across the world; his penchant for publicity ensured that his name immediately conjured up the image of the little general in black beret with two cap badges – and who won battles. But was Montgomery really Britain's best general of the war, or was his reputation the product of wartime propaganda, of Winston Churchill's comment that it could almost be said that before Alamein Britain never had a victory and after Alamein never had a defeat?

Montgomery was an unlikely heroic figure. Small, sharp-featured and speaking with a slight lisp, he would not be the public relations' guru's ideal image. But there was an intensity in his gaze and an air of confidence about him that affected those who met him. Soldiers who came in contact with him found him an inspiring leader although he did not have the warrior appearance of Auchinleck, or Slim or even Alexander. What seemed to drive Montgomery was a determination to be thoroughly professional and to take the business of soldiering seriously. His Great War experience – he was wounded, decorated for gallantry and served as a staff officer – convinced him that the successful officer and leader had to work hard. Without mastering the profession of soldiering no man could lead others successfully was Montgomery's firm conviction; he dedicated his adult life to mastering that profession.

Montgomery was also an unlikely soldier. Although there were many soldiers in his family's history – including the American patriot General Richard Montgomery, and the Anglo-Irish Montgomery family may have been descended from a Norman noble, Roger de Montgomerie, an army commander under William the Conqueror – the young Bernard did not seem destined for the military life. His decision to enter the Army class at St Paul's School, London surprised his family. Bernard Law Montgomery,* born in London on 17 November 1887 to the Reverend Henry and Mrs Maud Montgomery, was the fourth child, and third son, of the vicar of

---

* The Law came from another Donegal family, that of the Reverend Samuel Law whose sister Mary had married David Montgomery in the eighteenth century.

Kennington and his wife. But the family's roots were elsewhere, in County Donegal, where Henry and Maud had spent their honeymoon at New Park House on the edge of Moville on Lough Foyle. Bernard Montgomery's youngest brother, Brian, was later to write that 'We come from an old Irish family the roots of which are wide-spread and whose history is long.'

The family had settled in Ireland in the seventeenth century, putting down roots in southwest Donegal, between the fishing port of Killybegs and the village of Killaghtee. However, in 1758, Samuel Montgomery, a prosperous Londonderry wine merchant, bought an estate near Moville, some twenty miles from the city, from the marquess of Donegal and built New Park House on a sixty-acre demesne. Samuel married Ann Porter, daughter of Marino Porter, surveyor of nearby Greencastle. Although making his home at Moville, he continued his business connections with Londonderry and was chamberlain of the city for some years until his death in 1703. (In 1943 General Montgomery would describe himself as a 'Derryman' to soldiers of 9th (Londonderry) Heavy Anti-Aircraft Regiment at Tripoli in Libya.)

Although the Montgomery family continued to have its seat at Moville, it sent its sons to India with the Army and to various parts of Ulster as clerics of the Church of Ireland. Thus Henry Montgomery's decision to become a clergyman, of the Church of England, was seen as a natural choice for a Montgomery. It meant, however, that most of his children were born in England rather than Ireland. Three were born in Tasmania for, in 1899, Henry was appointed bishop of Tasmania, the one-time Van Diemen's Land, and his family accompanied him to the colony, soon to become part of the Commonwealth of Australia. While in Tasmania Bishop Montgomery also served for a year as bishop of Melanesia. Such was the success of his work, and his reputation in propagating the gospel, that Bishop Montgomery was offered the post of secretary to the Society for the Propagation of the Gospel in Foreign Parts (SPG). This meant a return to London and the family arrived in England at the end of 1901.

Bernard passed the examination for entry to St Paul's School at Hammersmith and on his first day, in January 1902, chose to enter the Army class, to the astonishment of his parents. Asked why he made this choice he answered that he wanted to be a soldier – which was news to all who knew him. In this choice he was to display a stubbornness that would remain with him throughout his life. From St Paul's he entered the Royal Military College, Sandhurst in 1907 where his military career very nearly came to an abrupt end following a bullying incident in which another cadet officer was burned and hospitalized. Although Montgomery was responsible the injured cadet refused to name his tormentor but Montgomery was identified as the culprit even with no direct evidence against him. He was demoted to the ranks – he had been a cadet corporal – and asked to leave Sandhurst. Although his career was saved by his mother's intervention he was not allowed to choose the regiment into which he would be commissioned.

Bernard Montgomery had hoped to be commissioned into the Indian Army where his lack of private means would not be an obstacle but was, instead, commissioned into an English county regiment, the Royal Warwickshire, and posted to the 1st

Battalion, then at Peshawar in India's North-West Frontier Province. This was fortunate since service in India made fewer demands on a young officer's pocket than home service and the Warwicks were not one of the more expensive regiments. Before long Second-Lieutenant Montgomery had been identified as a promising officer who was already showing signs of the professionalism that would be his hallmark throughout his career.

On 4 August 1914 Britain declared war on Germany. Montgomery's battalion, now back from India, went to France with the British Expeditionary Force (BEF). Just over two weeks after the first clash between British and German forces, a telegram was delivered to Bishop Montgomery at New Park House:

> Regret to inform you that Lieutenant B.L. Montgomery, Warwickshire Regiment, is reported missing. This does not necessarily mean that he is killed or wounded. Further information when received will be telegraphed immediately.

The BEF and the French armies were retreating before the invading German armies and many men had been killed, wounded or captured. There was considerable confusion and many stories of heroism, including the war's first Victoria Crosses; the first was earned posthumously by a young Irish Royal Fusiliers' officer, Maurice Dease. Bernard Montgomery had also demonstrated considerable personal courage, in stark contrast to his commanding officer who abandoned the survivors of two of his companies and, with the rest of his battalion, retreated fifteen miles to St Quentin where he prepared to surrender. He and another officer were later dismissed for incompetence.

Montgomery was in one of the abandoned companies but he and his fellow survivors were able to rejoin their battalion a few days later, after the telegram had been sent to his father at Moville. This was the young subaltern's first experience of battle. His second came in the first battle of Ypres in October, during which he earned the Distinguished Service Order (DSO), a decoration second only to the Victoria Cross as a gallantry award. At the village of Meteren Montgomery, carrying a sword, led his men in a bayonet charge. With no training in swordsmanship, Bernard threw away his sword to fling himself at a German soldier who was about to shoot him and kicked the man, as he later delicately described, 'as hard as I could in the lower part of the stomach'.

The attack was successful and the objective was taken, but as Montgomery stood up in pouring rain to re-organize his platoon he was shot in the chest. He lay in the open and remained still, feigning death, so as not to attract any further enemy attention. One of his soldiers ran over to tend him but was shot by a hidden sniper and collapsed over Montgomery. The German continued to shoot and Monty was hit in the knee while the unfortunate soldier who had gone to his aid 'received many bullets meant for me'. Their comrades, assuming that both were dead, left them where they lay until darkness when stretcher-bearers recovered the bodies. The soldier was dead but Montgomery was clinging to life. At the Advanced Dressing Station the doctors thought he had no chance of survival and ordered a grave to be dug since the ADS was preparing to move. However, when the time came for the move Montgomery was still alive and was placed in an ambulance and removed to a hospital. After treatment he was evacuated to England and did not return to France until early 1916.

Montgomery did not return to the Warwicks but was instead appointed brigade major of an infantry brigade that was preparing for the Somme offensive, which opened on 1 July 1916. For the rest of the war he was to carry out such staff roles and never returned to front-line battalion service. By November 1918, when the war ended, he was chief of staff of 47th (London) Division and just short of his thirty-first birthday. He had seen much in the past four years and considered himself able to think clearly, although his 'mind was still untrained'. What he had seen convinced him that much was wrong. He believed that there was little contact between generals and soldiers and wrote that he never once saw the British commander-in-chief and only saw an army commander on two occasions. He was critical of the higher staff for being out of touch with the soldiers and, in his *Memoirs*, states that the war

> led me to believe that the staff must be the servants of the troops, and that a good staff officer must serve his commander and the troops but himself be anonymous.

He also commented that he had been appalled at the casualties incurred and the apparent disregard for human life shown by some generals, although he excused General Plumer from this criticism. And he recounted the story of a senior staff officer who, before returning to Britain, asked to visit Passchendaele ridge and was shocked at the conditions there to the extent that he asked if soldiers had had to fight in such conditions. Upon receiving an affirmative reply the staff officer is alleged to have said: 'Why was I never told about this before?' The story may be apocryphal but Montgomery accepted it as true and commented

> The fact that the Chief of Staff of the British Armies in Europe had no idea of the conditions under which the troops had to live, fight, and die, will be sufficient to explain the uncertainties that were passing through my mind when the war ended.

For him the lesson of the war was that the profession of arms required a degree of dedicated study that few officers seemed to appreciate; he resolved that he would apply himself to that profession, mastering it to the exclusion of all else. He began by attending the Staff College at Camberley as a student on the 1920 course. Entry to the first two courses after the war – 1919 and 1920 – was by invitation only, based on an officer's wartime reputation but Montgomery did not receive an invitation. Undaunted by this, he put his case to General Sir Willie Robertson, Commander-in-

Chief of the British Army of Occupation in Germany; Robertson, a former Staff College commandant, obtained the necessary invitation.

From Camberley Montgomery was posted to Ireland, as Brigade Major of 17 Infantry Brigade in Cork. This took him into another war, that against the IRA in Munster. In many respects Monty considered this worse than the Great War; he described it as degenerating into a murder campaign and was pleased when it ended. Although the brigade's soldiers became very skilled in fighting a guerrilla foe, Monty thought such operations to be 'thoroughly bad for officers and men; it tends to lower their standards of decency and chivalry'.

Montgomery returned to Staff College as an instructor and earned a reputation that followed him to the Staff College at Quetta in India where he was also an instructor. At both establishments students were impressed by his logic, precise explanations and the way in which he encouraged analytical thinking. His reputation made him the War Office's choice to rewrite the manual of infantry training. This was not to be a solo effort; a committee was charged with approving the manual but Montgomery refused to accept their proposed changes and even suggested disbanding the committee, allowing him to finish the work alone. There must have been many who were surprised when his proposal was accepted. Monty went on to complete the final draft, excluding the suggested amendments, and commented that the finished work was considered excellent, 'especially by its author'. That single-mindedness later displayed by Montgomery as a commander was already obvious to those who knew him, one officer describing him as being 'known as a rather difficult and peculiar character'.

The aim of any infantry officer is to command a battalion of his own regiment and Montgomery achieved that when he was appointed to command 1st Royal Warwicks in England, Palestine, Egypt and India, following which he joined the staff at Quetta. He had also married the widow of a brother officer and was extremely happy as a married man. However, his wife died tragically while Montgomery was commanding a brigade in Britain and, following this loss, he devoted even more time and energy to his profession. During the Arab Rebellion he commanded 8th Division before being given command of 3rd Division in Britain, which was assigned to the British Expeditionary Force. Major-General Montgomery was to take it to France as part of II Corps, commanded by Sir Alan Brooke.

There was no immediate German attack on France as had occurred in the Great War and it was not long before journalists dubbed this waiting period 'the phoney war' while some soldiers called it the 'sitzkrieg'. However, there was little sitting about in Montgomery's division as he embarked on a rigorous training programme to improve 3rd Division's standards. That he was successful was demonstrated when the BEF was forced to retreat and Montgomery showed a mastery of that most diffi-cult of military manoeuvres, disengaging from contact with the enemy. Perhaps his most outstanding achievement came when he was asked to sidestep his division from one flank of the retreating BEF to the other. In darkness, and at very short notice, he moved his men as he had been asked, passing three other divisions in doing so and moving a few miles behind a constantly changing front line. His corps commander, Brooke, later described this as

> a task that might well have shaken the stoutest of hearts, but for Monty it might just have been a glorious picnic. He told me exactly how he was going to do it and was as usual exuberant in confidence.

Brooke identified one of Montgomery's most noticeable characteristics when he wrote about his confidence. In this instance it was entirely justified, based on the knowledge that he had trained 3rd Division in just such a night manoeuvre. And he retained the confidence of his men by staying in close contact with them throughout the training period and the retreat.

Before the BEF left France Montgomery was appointed to succeed Brooke in command of II Corps, the latter having been recalled to Britain to organize a new BEF. As corps commander he continued to exercise a calm but firm control and Lieutenant-General Brian Horrocks, who took over command of 3rd Division, noted this when he described how, after three weeks of continuous fighting, everyone was exhausted except Montgomery.

> During the retreat he insisted on having meals at regular hours and never missed his normal night's sleep. Consequently, when we arrived at Dunkirk he was as fresh as when he started. I saw him every day and he was always the same: confident, almost cocky you might say, cheerful and apparently quite fresh. He was convinced that he was the best divisional commander in the British Army and that we were the best division. By the time we reached Dunkirk I had come to the same conclusion.

Montgomery had shown no apparent fear of the German army. Instead he had observed its methods closely and subsequently provided his analysis to the Bartholomew Committee, the War Office committee that studied the campaign with a view to improving British fighting standards. The subsequent Bartholomew Report owed much to Montgomery.

In July 1940 Montgomery was appointed to command V Corps, succeeding Claude Auchinleck, who became General Officer Commanding (GOC), Southern Command and Montgomery's superior. With the Army's priority the defence of Britain against invasion, Montgomery threw himself into this task with characteristic vigour. However, he clashed with Auchinleck over the best tactics to use against invasion. Montgomery considered that any invader should be allowed to come ashore but would be engaged and defeated as they tried to move inland. Keen to have his soldiers fired with an offensive spirit, Montgomery did not want them sitting in defensive positions and adopting a defensive mentality. Auchinleck, however, believed that any invader had to be met and defeated on the beach. Montgomery appealed to Churchill who was impressed with and approved Monty's mobile counter-attack scheme. Had the Germans invaded in 1940 this strategy could hardly have succeeded against a well-equipped foe with large numbers of tanks but it was good for morale, especially after Dunkirk. His success on this argument seems to have inspired Montgomery with a certain disdain for Auchinleck that was to be even more apparent in the years ahead.

Alan Brooke, Monty's old mentor from BEF days, became Chief of the Imperial General Staff (CIGS) on Christmas Day 1941 and subsequently appointed Montgomery to command First Army, then being created for the invasion of French North Africa. But, following Eighth Army's retreat to the El Alamein line in July 1942, there were major changes in command in Egypt with Auchinleck losing his post as Commander-in-Chief, Middle East in favour of Sir Harold Alexander and 'Strafer' Gott taking command of Eighth Army. Churchill overruled Brooke on this latter appointment but Gott was killed before he could take over Eighth Army and Brooke was then able to recommend his man for the post: Montgomery.

Arriving in Egypt on 12 August 1942, Montgomery assumed command of Eighth Army before he was due to do so and set about creating an army in his own image. According to him, Eighth Army was in disarray and suffering from low morale, an argument countered by Alexander's comments that although 'baffled' the army was in good spirits. Both assessments were made after visiting the same soldiers; but Alexander never attempted to create a personal myth and his assessment is likely to be the more accurate. Certainly none of the Eighth Army veterans whom I have interviewed over the years recognize themselves in Monty's assessment. What they do accept, however, is that their German foe, Field Marshal Erwin Rommel, was better known to the average British soldier than any British general. Recognizing this, Auchinleck had begun moves to counter the Rommel legend but Montgomery went one step further and decided to create a counter legend, that of Monty the victorious general.

As Eighth Army prepared for an offensive to drive the Axis out of North Africa, its new commander set about winning the confidence of his soldiers. Montgomery did this by visiting as many units as he possibly could; he thus made himself known to the majority of soldiers under his command. His method was simple: after a formal parade he would mount a platform or the bonnet of a jeep and invite all those on parade to gather around him and, perhaps, to remove their headgear. (The latter, he told them, was so that he might recognize them when next he saw them; no one believed him but it was a good public relations exercise.) In this informal setting he would then tell them what his plans were, how they fitted into them and how important their role was. Even when inspecting soldiers on a formal parade he paid less attention to the effort put into polishing boots and brasses than to the way in which a soldier bore himself. Monty, as he became known, would look into a soldier's eyes with an intensity that could unnerve but left the soldier convinced that this little general meant business, knew what he was about and could be trusted.

He went even further by experimenting with various pieces of headdress to make him appear distinctive. The first was an Australian bush hat decorated liberally with cap badges but this proved a little too theatrical – except when visiting Australians – and he finally settled for the black beret of the Royal Tank Regiment. He kept the tankies' badge and added his own general's badge. Before long the popular image of Monty in Eighth Army and beyond was that of the general with the black beret and two badges. Whether he would have chosen the Royal Tanks' beret had he known that it had been adopted on the recommendation of Eric Dorman-Smith, an officer for whom Montgomery had neither respect nor love, is a moot question.

This change of image was hugely successful and, for Eighth Army and the British public, Monty became a powerful source of morale. One of his senior staff described him as the dynamo of Eighth Army, an apt analogy as he gave that formation a strong sense of purpose and invincibility akin to an electric charge. Eighth Army became Monty's team and the first great proof of that came with the final battle of El Alamein, which opened on 23 October 1942 with the heaviest artillery bombardment since the Great War. In early November, Italo-German forces withdrew from their Alamein positions and began a retreat that would take them to Tunisia. At El Alamein Montgomery had refused to be stampeded by Churchill into an offensive until he had made all the preparations necessary for victory and when Eighth Army finally moved on that October Friday night it enjoyed superiority in artillery and tanks, if not in infantry. And the Desert Air Force, with which close liaison had been maintained, provided mastery of the air over the battlefield, as well as much of the intelligence for the planners through aerial reconnaissance. However, in the euphoria of victory, the flaws in Montgomery's plans were overlooked; there had been no appreciation of the limits of tanks, in spite of advice from armoured commanders, and the opportunity to destroy Panzer Armee Afrika by rapid pursuit was lost in the closing phase of the battle.

However, the victory at El Alamein was deeply significant. Coming after the US Navy's defeat of the Japanese at Midway in the Pacific and just before the Red Army's destruction of Sixth German Army at Stalingrad, it marked one of the turning points of the war. At home, Churchill ordered church bells to be rung to proclaim the victory and, in a speech at London's Mansion House, declared: 'This is not the end. It is not even the beginning of the end. But it is, perhaps, the end of the beginning.' The North African campaign continued until May 1943 when General Jürgen von Arnim surrendered all Axis forces in the region; some 250,000 men marched into captivity. For Montgomery it represented revenge for Dunkirk, something he had yearned for since June 1940; now he had inflicted on his enemies a Dunkirk without an evacuation. He was lauded as one of Britain's greatest generals.

Eighth Army's soldiers had little doubt about his ability and were confident under his command, believing that his careful preparations for battle gave them more chance of survival and victory. They also knew that he was not be found in a comfortable headquarters well behind the lines but close to the fighting and sharing much of their danger. This bred a confidence in Eighth Army that made it the finest British field army since the Peninsular War. When King George VI visited the army with Churchill in February 1943 the prime minister told the monarch that Eighth Army's men were 'perhaps the best troops in the world'. Churchill also told the house of commons that he had never seen men march with 'the style or air of the Desert Army'.

Following the North Africa campaign, Montgomery was to lead the British element in Operation HUSKY, the invasion of Sicily. His command in Sicily was to be a new field army, Twelfth Army, but on his insistence the title Eighth Army was retained and thus it was Eighth Army alongside Seventh US Army – 15 Army Group – that invaded and then occupied Sicily after a campaign of less than six weeks. But it had been a tough campaign and the German defenders had managed to evacuate much of their strength, including heavy weapons, to Italy. The campaign had also been marred by rivalry between Montgomery and Seventh Army's commander, General George S. Patton. Both were egotists and each wanted the glory of entering the Sicilian capital, Messina, first. This was the first occasion on which Montgomery had clashed with an ally but it would not be the last.

The Sicilian campaign was followed by the invasion of mainland Italy. Montgomery's Eighth Army, landed in the toe of Italy and in the instep, at Taranto, fought through the Calabrian peninsula before being directed up the east coast. According to Monty, Rome was to fall by Christmas. That did not happen and, shortly after Christmas, he laid down command of Eighth Army to return to Britain to assume command of 21 Army Group for the invasion of northwest Europe.

On his return to Britain, Monty set about making himself known to the soldiers in his command and visited every formation that would serve under him for the invasion. These included American troops of Omar Bradley's First US Army, many of whom wrote home in glowing terms of their impressions of him. He was also received in private audience by King George VI who was not impressed by Monty's style of dress; the black beret with its two badges was, of course, improper. Forewarned of the monarch's objection to his trademark beret, Montgomery pre-empted any criticism by launching into a detailed appreciation of the importance of morale, and citing his black beret as a means of creating a bond between commander and troops. He even told the King that his beret was worth at least an army corps in morale terms and that it was vital that he should continue to wear it until the war had ended. No royal objections were forthcoming.

Montgomery's priority was the planning for Operation OVERLORD, the invasion of France, which was only a few months in the future, at the beginning of May 1944. Believing that he had built up a good staff team in Eighth Army, he brought many of them with him to 21 Army Group and cut loose men who had laboured for long months on the invasion plans. His planning staff inherited a plan drawn up under Major-General Frederick Morgan who had been designated as Chief of Staff to the Supreme Allied Commander, or COSSAC. Morgan's team had been instructed to identify an invasion area and prepare a plan for the operation but had been forced to work under a series of constrictions, the worst of which was an allocation of landing craft far below that deemed necessary for success. As a result, what was known as the COSSAC plan fell short of Morgan's ideal but Morgan had made this clear, while pointing out how he would have liked to expand the operation. Montgomery and Eisenhower, now appointed Supreme Commander, were aware of these shortcomings but the circumstances surrounding them did not prevent Montgomery criticizing Morgan's efforts and making fresh recommendations for the OVERLORD landings.* These included widening the landing area, to include the inside corner of the Cotentin peninsula, increasing the number of divisions in the first assault, and having two corps headquarters to control the invading troops. All this required additional landing craft but Eisenhower, Montgomery and Churchill were able to obtain the increase. So that the extra landing craft would be available and their crews trained, Eisenhower also obtained a postponement of the date for OVER-LORD; it was now to take place in June, with the exact date being at Eisenhower's discretion.

In the initial phase of the Normandy fighting, Eisenhower's headquarters would remain in England with Montgomery commanding all ground forces until Eisenhower moved to France. Eventually this placed Monty at the head of two army groups – 12 US Army Group as well as 21 Army Group – including four field armies. This was a massive vote of confidence in Montgomery as a field commander since it meant that Eisenhower regarded him as the general best equipped for the task. And this was in spite of the fact that Montgomery had already criticized Eisenhower's abilities as a commander; although he admired Eisenhower's ability to work with people, Monty considered him an amateur in the field of command.

German opposition in Normandy proved tougher than expected and Allied success owed much to having fooled the enemy into believing that the invasion was only a diversion with the real assault to come in the Pas de Calais, led by George Patton. Even with a full army held back to defend the Pas de Calais area, the Germans in Normandy forced the Allies into a series of bloody encounters in which the advantage usually lay with the defenders, especially in the close bocage country-side. Montgomery had told a briefing on 15 May in London that the cities of Bayeux and Caen would be taken on D-Day, the latter opening the way to ground suitable for the construction of airfields for the Allied tactical air forces. Bayeux did fall on 7 June, D-Day +1, but Caen proved a more formidable obstacle and it was more than a month before British troops took the city. This delay led to much criticism of Montgomery, not only from US commanders but also from some British commanders, including Eisenhower's deputy, Air Marshal Tedder, who wanted to see Montgomery removed; the two men did not agree on strategy and Tedder was angry about the failure to take the ground beyond Caen for airfields. Montgomery argued

---

* Strictly, OVERLORD did not begin until the first troops set foot on the beaches and did not end until the Germans surrendered in May 1945. Transporting the invasion force, and protecting it, was a naval operation known as NEPTUNE. The overall plan might better be described as NEPTUNE/OVERLORD.

that he never intended to take Caen on D-Day and that his strategy was unfolding as he planned by drawing the bulk of German forces on to the left flank, held by the British and Canadians, thereby allowing the Americans to break out in the west and begin swinging the Allied line towards the Seine. That events did follow this pattern seemed to support Montgomery's argument but this was as much a matter of serendipity as of planning and probably owed more to the initiative of American commanders, especially Patton and Bradley, than it did to Monty. But it should be noted that Bradley acknowledged that Montgomery allowed the Americans to exercise their initiative and did not try to keep them under firm control.

Dissatisfaction with Montgomery at this time was not confined to military commanders. Churchill was also frustrated with the lack of progress in Normandy and Montgomery came under pressure from the prime minister to produce results; Churchill had been present at the May briefing when Monty predicted the fall of Caen on D-Day. Only the intervention of Brooke, the CIGS, saved Montgomery from possible serious repercussions. It was Brooke, Monty's mentor, who advised him to perform two rare acts of diplomacy – one with Churchill and the other with Eisenhower – that ensured his future. Brooke considered Monty to be Britain's best tactical general since Wellington but was aware that his dealings with his allies were abrasive.

Once again, however, Montgomery had displayed his lack of appreciation of armour. In the words of one historian of the British Army in the Second World War, he demonstrated a 'failure to comprehend what tanks can and cannot reasonably be made to do'. This was evident from the plans for EPSOM and, especially, GOOD-WOOD; the latter was a deeply-flawed attempt to use a corps of armour to force a way out of the bridgehead without adequate artillery and infantry support. It evoked some reminders of El Alamein, especially in the huge traffic congestion inherent in the plan. Many armoured soldiers became cynical about Montgomery as a result, especially when he told them that their tanks were superior to those of the enemy.

The Allied breakout from Normandy came in August, following operations by all four field armies, First (Canadian), First (US), Second (British) and Third (US) that pushed the Germans out of Normandy with heavy losses in men and equipment. Thereafter, the Allies moved with great speed through France and into Belgium. Paris was liberated on 25 August and Brussels on 3 September, the fifth anniversary of the outbreak of war. Some believed that the war could be over by Christmas. Monty was in that number and had conceived a plan to achieve that end.

Montgomery wanted to deliver an 'almighty crack', as he described it to Brooke, by pushing concentrated Allied forces in a strong thrust to the north of the Ruhr, the industrial heartland of Germany. Some of his critics have argued that he intended to use a pencil-thin advance but his plan was for an advance by some forty divisions. This went against American thinking, which favoured a strategy of moving forward on a broad front. Montgomery countered that this left the Allies with a relatively weak front vulnerable to counter-attacks. The German attack on the Americans in the Ardennes – the battle of the Bulge – bore out his argument; but his own strategy was also flawed. No major attack on a narrow front had succeeded in either world war once the enemy regained his equilibrium, something the Germans were especially good at doing. What he was proposing was also probably beyond the tactical skills of most Allied generals and was closer to the post-war doctrine of deep battle. The American view prevailed and the Allies continued their broad front advance.

On 1 September 1944, Montgomery was promoted to field marshal, a compensation for the fact that Eisenhower had now brought his headquarters to the continent and Montgomery had reverted to commanding only 21 Army Group. That month Monty also launched what has been described as the greatest mistake of his career: Operation MARKET GARDEN. This was really two separate operations: MARKET, an attack by First Allied Airborne Army on the bridges of Eindhoven, Grave, Nijmegen and Arnhem; and GARDEN, a thrust along the road connecting those towns by XXX Corps of Second British Army. The concept was that the airborne troops would lay 'carpets' at the bridges and the ground forces would take the ground between the carpets, linking all together to provide a path into the Reich. Montgomery's staff opposed the plan because of the logistical difficulties involved but the Field Marshal seemed slow to appreciate the price of failure, pointing instead to the possible rewards of success. He did not appreciate that failure could endanger the entire Allied strategy. The fruits of success could have been great; Eisenhower wrote that 'We shall soon, I hope ... be in possession of the Ruhr, the Sahr and the Frankfurt area ... Berlin is the main prize.'

MARKET GARDEN did not succeed on a strategic level; its main aims, to turn the flank of the 'West Wall', isolate Fifteenth German Army and encircle the Ruhr, were not achieved and such success as attended the venture was restricted to a tactical level. Two divisions of First Allied Airborne Army took their objectives, but the British 1st Airborne Division, on the orders of Lieutenant-General Lewis Brereton, commanding the Airborne Army, was dropped too far from Arnhem bridge. Interestingly, Montgomery later wrote: 'I take the blame for this mistake.' XXX Corps was also delayed by strong opposition and the failure of 101st Airborne Division to seize the Son bridge before the Germans demolished it. That XXX Corps was to advance on a front that was the width of a single road was a serious flaw; it seemed that, once again as at El Alamein and in GOODWOOD, Montgomery's appreciation of mobile warfare left something to be desired. Thus the troops at Arnhem were isolated. Ten days later they were forced to surrender, although many managed to break through the enemy lines to safety. Montgomery's gamble had failed but the mystery is that, having gambled so much, he had not given the attention to detail in planning and execution that was his trademark. MARKET GARDEN was mounted in haste, contrary to his normal *modus operandi*. One of his staff also noted his lack of grip during the battle. The Monty dynamo could not have been operating at full power, or had his eagerness to encircle the Ruhr blinded him to the problems inherent in his plan?

Parallel to the Arnhem error was Montgomery's failure to appreciate the strategic importance of clearing the Scheldt estuary so that the port of Antwerp, taken by the Allies on 4 September, could be brought into operation to shorten the supply lines of the two army groups. Even had MARKET GARDEN succeeded the supply problem would have remained. It is remarkable that neither Montgomery nor Eisenhower seemed to understand the importance of clearing the Scheldt, in spite of the exhortations of Admiral Ramsay, the Allied Naval Commander-in-Chief.

As Allied armies advanced slowly towards Germany, relations between Montgomery and the Americans continued to deteriorate. On 16 December the Germans launched a major counter-attack in the Ardennes, driving a huge bulge into the American front. Bradley's 12 US Army Group was split with Bradley cut off south of the German attackers; some 15,000 US soldiers were captured and Bradley went to earth for fear of being taken prisoner. Eisenhower, therefore, asked Montgomery to assume command of all US forces on the northern flank of the Bulge, including First and Ninth US Armies. British and American troops fought together under Monty's command – and he ensured that as many as possible knew that he was in command – and the German offensive was broken. Eisenhower expressed his gratitude to Montgomery.

> Thank you again for the way you pitched in to help out during the German thrust. Someday I hope I can show my appreciation in a more lasting manner.

Ninth US Army remained under Montgomery's command as the Allies prepared to cross the Rhine. On 23 March 1945 Operation PLUNDER began. Monty sent a message to all his soldiers.

> 21 Army Group will now cross the Rhine ... And having crossed the Rhine we will crack about in the plains of Northern Germany, chasing the enemy from pillar to post. The swifter and the more energetic our action, the sooner the war will be over, and that is what we all desire: to get on with the job and finish off the German war as soon as possible ... May 'The Lord mighty in battle' give us the victory in this your latest undertaking, as He has done in all our battles since we landed in Normandy on D Day.

Following the Rhine crossing the Allied armies advanced into northern Germany but Monty's behaviour after the battle of the Bulge was about to rebound on him. In the wake of that battle he had called a press conference during which he claimed that he had predicted such an offensive by the Germans. This earned him Bradley's undying enmity. But it had more serious repercussions after the Rhine crossing when Monty proposed an advance on Berlin by 21 Army Group. With three armies under command it is possible that he could have taken Berlin but Ninth Army was then removed from his control and all US forces were directed to swing right towards southern Germany. Had both army groups operated north of the Ruhr a western advance to Berlin might have been possible; but, as the US armies wheeled southwards, Eisenhower sent a message to Stalin telling him that Berlin was to be left to the Red Army. Montgomery's 21 Army Group could no longer advance on Berlin and its official objectives were changed so that the Soviets would not overrun Denmark. Thus British and Canadian forces raced across northern Germany to the Baltic to prevent Soviet troops entering Denmark. They succeeded, but only by a matter of hours.

On 3 May Field Marshal Keitel sent a message to Montgomery's headquarters on Luneburg Heide to seek negotiations for surrender. Keitel was told that only unconditional terms were available and he accepted this. Montgomery took the official surrender on 4 May. Although the document signed by the Germans should have been sent to Allied Supreme Headquarters, Monty had photostatic copies made and kept the original 'and I will never part with it; it is a historic document'.

The war in Europe was over but Montgomery's military career still had many years to run. In the New Year Honours' List of 1946 he was created Viscount Montgomery of Alamein while, later that year, he succeeded Brooke, now Lord Alanbrooke, as Chief of the Imperial General Staff. He was a difficult CIGS, constantly at loggerheads with his fellow chiefs – John, the First Sea Lord, and Tedder, Chief of the Air Staff, who had plotted to have Monty removed in Normandy – and tended to send deputies to the Chiefs of Staff meetings. Matters were not helped by his popularity in the country – he was probably more popular than Churchill who had been voted out of office in 1945. Monty's habit of antagonizing others was not restricted to service chiefs: he also antagonized Attlee, the prime minister, and Ernest Bevin, the foreign secretary, especially through his habit of using his reputation to elicit invitations to visit various countries where he would give press interviews or make speeches in which he put forward personal views rather than the government line on which he had been briefed. This made him unpopular with the government but there was one occasion when his cavalier behaviour had far-reaching consequences and led to the establishment of the North Atlantic Treaty Organisation (NATO). This occurred in late-1946 when he travelled to North America.

Montgomery had been warned not to meet Canadian or American politicians but, typically, arranged invitations to do just that, which he said he had to accept as a matter of courtesy. In the wake of Churchill's 'Iron Curtain' speech at Fulton, Missouri, in March 1946, Monty persuaded both Canadian Prime Minister, Mackenzie King, and US President, Harry Truman, that the West needed to face up to the Soviet threat. He sent a signal to his vice-chief that 'the Heads of State of Canada and America have both expressed their wish that we should cease to be on merely friendly terms, but should get down to full and frank discussions on all defence matters', and suggested that 'the necessary action' should be taken in London. Attlee was amazed and angry; he would have sacked any other CIGS who had done the same but sacking Monty would have put him in the house of lords with an excellent public platform from which to expound his thoughts. Attlee, therefore, went along with his CIGS's ideas and began a series of secret military and political conferences that led to the creation of the Western European Union (WEU), and then to NATO. A committed believer in a European defence strategy for Britain, Monty had his way.

Having finished his term as CIGS, Montgomery was appointed Chairman of the WEU Chiefs of Staff Committee before, in April 1951, becoming Eisenhower's deputy at the newly-established Supreme Headquarters, Allied Powers Europe (SHAPE). He served until 1958 as Deputy to four different Supreme Commanders and his presence helped convince the continental nations that, at last, Britain had abandoned her centuries old maritime strategy in favour of a continental strategy designed to provide peace and security in Europe.

Montgomery finally retired from soldiering in 1958, after fifty years in the Army, to become something of a media personality. He published his *Memoirs* and presented a highly successful BBC television series. The former were serialized in the press and sales of both the book and newspapers were record breaking. However, the book brought criticism, even though the legend of the victor of El Alamein was still fresh. There were those who felt that he had been unfair to Auchinleck and his handling of the desert campaign in the summer of 1942, including a young historian called Correlli Barnett who put his criticism into the form of a book, *The Desert Generals*, that placed those who had preceded Monty in North Africa in a different perspective. Although Barnett agreed that Montgomery had ensured victory at El Alamein by careful, painstaking preparation, he accused him, nonetheless, of myth-making. Another critic was Eric Dorman-Smith, who had been Auchinleck's senior staff officer but was later dismissed from command. Dorman-Smith forced a revision in subsequent prints of the memoirs by threatening legal action.

However, the legend remained. Many who served under Montgomery in Eighth Army would hear no criticism of him. Vain, egotistical and pompous he may have been, but he led them to victory and instilled in them a firm belief in their ability as soldiers and as an army. And perhaps he recognized his own weaknesses when, in the foreword to his memoirs, he wrote:

> I recognise that I have often been a controversial figure. But my thoughts, actions, mistakes have been human. Throughout my life and conduct my criterion has been not the approval of others nor of the world; it has been my inward convictions, my duty and my conscience. I have never been afraid to say what I believe to be right and to stand firm in that belief. This has often got me into trouble.

And, significantly, he chose to open his book with a quotation from the *Book of Job*:

> Yet man is born unto trouble as the sparks fly upward.

Almost three decades after his death the Monty legend has been subjected to considerable examination. He has probably had more books written about him than any other British general of the twentieth century but the image that he fostered so carefully has been altered. Today he is considered to be a good general but not an outstanding commander. At El Alamein he benefited greatly from the work of those who preceded him, but to whom he gave no credit, as well as to good intelligence, but his handling of the armour was so flawed as to raise doubts about whether he really knew what tanks could do. Operations GOODWOOD and MARKET GARDEN raised similar questions. Even his mentor Brooke considered the latter a mistake. In the immediate post-war years and for most of his own lifetime, Monty was regarded by many as being in the same league as Wellington or Marlborough and certainly as Britain's best general of the war. Few today would endorse such claims: Bill Slim is seen as a much better field commander and Monty's place in history is no longer close to that of either Wellington or Marlborough.

~ 2 ~

Auchinleck

In June 1942 the German-Italian Panzer Armee Afrika, under Erwin Rommel, the Desert Fox, defeated Eighth Army, captured the port of Tobruk and advanced into Egypt where it seemed as if Axis forces might punch their way through the final British defences into the Nile delta. Although the Axis strategic plan had been to seize the island of Malta before striking into Egypt, the euphoria surrounding the fall of Tobruk persuaded Rommel that Egypt could be his if he pushed on. Promoted to field marshal by Hitler, he was also permitted by the Führer to continue his advance. Both Hitler and Mussolini looked forward to the conquest of Egypt. The latter prepared for a victory parade in Cairo, having a white charger flown to Tripoli and a victory medal struck for Axis troops.

But Rommel's confidence was misplaced. Britain's Commander-in-Chief, Middle East, General Sir Claude Auchinleck, relieved Eighth Army's commander, Neil Ritchie, and assumed personal command. Countermanding Ritchie's orders for a stand at Mersa Matruh, Auchinleck ordered Eighth Army back to the line from El Alamein on the coast to the Qattara Depression in the south. On 1 July 1942 Panzer Armee Afrika hit that line but failed to break through. As battle raged, Auchinleck sent a defiant message to Eighth Army's soldiers.

> The enemy is stretched to the limit and thinks we are a beaten army. His tactics against the New Zealanders were poor in the extreme. He hopes to take Egypt by bluff. Show him where to get off.

In the following weeks Auchinleck fought the enemy to a standstill, tore victory from Rommel's grasp and saved the Middle East from Axis domination. The battles of July 1942 were the turning point of the desert war. Although Churchill and Montgomery claimed otherwise, the latter's victory at El Alamein in October/ November 1942 would never have happened without Auchinleck's achievements that summer. This was recognized by Rommel who later wrote that the Axis had lost the battle in July. Of the fighting on 26 July, Rommel commented that

> the price to Auchinleck [in casualties] had not been excessive, for the one thing that mattered to him was to halt our advance, and that, unfortunately, he had done.

In spite of his achievements, Claude Auchinleck, the Auk, is today one of the less well known of the major commanders of the Second World War. Auchinleck is a Gaelic name, meaning the 'field of the flat stone' and is shared with an Ayrshire village from which the family originated. And it was from Scotland that the Auchinleck family first came to Ireland during the reign of James I, settling in Fermanagh and Tyrone. The Reverend James Auchinleck, a seventeenth-century rector of Cleenish, was one of the earliest family members to gain prominence in Fermanagh. Most of the family found their living either from the land or as Church of Ireland clergy. The first to deviate from this tradition appears to have been John Auchinleck, Claude's father.

John Auchinleck was serving in the Royal Horse Artillery at Aldershot when Claude was born in 1884. When Claude was still an infant, Colonel Auchinleck was posted to Bangalore in India. He was accompanied by his family; this began Claude's long association with, and love for, India. In 1892 Colonel John Auchinleck died, leaving his widow with four young children and an Army pension of £40 per year. However, as the son of a deceased officer, Claude obtained a 'Foundationer' scholarship to Wellington College from where he went to the Royal Military College, Sandhurst in 1902. He was placed highly in the entrance examination, which gave him the opportunity to chose a career in the Indian Army; at that time it was the cadet's placing on entering Sandhurst rather than passing out that determined whether he could go to the Indian Army. Officers of that Army were better paid than their British counterparts and had much lower living expenses; a young subaltern in a British regiment needed a private income of about £100 per year to enable him to meet his expenses. Such were the Auchinleck family's circumstances that Claude could not afford to join a British regiment – his choice might well have been the Royal Inniskilling Fusiliers – and so he was commissioned into an Indian regiment, 62nd Punjab, which he joined in April 1904.

So much did Auchinleck enjoy serving with the Punjabis that he turned down an opportunity to transfer to 5th Royal Gurkhas, one of the Indian Army's most distinguished regiments. With 62nd Punjabis, Auchinleck served on the Tibetan border in a deployment to prevent Russian incursions into India. He was popular with his soldiers, Sikhs, Muslims and Rajputs, whom he got to know as individuals and learned to speak their language, a standard requirement of Indian Army officers. After 1909, when he became adjutant, he was responsible for recruit training. On home leave in 1912, Captain Auchinleck obtained an attachment to the Royal Inniskilling Fusiliers, in which his cousin, Daniel Auchinleck, was serving. It was a happy attachment and many years later the Auk became Colonel of the Inniskillings, an appointment from which he derived much pleasure.

When the Great War broke out in 1914 the Indian government agreed to send troops, including Auchinleck's regiment, to France. However, while they were at sea, Turkey entered the war and 62nd Punjabis disembarked in Egypt. Captain Auchinleck's first action was against Turkish forces attempting to occupy the Suez Canal area to sever Britain's principal trade route to India. Once the threat to the canal had been defeated, 62nd Punjabis moved to Aden and helped push the Turks out of the town of Sheik Othman. By the end of 1915 the battalion was in Basra for the Mesopotamian campaign.

In early 1916 the British and Indian defenders of Kut al Amara were besieged by strong Turkish forces. Attempts were made to break through and raise the siege. Fighting took place in foul weather conditions with heavy rain turning the Tigris valley into a swamp; it was also bitterly cold. By March 62nd Punjab Regiment had suffered such severe casualties that it was reduced to 247 men. In little over six weeks, two commanding officers had been killed in action and, for a time, Captain Auchinleck, as senior surviving officer, took command. The relief missions to Kut were unsuccessful and the town eventually fell to the Turks. However, the campaign made a lasting impression on Auchinleck who was appalled by what he had witnessed, later describing as 'absolute murder' the tactic of sending men in on point-less frontal attacks. He had also seen men die of diseases that might have been prevented by better medical care; and he had seen men die of cold because they had only thin tropical uniforms. In the issue of uniforms his own regiment was fortunate, as the commanding officer had had the foresight to use regimental funds to buy heavy serge uniforms for his soldiers before leaving India. Intended to allow Indian soldiers to cope with European conditions, the serge clothing had been a godsend in Mesopotamia.

His experience convinced Auchinleck of the value of good leadership, high morale and concern for soldiers' welfare. Already a popular officer, he was also a good leader. He looked like a warrior leader: over six-foot tall he was physically impressive. Now the lessons of war were to make him an even better leader and by the end of the war he had been promoted to major, been decorated with the DSO and had also been appointed OBE for his outstanding staff work. In 1919, as a lieutenant-colonel, he entered the Indian Army Staff College at Quetta where he outranked most students and several staff. However, he was critical of the College syllabus, much of which he found 'too theoretical' and with insufficient emphasis on administration and supply. The latter were matters that he had identified as being among the most serious shortcomings in the Mesopotamian campaign. In spite of his criticisms, he passed his course and was graded in the top ten students. Auchinleck returned to the College as an instructor in 1930.

Following his spell as an instructor at Quetta the Auk was appointed to command the Peshawar Brigade, one of the Indian Army's most coveted commands; this appointment indicated the esteem in which he was held. In 1933, during the Mohmand expedition, he commanded Mohforce, a formation including his own brigade, the Nowshera Brigade – another infantry brigade – a cavalry regiment, armoured cars, artillery and engineers with a Royal Air Force squadron in support. The Nowshera Brigade was commanded by another Irishman, Brigadier Harold Alexander. As the senior of the two brigadiers, Auchinleck held overall command; he was also district commander since the GOC was on leave in Britain.

For his part in the Mohmand expedition, Auchinleck was appointed a Commander of the Bath (CB). He had also met Bernard Montgomery for the first time. Monty, then an instructor at Quetta, came to observe operations on the frontier during the campaign. Ironically, in view of what was to happen in 1942, Montgomery described Auchinleck as 'the best man' he had met there. His period in command of the Peshawar Brigade over, Auchinleck was appointed Deputy Chief of the General Staff in India, with the rank of major-general, responsible for modernizing and training the Indian Army. Also included in his role was overseeing the Indianization of that Army; as Britain prepared for Indian self-rule more and more officers were to be Indians with the ultimate aim that the officer corps, as well as the rank and file, should be Indian.

Auchinleck's next post was that of GOC, Meerut District, which he took up in 1938. There then occurred one of those episodes of happenstance that affect greatly the career of an individual. He was appointed to the Expert Committee on the Defence of India, also known as the Chatfield Committee, since its chairman was Lord Chatfield. The Committee concluded its work in Britain after which Auchinleck chose to take a short period of leave before returning to India. He was in Britain when war was declared on 3 September 1939 and was immediately recalled to prepare 3rd Indian Division for service. Before long, however, he was ordered back to Britain to command IV Corps of the British Army. An Indian Army officer in such a post was unusual and a clear indication of the high regard in which Auchinleck was held; his earlier presence in Britain with the Chatfield Committee may also have played a part. IV Corps was to join the BEF in France in June 1940, which would have placed Auchinleck, Brooke, Alexander and Montgomery in the same theatre at the same time. However, on 9 April, as IV Corps was preparing to move to France, Germany invaded Denmark and Norway. The former was overrun quickly but an Allied Expeditionary Force was despatched to help the Norwegians.

During early operations in Norway there was a distinct lack of harmony between British land and sea commanders, as a result of which the Army commander was relieved and Auchinleck was ordered to Norway in his place. Immediately, he arranged to establish an advance headquarters in the War Office and for the next week he and his staff were busily engaged in 'collecting and collating information concerning Norway and the existing situation in that theatre'. During that week the Auk first encountered Winston Churchill, then First Lord of the Admiralty. The two met in a Whitehall corridor and Churchill told Auchinleck that he had thought the latter was already on his way to Norway. Auchinleck replied that he was awaiting written orders from the Chiefs of Staff. This brief and curt meeting was, perhaps, an augury of future relationships.

Auchinleck arrived in Norway to command a force with little chance of success. As he was travelling to Norway, the Germans launched their attack on the Low Countries on 10 May. Norway became a sideshow. The situation was worsened by the fact that inter-Allied relations were not ideal; for example, the Norwegians wanted more anti-aircraft guns than either the British or French could give them. Nonetheless, Auchinleck believed that he could stop the Germans and, on 24 May, sent a special order of the day to his troops:

It is our firm intention to stop the further advance northwards of the enemy and to round up their forces in the Narvik area. We then intend to turn the tables on them and to do to them what they have been trying to do to us.

Our brave allies, the French, have already carried out a brilliant landing operation from boats near Narvik and bundled the enemy out of his forward positions; they are pressing forward steadily in the most difficult country and have the upper hand.

We ask every one of you to give of his best and make up his mind that the enemy has got to be beaten – and beaten thoroughly.

As he wrote that exhortation, Auchinleck was not to know that the British Chiefs of Staff had already decided to give up Norway. On 25 May the naval commander received a telegram from London that told him 'to evacuate Northern Norway at earliest moment'. With the BEF in France on the retreat, the forces in Norway were now needed urgently to defend Britain. This order forced Auchinleck into an invidious position. Since he could only ensure safe evacuation of his forces from Norway if the Germans were unaware of his intentions, he had to implement a deception plan to mislead both Germans and Norwegians. (Such was his concern about the leaking of information from Norwegian sources to the Germans that he often spoke in Pushtu or Urdu in telephone conversations with his officers.) Knowing that the Germans would not believe the Allies were evacuating Norway if they attacked Narvik, he planned an assault on that city. Narvik fell to a force of French, Norwegians, Poles and British on 28 May but over the following week Allied forces were evacuated from the country.

En route home Auchinleck wrote his report on the campaign. It was a typical example of Auchinleck's bluntly honest nature and criticized British intervention in 'an undeveloped and wild country such as Norway' with troops who had not been trained thoroughly for such conditions and equipped to fight there.

Improvisation in either of these respects can only lead to failure ... To commit troops to a campaign in which they cannot be provided with adequate air support is to court disaster.

The campaign, and the honesty of his report, did nothing for Auchinleck's relationships with Churchill, who had become prime minister on 10 May. Nor did admiration for the French go down well with the War Cabinet who thought that he had been too long in India and had, therefore, misjudged the situation in Norway. Even so, he was kept in Britain and appointed GOC, Southern Command, responsible for an area where invasion was expected.

One of Auchinleck's subordinate commanders was Major-General Bernard Montgomery, who proved a difficult individual. The two clashed over the tactics to be adopted should the Germans invade. The Auk planned to meet the enemy on the beaches and destroy them as they landed while Montgomery preferred to allow them off the beaches, meeting them in battle with his main force, which he wanted to keep in reserve, as they moved inland. Montgomery went over Auchinleck's head to present his plan to Churchill. The prime minister considered Monty's plan imaginative and it was certainly good for morale. By comparison the Auk's looked dull and uninspired.

Since the Germans never invaded Britain it may be argued that the disagreement was unresolved. However, there is an interesting parallel. In 1944 Field Marshal Rommel wanted to attack the Allies as they landed on the beaches in Normandy but his superior, Field Marshal Gerd von Rundstedt, adopted Monty's view which led to a compromise in the deployment of German armour that ensured that little armoured opposition was met by the Allies on D-Day. Later attempts to stop the Allies were unsuccessful. Had the Germans landed in Britain and moved off the beaches, it is unlikely that they could have been stopped by Monty's tactics, especially as the British Army was desperately short of tanks.

It is possible to make another comparison between Auchinleck and Rommel. The latter possessed what the Germans called *Fingerspitzengefuehl*, literally a sixth sense transmitted through the fingers. Auchinleck would prove that he, too, possessed such a sixth sense. In his accounts of the desert war, Rommel paid many tributes to Auchinleck's abilities and ascribed Axis defeat in the campaign to the fighting along the El Alamein line in July 1942 when the latter took direct command of Eighth Army.

In late 1940 General Auchinleck returned to India as Commander-in-Chief. He was soon called upon to support British forces involved in suppressing the Nazi-supported Rashid Ali rebellion in Iraq, formerly Mesopotamia, where he sent a force from India. This earned him praise from Churchill who commented:

> His appointment as Commander-in-Chief in India had been generally acclaimed. We had seen how forthcoming he had been in sending troops to Basra and the ardour with which he had addressed himself to the suppression of the revolt in Iraq.

Churchill also decided that Auchinleck was the man he needed in the Middle East to succeed General Wavell. In June 1941 Wavell's Operation BATTLEAXE had been fought to a standstill by Rommel's forces on the Libyan frontier. Although Wavell had asked for more time to prepare his new tanks for desert warfare and to train his soldiers, Churchill had pressurized him into launching the attack before Wavell deemed it wise. When BATTLEAXE failed, Churchill chose to blame Wavell and to replace him as C-in-C, Middle East. On 21 June Wavell and Auchinleck swapped jobs. Churchill wrote to Auchinleck to tell him of the change and to suggest that:

> You should confer with [Wavell] upon the whole situation and should also concert with him the measures you will take in common to arrest the eastward movement of the German armies which is clearly impending.

Wavell and Auchinleck spent a week discussing the Middle East situation before, on 7 July, the latter assumed command. Not long afterwards, he received a lengthy letter of advice from General Sir John Dill, the CIGS, in which the latter pointed out the political pressures that might be brought to bear on the Auk's new command. He also advised him on the best way to deal with that pressure, noting that a commander should not wait for pressure, suggestion or even orders but should anticipate these and tell the government 'in the most secret manner' his assessment of the situation and his plans for dealing with it.

> He should point clearly to the risks he is prepared to accept and those he considers great. He should demand the resources he considers strictly necessary to carry out any project and he should make it clear what he can and cannot do in their absence.

In his letter Dill also emphasized that he would back Auchinleck's military judgements. Sadly, his own relationship with Churchill was deteriorating and it would not be long before the pressure on Auchinleck from Downing Street started.

Sir Francis de Guingand later described Auchinleck's arrival as

> a breath of fresh air ... he had an amazing personality, was most accessible, and appeared amazingly alert and competent. He certainly managed to get his personality around his headquarters in a very short time.

Auchinleck had no doubt that, with proper resources, his troops could beat Rommel. He refused to be intimidated by the Rommel legend that had permeated British forces in North Africa and intended to dispel the idea among his soldiers that Rommel was anything other 'than an ordinary German general'.

> The important thing now is to see that we do not always talk of Rommel when we mean the enemy in Libya. We must refer to 'the Germans' or 'the Axis powers' or 'the enemy' and not always keep harping on about Rommel.

The forces under Auchinleck's command were tired and weary from long service in the desert. Reinforcements were arriving from Britain but needed training and acclimatizion to desert conditions before going into action. More and better equipment was also needed and Auchinleck set out a shopping list for this. His requests were met, at least on paper, but the guns and tanks received were not up to the task demanded of them. The standard British anti-tank gun, the 2-pounder, was already obsolete but it would be November 1941 before the first 6-pounders rolled off the production lines. In theory, the 2-pounder, which was also fitted to many British tanks, could penetrate 40mm of armour, sloped at 30 degrees, at a range of 1,000 yards. In practice it was heavy with too high a profile, allowing enemy armour to stand off out of range and destroy 2-pounders before their gunners could open fire. 'It took aggressive handling and ingenious tactics to get a 2pdr close enough to a German or Italian tank to be sure of stopping it.' Needless to say, it also took tremendous courage and it is hardly surprising that at least two Victoria Crosses were awarded to anti-tank gunners in the desert, nor should it be surprising that both were posthumous awards.*

British tanks were divided into two classes, Infantry, or I-, tanks and cruisers. I-tanks were intended to support the infantry and were slow but well armoured although fitted only with a 2-pounder. At this stage the standard I-tank was the Matilda II. Cruisers were seen as the successors to the cavalry, capable of fast movement and tank-to-tank combat. The standard cruiser in 1941 was the Crusader; the Mark II had its armour improved to 50mm. Neither tank could match their most recent German counterparts, the Panzer Mark IV with a 75mm gun.† German anti-tank guns were more than capable of dealing with the British tanks while Rommel deployed 88mm anti-aircraft guns as anti-tank weapons, in which role they were lethal.

Reports from fighting units confirmed the inferiority of much British equipment and Auchinleck could see the problem for himself, as well as being acutely conscious of the morale aspects. However, when Auchinleck reported these facts to the War Cabinet, Churchill did not believe him. The prime minister and the War Cabinet were privy to regular reports of secret German signals that were being intercepted and decoded by the British ULTRA organization at Bletchley Park and these included pleas from Rommel to Berlin for more men, tanks and artillery. Churchill chose to believe Rommel's side of this story without considering the possibility that the latter was exaggerating his difficulties, a judgement Churchill would have been very quick to make about one of his own generals. The truth about the inferiority of British equipment was to be found in Britain where a captured German tank, shipped from Egypt, was available for examination. However, nine months passed before a report on the tank's armour proved that no existing British anti-tank gun was capable of penetrating it.

In spite of these difficulties Auchinleck prepared for further action. One of his decisions was to authorize the establishment of a small, hard-hitting, special unit to operate behind enemy lines. This became the Special Air Service Regiment and was reputed to have destroyed more enemy aircraft on the ground in one night than the Desert Air Force had done in the air over some months. And yet Churchill continued to consider the Auk as unimaginative, in stark contrast to the opinion held by many of his staff in Cairo who considered him too imaginative to be a good commander.

---

* These were Lieutenant Ward Gunn, Royal Horse Artillery, and Private Adam Wakenshaw, Durham Light Infantry.
† The Panzer Mark III was equipped with a 37mm gun that could not penetrate the armour of a Matilda. This was later upgunned with a 50mm weapon. The Panzer Mark II was armed only with a 20mm gun and, as a light tank, was suitable solely for reconnaissance duties. (Hogg & Weeks, *The Illustrated Encyclopedia of Military Vehicles*, pp. 78-9.)

By late September 1941 British forces in the desert had been built up sufficiently to form a new army: this was the famous Eighth Army whose first commander was General Alan Cunningham, who had liberated Abyssinia from the Italians. Eighth Army included XIII Corps, formerly Western Desert Force, and XXX Corps, a new armoured formation, and with this army Auchinleck launched Operation CRUSADER on 18 November 1941. This major offensive against Axis forces in Libya was also intended to relieve the besieged port of Tobruk. In a series of very bloody, confusing battles, which are some of the most complex actions of the war, Eighth Army's armour suffered heavily but Rommel was forced to withdraw. Tobruk was relieved, the port of Benghazi was captured and tens of thousands of German and Italian soldiers became prisoners.

In the course of the fighting Auchinleck had been forced to dismiss Cunningham who was worn out from long service in the Middle East and the strain of command. Major-General Neil Ritchie was given temporary command of Eighth Army but, unfortunately, a message from Auchinleck to Churchill to that effect was reported to the house of commons as if it were a permanent appointment and so Ritchie became, by default, Eighth Army commander. The choice had not been an easy one for Auchinleck and, as the campaign unfolded, it proved a bad one. Auchinleck had been slow to sack Cunningham; he did not like removing officers who were loyal to him, as Cunningham undoubtedly was, and believed in reciprocating that loyalty. In his letter to Cunningham, Auchinleck suggested that the army commander should ask to be placed on the sick list. He finished by writing:

> You may not believe me when I tell you that I have nothing but sympathy, but it is true all the same. I feel my responsibility very deeply.

As ever, Rommel was quick to recover from the setbacks of CRUSADER. In early January 1942 a convoy delivered fifty-five tanks, twenty armoured cars and some anti-tank guns to Tripoli, while Hitler had ordered the transfer of an entire Luftwaffe Fliegerkorps from Russia to Libya. Thus strengthened, Rommel launched a fresh offensive from the El Agheila position in late-January. In a fast-moving assault, much of the ground taken by Eighth Army in November and December was lost and Ritchie's command was forced back to a series of defensive positions stretching from Gazala to Bir Hakeim, known as the Gazala line. Once more, Auchinleck felt pressure from Downing Street as Churchill urged a speedy riposte against Rommel's Panzer Armee Afrika. But Eighth Army had not only suffered heavy losses in the recent retreat but had also lost three divisions to the Far East to oppose the Japanese;* elements of the Desert Air Force were also transferred. Against this

---

* Only one of these was British: 18th Division was en route to Egypt but was diverted to Singapore where it was captured by the Japanese. Two Australian divisions, 6th and 7th, were recalled to Australia. In addition, 17th Indian Division, due to move to the Middle East, was retained in India. Seven bomber squadrons were also transferred out of the Middle East as were a number of fighter squadrons. An armoured brigade was also sent to the Far East.

background, Auchinleck told Churchill that he needed more time to prepare for an attack. Eventually, and against his own judgement, he conceded to the prime minister's demands and planned an offensive for the end of May, with the aim of easing pressure on beleaguered Malta.

However, Rommel attacked first. On 27 May Panzer Armee Afrika struck at Eighth Army's positions on the Gazala line. Despite gallant and determined opposition from British troops, and from the Free French at Bir Hakeim, Rommel's forces broke through. There followed a series of bloody and bitter battles and skirmishes that saw a number of British units wiped out. It seemed that setback followed setback for Eighth Army that June, especially when on Auchinleck's birthday, 21 June, Tobruk fell to Rommel. Almost 35,000 British and South African soldiers marched into captivity. Churchill was attending a conference in Washington and was given the news of the loss by Roosevelt. He was stunned: Tobruk had withstood siege from April to November the previous year and had become a symbol of Allied defiance. Churchill had believed that the port could hold out yet again. But the Royal Navy had lost heavily in 1941 while maintaining the Tobruk garrison and was not prepared to do so again. Nor would Auchinleck have asked them. Most of the port's landward defences had been stripped, with many of the mines transplanted to the Gazala line. Eighth Army now withdrew to the Mersa Matruh position, which had been designed in 1940 as Egypt's last line of defence. However, Auchinleck was concerned that Rommel could outflank and roll up Eighth Army at Matruh and urged Ritchie to pull back to the El Alamein–Qattara Depression line, which could not be outflanked.

But Ritchie was already preparing to stand and fight at Mersa Matruh while Churchill was fighting his own battle at home. He had returned from Washington to face a vote of no confidence in the house of commons:

> That this House, while paying tribute to the heroism and endurance of the Armed Forces of the Crown in circumstances of exceptional difficulty, has no confidence in the central direction of the war.

Although Churchill survived the vote, he did so with Aneurin Bevin's rejoinder ringing in his ears: that he had won debate after debate while losing battle after battle.

In North Africa, Auchinleck decided once again to take command of Eighth Army. Rommel would not be engaged at Mersa Matruh but would be drawn into attacking the El Alamein line. He went up to Eighth Army headquarters at Ma'aten Baggush and relieved Ritchie.

> I told Ritchie that the situation was such that nobody but I could be saddled with the responsibility and that therefore I was taking over from him.

Although Auchinleck believed that Eighth Army would come under attack in a matter of hours, there was no sense of panic in his headquarters. Tedder, commanding the Desert Air Force, later wrote:

> That evening Auchinleck called me to the ops room … I was much impressed by the contrast between his calm authority and Ritchie's fumbling. Auchinleck had grasped the essentials of a most confused situation in about two hours … I felt that passive bewilderment was being replaced by active command.

Before daylight on 26 June the Auk issued an order to Eighth Army's corps commanders, which he also passed to Brooke, the CIGS.

> At all costs, even if ground has to be given up, I intend to keep Eighth Army in being and to give no hostage to fortune in the shape of immobile troops holding localities which can be isolated.

Over the following four days, Eighth Army impeded Rommel's advance while the defences of the El Alamein line were being strengthened. On the afternoon of 30 June, tanks of Afrika Korps met the first outposts of that line and were stopped by the tenacious British defence. Rommel prepared to renew the attack but now made a serious mistake. It is a principle of all commanders that time spent on reconnaissance is seldom wasted. Rommel spent little or no time on reconnaissance and his soldiers were about to pay for that error. On the other hand, Eighth Army would benefit.

Rommel resumed his attack at 3.00am on 1 July but 15th Panzer Division met a British brigade at Deir el Shein and was fought to a standstill; the Germans had no idea that the brigade was there. When British tanks arrived the panzers were chased from the battlefield. The other armoured formation of Afrika Korps, 21st Panzer Division, was also stopped and the Korps' 90th Light Division was forced to dig in. Auchinleck had compelled Rommel into a battle of attrition, which put the latter at a severe disadvantage. German troops moved forward again on the 2nd but were pounded by the Desert Air Force, British artillery and tanks and, by the end of the day, Afrika Korps had only twenty-six tanks left. On the 3rd the battle continued and by that evening the strength of the German divisions was down to some 1,500 men each while the Italian Ariete Division had only five tanks and two guns to call on. Rommel sent a signal to Berlin saying that the offensive was over.

Auchinleck had taken charge of the battle and his handling had been superb. He had shown himself to be more than a match for Rommel and had used innovative thinking in deploying his forces. Breaking away from the traditional divisional system he had created battlegroups including infantry, armour and artillery. Since the war he has been criticized for splitting his forces into penny packets but the battlegroup system has now been used for decades by British, French, German and American armies. In his own defence Auchinleck said that circumstances dictated the tactics employed since infantry and artillery in solid divisional masses could not match armour unless they were dug in with secure flanks. Even then enemy armour could penetrate the defences and 'play hell behind' unless opposed by British armour, which had not been there to begin with. In his view the controversy over battlegroups was 'rubbish'.

The New Zealander, Brigadier Howard Kippenberger, a severe critic of the British command system, wrote that:

> The brigade group organisation had many advantages for desert warfare, particularly in mobility and quick readiness for action.

Fighting continued on the El Alamein line throughout the month. On 10 July Eighth Army attacked the area of Tel el Eisa, the Hill of Jesus, held by the Italian Sabratha Division. A German general, Frido von Mellenthin, later described the ensuing confusion.

> I was considerably startled early on the morning of 10 July to see hundreds of Italians rushing past the HQ in the final stages of panic and rout.

By the end of the day Eighth Army held Tel el Eisa. And so it continued throughout July; by the end of the month Rommel had accepted that he was beaten and he wrote to his wife:

> It can't go on like [this] for long otherwise the front will crack. Militarily this is the most difficult period I've ever been through ... the enemy is using his superiority, especially in infantry, to destroy the Italian formations one by one and the German formations are too weak to stand alone. It's enough to make one weep.

One of Rommel's staff officers later told a British officer:

> We were very much impressed and very much disturbed by the way you attacked us all through July. You very nearly succeeded in breaking through our position several times between the 10th and the 26th. If you could have continued to attack for only a couple of days more you would have done so. July 26th was the decisive day. We then had no ammunition at all for our heavy artillery and Rommel had determined to withdraw to the frontier if the attack was resumed.

Although Auchinleck had fought Rommel to a standstill and thereby gained a victory, Churchill did not perceive the situation thus and demanded that Eighth Army move to the offensive. He also wanted Auchinleck to come to London to discuss plans but the Auk refused to leave while fighting continued at El Alamein. An angry Churchill therefore decided to visit Egypt himself. Although Brooke had been planning such a visit he had hoped that the prime minister would not accompany him and, although both made separate travel arrangements, they arrived in Egypt within hours of each other.

Churchill visited Auchinleck at Eighth Army's tactical headquarters on Ruweisat Ridge where he was unimpressed by the spartan living conditions and the flies infesting the area. This was in stark contrast to the RAF mess by the sea where a special meal, from Shepheard's Hotel in Cairo, complete with silverware and napery had been provided for the visitor. Churchill and Auchinleck agreed that a new commander was needed for Eighth Army; the latter suggested Montgomery in spite of the difficulties he had experienced with Monty in England. Brooke also wanted Montgomery and was unimpressed when he learned that a senior staff officer in Cairo thought he was a candidate for the post; Auchinleck had considered the man as an interim commander until someone of the right calibre could be found. Churchill considered Major-General 'Strafer' Gott to be the most suitable to command Eighth Army although Brooke thought Gott to be worn out, an assessment with which Gott probably agreed.

The outcome of the visit was that Churchill decided to appoint Gott to Eighth Army and to offer Auchinleck a new post, that of Persia–Iraq, which was really one half – the quieter half – of Middle East Command. Auchinleck refused the appointment and was dismissed as C-in-C, Middle East, to be replaced by General Sir Harold Alexander. Gott was killed when the aircraft in which he was flying was shot down by German fighters and Montgomery was ordered out from England to command Eighth Army.

Montgomery received a briefing from Auchinleck on the Middle East situation and on Eighth Army's plans. Monty's version of what was discussed at that briefing would lead to controversy and to his having to include an apology to Auchinleck in copies of his *Memoirs*, following the first print run. According to Montgomery, Auchinleck had been preparing to withdraw into the Nile Delta while he, Monty, was determined that there would be no retreat from the El Alamein line. There is an element of truth in Montgomery's claim since Auchinleck, as Commander-in-Chief was responsible for more than Eighth Army and it would have been irresponsible of him not to have contingency plans for withdrawal. Auchinleck realized that the vital British and Allied interest in the region was the oil of the Persian Gulf and, in mid-1942, there was a danger of a German attack through the Caucasus into Syria and Palestine to link up with Panzer Armee Afrika. Even while preparing to meet the latter, Auchinleck had strengthened Ninth Army in Palestine.* Rommel had been an advocate of such a strategic pincer movement, which had also attracted Hitler; the concept was known as Plan ORIENT. Montgomery seems to have failed to see the greater strategic picture of which Auchinleck and Rommel were both aware.

In claiming that he ordered that there would be no plans for retreat from El Alamein, Montgomery was again being less than honest. Such plans remained but, since they were the responsibility of Alexander's Middle East headquarters, Montgomery was able to disclaim them. Nonetheless, in late August, South Delta Force was created to defend the Nile delta and Cairo from a sudden Axis attack.

* Among the units reinforcing Ninth Army in the summer of 1942 was 9th (Londonderry) HAA Regiment in which the author's father was serving. The regiment returned to Eighth Army after the Battle of El Alamein.

Montgomery must have been aware of this contingency plan since one of the formations involved, 51st (Highland) Division, was due to join Eighth Army. Auchinleck
was not the defeatist that Monty tried to assert. There may well have been defeatists
at Middle East headquarters but the Auk was not of their number. At the end of June
he had told his chief of staff, and fellow-Irishman, Eric Dorman-Smith that 'these
damn English have been taught for too long to be good losers. I've never been a good
loser, I intend to win.'

Relieved of his command, Auchinleck returned to India without an active job but, in
June 1943, he was appointed C-in-C, India for the second time. In that position he
was responsible for the supply of all South-East Asia Command (SEAC) as well as
the Chinese armies in Burma. His abilities proved an invaluable asset to Allied forces
in that theatre and contributed significantly to their eventual success. On 1 June 1946
he was promoted to field marshal.

Indian independence was now much closer and Lord Mountbatten succeeded
Field Marshal Lord Wavell as Viceroy of India. Under Mountbatten the move to
independence was accelerated but differences between political leaders and religious
conflict between Hindus and Muslims led to the partition of the sub-continent.
Auchinleck opposed what he saw as Mountbatten's unnecessary haste and advised
the Viceroy that his plans would lead to bloodshed. That advice was ignored and as
many as two million died; only intervention by British and Indian troops prevented
the death toll from rising even higher. Auchinleck was now appointed Supreme
Commander, India and Pakistan, a difficult and thankless post in which he had to
oversee the break-up of the old Indian Army; his own regiment became part of the
Pakistani Army. It had been envisaged that both armies would act as a force for the
defence of the sub-continent but the bitterness of partition ensured that this could not
happen. Auchinleck was left in an invidious position: Indians accused him of being
pro-Pakistani and some senior Indian officers treated him with suspicion. And from
Britain, Montgomery, his old rival, now CIGS, wrote to Mountbatten to suggest that
Auchinleck be retired. But the Auk himself had asked to be relieved.

A few weeks later Mountbatten told Auchinleck that his time as Supreme
Commander was over. But there were many Indians who continued to admire the
Auk. That admiration was increased by his treatment of prisoners from Subhas
Chandra Bose's Indian National Army (INA), which had fought for the Japanese.
Some INA officers were court-martialled for murder and waging war against the
King-Emperor and their trial, which lasted almost two months, became a political
issue. Although the men were sentenced to transportation for life, Auchinleck refused
to confirm their sentences, arguing that such would make them martyrs. He also
opposed prison sentences. His action inspired one leading Indian to write to him:

> Your action with respect to the INA officers has proved that there are still
> some in this world who believe in the almost forgotten-in-practice saying that
> 'to err is human and to forgive divine'. A fitting tribute will be the Nobel Prize

for Peace for you, for I sincerely feel that your action has contributed more to peace than any other single act in India during the last few years.

However, the Nobel Prize did not come his way, although he would have been a much worthier recipient than some who have received that prize. He also refused a peerage on the grounds that presiding over the dissolution of the Indian Army was not something to be proud of. In any case, he had no great regard for titles and of peers he said that 'there are too many of them, at least that sort of peer'. In December 1947 he left India.

Claude Auchinleck rarely received the recognition that he deserved, a state of affairs for which Churchill and Montgomery were largely responsible. Later, Churchill did give the Auk some credit and acknowledged that he had wronged him. At a function in the London in the early 1950s, when he was again prime minister, Churchill approached the Field Marshal and told him that he had wronged him in 1942. Typically, Auchinleck's response was straightforward and honest: 'I know, Prime Minister,' he said.

This shy and honest man was a brilliant general who was very popular with his soldiers. One general who served under Auchinleck and Montgomery said of the former that

> His command was too big and too much was expected of him. Yet he was a most attractive commander with a great sense of humour, individually a born leader.

For many years after the war the legend of Montgomery overshadowed the Auk to such an extent that his achievements, and those of Eighth Army under his command, were ignored and in danger of being forgotten. In fact, Montgomery made certain that the Eighth Army clasp to the Africa Star campaign medal would only be awarded to those who served under Monty. Those whose service fell between the creation of Eighth Army and Montgomery's assumption of command were denied that distinction. This injustice has never been put right. Nor did Montgomery ever acknowledge how good a commander Auchinleck was. But the Germans were aware of his qualities and Rommel certainly knew, for he accepted the Auk as his equal and knew that Auchinleck would always have something up his sleeve – Auchinleck possessed *Fingerspitzengefuehl*. Typical German feeling is summed up in this comment.

> If Auchinleck had not been the man he was and by that I mean the best Allied general in North Africa during the war, Rommel would have finished Eighth Army off.

In truth, as Rommel wrote, the real turning point of the desert war was the first battle of El Alamein in July 1942 and the man responsible for that, and, therefore, ultimate victory in Africa was the Auk – General Sir Claude Auchinleck.

~ 3 ~

Alexander

In Winston Churchill's eyes the finest of his wartime generals was Field Marshal Alexander, whom Churchill regarded as a *beau sabreur*. Alexander epitomized both leadership and courage, which were illustrated effectively during the retreat in Burma. General Bill Slim recorded an incident when he and Alexander were visiting a brigade headquarters that came under attack from Japanese aircraft. According to Slim, Alexander

> as usual, was quite unperturbed and refused to take shelter in a trench, as I did very briskly enough, preferring to stand upright behind a tree. I was very annoyed with him for this, not only because it was a foolhardy thing to do, but because we had been trying to stop the men doing it … This was not the only time I found the Army Commander's courage above my standard.

This incident was not unique. Alexander's personal courage became legendary. Amounting almost to a reckless disregard for his own safety, it was one of the most distinguishing features of Churchill's favourite general throughout his long military career.

Alex, as he was better known, came from a family with roots in Ireland stretching back several centuries. Originally of Scottish planter stock, Alexanders settled in County Donegal before moving to Londonderry where they became prominent in business and provided aldermen of the city. The family's prosperity allowed them to purchase a large house on the west bank of the Foyle, north of the city. In the late-eighteenth century an ancestor made a fortune in India and built a new residence, Caledon Castle, in County Tyrone, which became the family seat. That same ancestor, James Alexander, became the first earl of Caledon in 1801. Ninety years later, in December 1891, Harold Alexander was born in London and was brought to Caledon a few days later. His father, who had served in the Life Guards and Royal Inniskilling Fusiliers, died when Harold was six years old. The young Harold spent his early years at Caledon with summer holidays in Donegal.

Educated at Harrow, he entered Sandhurst and in 1911 was commissioned into the Irish Guards with whom he would have a lifelong association. He was not an outstanding cadet at Sandhurst although he excelled at athletics and won the Irish

Mile championship. Had the Great War not intervened he may have participated in the 1916 Olympics. Alexander's regiment was even younger than he. Formed in 1900 at the express command of Queen Victoria to 'commemorate the bravery shown by the Irish regiments' in the South African War, it had yet to see service, although some of its first soldiers had been despatched to South Africa towards the end of the Boer War. Nonetheless, the regiment had a fine conceit of itself and a strong sense of identity. Its soldiers were mostly Irish or had been born into Britain's Irish communities. Known as the 'Micks', Alexander found them

> bosom friends. In the Micks there is a great feeling of matiness between officers and men. The Irish love their leaders, as I found as a boy, and they have natural good manners.

Before long the regiment was at war, going to France with the BEF in the first weeks of the Great War and being engaged in the first battle of Ypres in which heavy losses were sustained. Alexander had a remarkable war record. In late-1914 he was awarded the French Legion of Honour, which was followed by two British gallantry decorations, the Distinguished Service Order and Military Cross. Many contemporaries averred that he ought to have received the Victoria Cross, which they believed he had earned several times. Alex was also Mentioned in Despatches five times, was twice wounded, on one occasion seriously, and was in action throughout the war save for occasions when he was recovering from wounds. In a year he progressed from commanding a platoon as a lieutenant to commanding a battalion and became one of the Army's youngest lieutenant-colonels. For a few days in 1918 he even commanded a brigade.

Alexander's reputation was outstanding, especially amongst the guardsmen who admired his easy manner and apparent lack of fear. His popularity was attested to by the historian of the Irish Guards in the Great War, none other than Rudyard Kipling, whose son had been killed while serving in the Micks. Of Alexander, Kipling wrote that he possessed the

> gift of handling the men on the lines to which they most readily responded. At the worst crises he was both inventive and cordial and, on such occasions as they all strove together at the gates of death, would somehow contrive to dress the affair in high comedy. Moreover, when the blame for some incident of battle or fatigue was his, he confessed and took it upon his own shoulders in the presence of all. Consequently his subordinates loved him, even when he fell upon them blisteringly for their shortcomings; and his men were all his own.

One Irish Guard confirmed Kipling's analysis in an interview with Alexander's first biographer.

> We saw at once that he was an extraordinary young man. There was originality in everything he did. He appeared to be able to lead and control men

by the power of his personality. He was entirely free from fear, superior airs or snobbery. Being an athlete who knew how to train and look after himself, he was fitter than anyone else in the Regiment. He was the most perfect man, morally, physically and mentally that I have ever met. These things enabled him to be superb in face of danger and tight corners. For his own safety he never gave a thought.

Alexander seemed to crave danger. Although the November 1918 armistice brought hostilities in western Europe to a close this was not so in Russia, which had made a separate peace with Germany a year earlier. In the wake of the revolution and the turmoil created by the Great War, Russia was attempting to export Bolshevism to neighbouring countries, some of which appealed to the victors of the late war for assistance. A British Military Mission was despatched to eastern Europe and Lieutenant-Colonel Alexander volunteered to serve in that mission, travelling to Poland and then to Latvia where he was appointed to command a brigade of troops forming part of a small army, the Landeswehr, which was fighting to keep Bolshevik influence out of Latvia.

The Latvian situation was confusing, with Germans, Bolsheviks, Latvians and Estonians all engaged in the campaign. Alexander's diplomatic skills proved vital as he was called upon to reassure the Germans in his brigade that they would not be sacrificed by their allies through being forced into a suicidal battle with the Bolsheviks. He succeeded in gaining the confidence of his German soldiers and in making the Landeswehr the most professional formation in the campaign. In October 1919 Alexander's men captured Lievenho, a fortified village, before advancing another ten miles; the brigade also held off a Bolshevik counter-attack over three days. In spite of political difficulties, military threats and misunderstandings, the Landeswehr remained loyal to Alexander.

A major offensive opened in early 1920 that saw the Bolsheviks pushed out of Latvia by March. Alexander, who had been wounded in October 1919, gave up his command as negotiations on new frontiers opened. He returned to British service and in 1922 was commanding a battalion of Irish Guards in Constantinople, now Istanbul. The Micks spent eighteen months there, during which they prepared for invasion by the Greeks; fortunately, this never occurred.

In 1926 Alexander entered Staff College as a student. With an established reputation he was not only older than most of his fellow students but also outranked them. In addition, he outranked most of the staff, including Bernard Montgomery. One fellow student was Douglas Wimberley, who would command 51st (Highland) Division in the battle of El Alamein. Wimberley found Alexander to show no signs of being pleased with himself because of his prowess in war but instead showed 'simplicity, directness and kindness'. He earned the respect of all at the College.

Alexander returned to active campaigning with the command of the Nowshera Brigade on India's North-West Frontier. This was a much-coveted command and an indication that he was being groomed for greater things. Many years later, a fellow

Irishman, Sir Gerald Templer, a most astute observer and judge of men, recalled Alex's days on the Frontier.

> We all felt in those days that the two up and coming men in the Army, one on the British side and one on the Indian, were Alex and Claude Auchinleck. And now they found themselves commanding brigades side by side.

Auchinleck was, of course, commanding the Peshawar Brigade, which was only twenty miles away. In typical fashion, Alex studied Hindustani, which gained him the respect of his Indian soldiers. He also led them in two campaigns in the frontier area and proved a better commander than many veterans of the region. His brigade chaplain recalled that

> they said that he never ordered them to go anywhere where he had not first been himself. At daybreak they had watched him crawling along a ridge where they would later have to follow, and they boasted how he had marched with them along the valleys.

Alex was promoted to command 1st Division in Britain at the beginning of 1938 and, in September 1939, took the division to France as part of the BEF's I Corps. Major-General Alexander had ensured that his division was trained to the highest standards and maintained a strict training programme in France as the BEF waited for a German attack. He could be ruthless when necessary, sacking one battalion commander whom he considered was not taking his job seriously enough. On 10 May 1940 the Germans launched their offensive and the BEF moved forward into Belgium. Before long, however, both British and French armies were retreating as the Belgian army collapsed and French morale started crumbling. In the chaos of retreat Alexander and 1st Division performed coolly and so well did Alex do his job that he was promoted to command I Corps in the final days of the campaign. Such was his reputation that all were confident that he could be relied upon to cover the BEF's evacuation from France.

Alexander was also confident that he would extricate his soldiers from France. When he assumed command of I Corps he declared that it was his intention, at all costs, to ensure the corps' evacuation from France; he would not be surrendering. He recognized the seriousness of the situation in the Dunkirk perimeter, into which much of the BEF had withdrawn, realized that it would be impossible to hold on beyond the night of 1 June and informed the French that he intended to complete evacuating his men without delay. The last British personnel were embarked before midnight of 2 June. There then occurred an episode that has gained almost mythical status but which reveals the concern that Alex felt for his soldiers and shows why he was so well loved and respected by them.

Alexander took a small motorboat in which he travelled the length of the beaches and through the harbour complex to check for stragglers. Using a loudspeaker he called out 'Is anyone there?' in English and French, but received no reply. His self-imposed task complete, he boarded a destroyer for the crossing to Dover. What he had done had been most unusual for such a high-ranking officer, and extremely dangerous; once, again, however, Alexander spurned danger. Nor was the danger behind him when he boarded ship; for much of the homeward journey the destroyer was bombed and machine-gunned by enemy aircraft. Alexander's behaviour at Dunkirk made him a national hero and, in particular, earned him the respect of the new prime minister, Winston Churchill. The latter came to regard Alex as the Army's finest general and was impressed by his personal courage as well as his ability as a commander. Doubtless, Alexander's personal charm also influenced the premier.

As the Army re-organized in Britain, Alexander was confirmed in his command of I Corps and set about preparing to meet the expected German invasion. He paid close attention to the training of his soldiers but was criticized for 'sadly mishandling' his armoured units during Exercise BUMPER, a major anti-invasion exercise. His critic was his superior, General Brooke, Commander Home Forces. Brooke was to be a regular critic of Alexander; the fact that the two families came from the same region of Ireland made no difference to their relationship. Then, in December 1940, Alexander became GOC Southern Command, succeeding Auchinleck. Less than two years later he would again succeed Auchinleck, but in less pleasant circumstances. In the meantime, however, Alex's reputation from Dunkirk was to lead to another posting to command a retreating army.

When the Japanese invaded Burma the small British force in that country had no option other than to retreat towards India. Alexander was sent to command the retreating Burma army, made up of British, Indian, Burmese and Chinese troops. This appointment was one that could have destroyed his military career since defeat in Burma was inevitable and commanders of defeated armies often become scapegoats. Alexander was told to make the best of the situation and bring his command out of Burma. His reaction was typical: 'I will do my duty,' he said. That duty was to extract as much of the army as possible from Burma into India where it could then defend the frontier against Japanese aggression and begin preparing to retake Burma.

During the Burmese campaign Alexander made one serious error in misjudging the speed at which the enemy was advancing. As a result he delayed at Rangoon, the capital, and might have lost the campaign by so doing had the Japanese commander not erred also by adhering rigidly to a plan to outflank Rangoon from the west. That allowed Alexander to withdraw to the north. Part of the reason why Alex delayed at Rangoon was that General Wavell had ordered him to hold the city; but that was an impossible task that could so easily have ended in disaster. Once again retreat and adversity brought out the best in Alexander. Slim commented on his personal courage as together they brought back to India and safety a shattered and poorly supplied army with no air support. And there was a tough test for Alex's diplomatic skills when he encountered a hostile ally in the form of the American General Joseph Stilwell, better known as 'Vinegar Joe', a soubriquet first applied by US Army officers. As the nickname suggests, Stilwell was a dour individual: he hated many of his fellow US officers; he hated the Chinese, even though he commanded Chinese forces; he hated all his allies, including the British – perhaps especially the British – and he seemed to take every opportunity to make this clear. A typical Stilwell outburst was 'God damn them, they left Rangoon and didn't tell the liaison officer – the bastards have promised us gas for trucks and haven't delivered'. Despite being repulsed by Stilwell's phobias, Alexander behaved in his habitual gentlemanly and patient manner when dealing with his difficult ally. Sadly, Stilwell's behaviour had the effect of leaving Alexander with a low opinion of Americans generally.

The British had no advantages in this first Burma campaign. Total air superiority was enjoyed by the Japanese who also demonstrated more skill in jungle fighting. More accurately, they showed that they were prepared to use the jungle whereas traditional British military wisdom had dismissed the jungle as a battleground. Japanese units were, therefore, able to outflank British units, which were then forced to withdraw. Eventually the remains of Burma Army entered India and Alexander's task was complete. He returned to Britain with his second retreat and second defeat behind him, a reputation that no general would relish. Yet his standing in Churchill's eyes was undiminished. Although Churchill had been ruthless in sacking defeated generals before, Alexander received no rebuke but remained the prime minister's favourite general.

Alexander's Commander-in-Chief in India and Burma, General Sir Archibald Wavell, had been relieved by Churchill as C-in-C Middle East in June 1941 and it may have been Wavell's presence that protected Alexander from any blame for the defeat in Burma. Churchill once again vented his anger on Wavell, claiming that Wavell had lost Athens, Singapore and now Rangoon in little over a year. But it may also be that it was Churchill's genuine respect for Alex that ensured that no blame fell on him; he was the only general whom Churchill never seemed openly to criticize.

Churchill's faith in Alexander was underlined in July 1942 with the appointment of Alex to command the British task force for Operation TORCH, the invasion of French North Africa. That appointment proved short-lived due to circumstances elsewhere in North Africa. At the eastern end of the Mediterranean, Axis forces under Rommel had driven Eighth Army back to the El Alamein line where a spirited defence, conducted by General Auchinleck, brought Panzer Armee Afrika to a stop on 1 July. In the retreat to El Alamein, Tobruk, which had held out for eight months in 1941, had fallen to Rommel* and Churchill had had to face a 'no confidence' vote in parliament. Having survived that vote, Churchill decided to go to Egypt to assess the situation at first hand. This was much to Brooke's chagrin; he had hoped to travel to Egypt himself without the prime minister. Although the two men travelled separately they arrived in Cairo within hours of each other and Brooke was not allowed the opportunity to inspect Middle East Command or Eighth Army without Churchill being present.

* Hitler promoted Rommel to Field Marshal for the capture of Tobruk, making him the youngest of that rank in the German army.

After a brief spell in Cairo and at Eighth Army headquarters in the desert, Churchill decided to remove Auchinleck from his post as C-in-C, Middle East and to appoint Alexander in his place. Following the death of General Gott, Churchill's appointee to command Eighth Army, Bernard Montgomery was chosen to fill that post. The combination of Alexander and Montgomery was to prove most successful. Alex considered Eighth Army the most important element of his command and made it clear to the staff of Middle East Command that Montgomery's army was their first priority. But his overall responsibilities were much greater; Ninth and Tenth Armies were also under his command and his regional responsibilities stretched north into Palestine and Syria, south to the Kenyan border and east to the border with Persia.

Alexander interposed himself as a buffer between Montgomery and Churchill, which allowed Montgomery to prepare without undue pressure from London for the offensive that would be the final battle of El Alamein. One of Churchill's reasons for removing Auchinleck from his post was the latter's insistence that he could not attack before September. Naturally, Churchill had expected more urgency from the new commanders but, instead, found that Montgomery was not prepared to move until October. Alexander supported Montgomery's plans and timing and his endorsement was sufficient to ensure that Churchill accepted the delay. Once again, Alexander's diplomacy proved crucial.

Since the war Montgomery has been portrayed as the general who won the desert war with Alexander's role overlooked. Many Montgomery supporters argue that Alex did as Monty told him to do, a story begun by Montgomery himself. But Alexander played a pivotal role, as a buffer against Churchillian pressure, as an advocate for Eighth Army and its commander, and in providing sound advice when it was needed. It was one of Alexander's senior staff, Richard McCreery, who would be Eighth Army's last commander, who ensured that an error in Montgomery's planning for Operation SUPERCHARGE was corrected, although it took the combined diplomacy of Alex and Freddie de Guingand, Monty's Chief of Staff, to ensure that Montgomery saw McCreery's suggestion as his own and therefore implemented it. In the final phase of the North African campaign, when the fighting had moved into Tunisia, Alexander gave a very clear example of how he could restrain Montgomery when he gave the major role in the advance on Tunis to formations of Lieutenant-General Anderson's First Army in preference to Eighth Army. But he managed to provide Montgomery with an explanation that Eighth Army was there at the end by transferring elements of that army to Anderson's command. And units that had been in Eighth Army were at the forefront of the final battles in Tunisia. Montgomery was thus able to claim that Eighth Army was also there. Honour was satisfied on both sides. Gregory Blaxland, an infantry officer under Alex's command, wrote that

> His final victory in Tunisia proved his versatility, being the perfect example of a knockout punch, and it was in fighting battles, rather than in planning campaigns, that his strength lay.

Alexander had become commander of the new 18 Army Group in February 1943 and was also Deputy Supreme Commander to the American General Dwight Eisenhower. Many of Alexander's doubts about American troops, caused by his experience of Stilwell in Burma, were reinforced by the initial poor performance of American troops in Tunisia, especially the debacle at Kasserine Pass. Those doubts were illustrated by the fact that the commander of II US Corps, Major-General George Patton, had to submit his tactical plans for approval to 18 Army Group's headquarters whereas Montgomery and Anderson were given much more freedom of movement. But working with Eisenhower, who was also extremely diplomatic, must have assuaged some of Alex's doubts and he certainly never expressed these publicly. Although he wrote to Brooke about his concerns, his diplomacy is also evident in his letter.

> We must tread very warily. If they think we are sneering at them – and God forbid that – or that we are being superior, they will take it very badly, as they are a proud people. We must take the line that we are comrades and brothers in arms, and our only wish is for them to share the horrors of war (and the handicaps) and reap the fruits of victory together.

That attitude shaped his future relationships with his American allies and led to a unique partnership in the Mediterranean theatre.

On 10 July 1943 Allied forces invaded Sicily in Operation HUSKY. The invading forces were Seventh US and Eighth British Armies, the former commanded by George Patton and the latter by Montgomery. Alexander commanded what was now 15 Army Group but his diplomatic skills were tested to the limit by his army commanders, both of whom possessed turbo-charged egos. A clash was inevitable: Patton felt that Alexander and Montgomery had conspired to assign a lesser role to Seventh Army; he considered that his command was being relegated to supporting Eighth Army. When Montgomery's command became embroiled in fighting in the mountains above Catania, Patton urged Alexander to allow Seventh Army to sweep for Palermo. From there, Patton drove for Messina which he reached just hours before Eighth Army. But, although Patton could claim to be first in Messina, the Germans had evacuated their forces to mainland Italy, with most of their equipment. The German plan had been for a fighting retreat leading to an evacuation and this had succeeded. In this they may well have been aided by Patton's strike for Palermo; the American had shown a desire to go for a geographical target rather than the military one of destroying the enemy's forces and while this might have been good for public consumption in the United States it may also have allowed many German soldiers to escape to fight another day, this time in Italy. It can be argued that Alexander should have curtailed Patton but this would have led to accusations of favouring Montgomery and wanting the greater share of the glory for the British. Moreover, the political considerations of fighting a coalition war had to be considered, especially as Britain was now the junior partner; this outweighed military realities.

After the Sicilian campaign the Americans agreed to the British plan to invade Italy, described by Churchill as the 'soft underbelly' of Europe. In September 1943, Allied troops invaded mainland Italy, landing at Reggio and Taranto in the very south of the country while, on the shin of Italy, Fifth Army landed in Operation AVALANCHE. Fifth Army, although officially an American formation under General Mark Wayne Clark, was virtually half-British. The invading force included a US corps and X British Corps, under Lieutenant-General Richard McCreery. Clark, who had very little combat experience,* was every bit as egotistical as his countryman George Patton who would probably have commanded Fifth Army had it not been for an incident in Sicily in which he slapped a shell-shocked American soldier in hospital and called him a coward. As the invasion fleet carrying Fifth Army to Salerno sailed for Italy the Italian government surrendered to the Allies and Italy was out of the war, although the country would change sides and fight with the Allies.

Anticipating an Italian surrender, Hitler had prepared for this eventuality. In Operation ALARICH, German forces took over the defence of Italy and a puppet Fascist government was maintained. Fifth Army came ashore at Salerno on 9 September but the reaction of Albert Kesselring, the German commander in southern Italy, was swift, furious and effective. Kesselring placed a ring of steel around the bay of Salerno and the invaders were pounded mercilessly by German artillery and tanks. Kesselring's commanders had identified the Americans as the weak link in the Allied army and launched a series of attacks against VI US Corps, commanded by General Dawley. This caused Dawley to panic and Clark even went so far as to propose lifting VI Corps from the beaches and putting them down again in the British sector. Alexander vetoed this crazy plan as did Admiral Cunningham whose ships would have had to carry it out. Instead, Alexander visited the beachhead to make a personal assessment, as a result of which he considered that Clark could handle the crisis but that Dawley was too weak. He told Clark that he did not want to interfere with his business, i.e., the running of Fifth Army, but that, with some ten years' experience in sizing up commanders, he felt 'I can tell you definitely that you have a broken reed on your hands and I suggest you replace him immediately'. That suggestion summarizes Alexander's method of command. He preferred to work by suggesting solutions rather than by ordering. This was generally successful, as in this case, but there were occasions when individuals such as Clark and Montgomery ignored his suggestions. Monty was apt to describe himself as the thinking partner in Alexander's command structure.

As well as recommending the relief of Dawley, Alexander also offered Clark the use of 82nd US Airborne Division, which was under Army Group command. Clark accepted and General Matt Ridgeway's highly trained paratroopers helped stabilize the Salerno front. They also helped close the gap between VI and X Corps, which the Germans had identified as another weakness on the Allied front. From the gulf of Salerno the firepower of the battleships *Valiant* and *Warspite* smote the hills around

* He had served in France where he was wounded during the Great War.

Salerno. Their heavy guns were augmented by those of many other ships and by artillery on shore, which included heavy anti-aircraft guns firing against enemy artillery positions. After more than a week of heavy shelling, and with the threat of Eighth Army advancing from the toe of Italy, the Germans finally withdrew and the Allies were able to break out of the beachhead. One German prisoner, a veteran of the Russian front, later described the bombardment as the worst he had ever experienced. Alexander's visit to the beachhead had been significant.

> As has been testified by Harding, Alexander had an extraordinary feel for a battlefield, even to the point of knowing where the enemy's shells would land. His presence on one, calm and unostentatious, had remarkable effect on both officers and men, and never did it wield greater influence than at Salerno, when the bridgehead was in jeopardy. There is ample evidence that his one brief but pervasive visit restored confidence and stability when both were dearly needed.

The German tactics at Salerno, although intended initially to push the Allies back into the sea, set the pattern for the Italian campaign. Italy proved to be a 'tough old gut' in contrast to the 'soft underbelly' of Churchill's imagination. During the winter of 1943–4, the Germans held the Allies along the Gustav line, inflicting heavy losses. Montgomery's aim of being in Rome for Christmas was not realized and he himself was called back to Britain to command 21 Army Group in the invasion of France. In an effort to break the deadlock, II Corps of Fifth Army landed at Anzio, south of Rome in Operation SHINGLE on 22 January 1944. But the operation failed to achieve its aim and the Germans continued to hold the Gustav line while an Anglo-American force was besieged in the Anzio beachhead.

The deadlock was finally broken in May 1944 with Operation DIADEM. In a deception plan masterminded by Alexander's Chief of Staff, Major-General A.F. (John) Harding, later Field Marshal Lord Harding, Eighth Army was sidestepped across Italy to the left flank, leaving only a corps on the Adriatic flank. Both Eighth and Fifth Armies then attacked the Gustav line which eventually broke, thanks largely to the work of the French Expeditionary Corps which advanced through the Aurunci mountains and forced the Germans to withdraw. The Monte Cassino position also fell and Eighth Army moved through the Liri valley in pursuit of the Germans. Alexander then ordered the Anzio force to break out from its bridgehead so that the full Allied might would be brought to bear on the retreating German armies, thereby smashing them. What Alex planned was a pincer movement that, if successful, could bring the campaign in Italy to an end in the summer of 1944.

Alexander's plan did not succeed. The reason was the attraction of a geographical objective to Mark Clark. Rome, the Eternal City, lay ahead of the Allies but both sides had accepted the Italian capital as an open city; the Allies had not bombed it and the Germans were not going to hold it. Alexander had no intention of driving his forces towards Rome, but Clark had. Fifth Army's commander disobeyed

Alexander and made for Rome, which fell to the Allies on 4 June 1944, two days before Allied troops landed in Normandy in Operation OVERLORD. Clark's glory was shortlived. He denied that he had disobeyed orders but after the war admitted to journalist Sidney Matthews that he had ordered American soldiers to open fire on any British troops who appeared to be heading for Rome. The kudos of being the liberator of this ancient city blinded Clark to the strategic imperative of destroying the fighting capability of Kesselring's forces in Italy.

However, Alexander never criticized Clark for his behaviour and refused to be drawn into criticism of him. Sir Rupert Clarke, Alex's ADC at the time, believed that 'The Chief must have been very angry' but that

> When Alex was asked about Clark's disregard for his orders, the Chief replied, 'I am for any line which the Army Commander believes will offer a chance to continue his present success'. It was so much in line with his self-less approach to his position, in which he believed that his job was to enable his Army Commanders to win their victories.

Rupert Clarke also noted that Mark Clark was

> Nobody's fool and knowing Alex as he did, Clark had clearly gambled that, providing his ploy came off, he would get away with it and bring great kudos to the American Army – and himself.

As Rupert Clarke states, Alexander was selfless to the point that he would not openly criticize his own generals, even long after the event, and nor would he respond to criticism of how he had handled operations from some of those same generals, even though he must frequently have been hurt by some of their comments. Those subordinate generals and his staff, such as Rupert Clarke, knew that Alexander was a true gentleman, and this quality was one of the factors that allowed him to command such diverse Allied forces effectively. Sixty years later it is easy to forget how many nations were included in Alexander's armies. There were soldiers from Britain – English, Scots, Irish, Welsh, Manx and Channel Islanders – Canada, New Zealand, South Africa, India, France, Morocco, Tunisia, Algeria, Rhodesia, Basutoland, Bechuanaland, Nepal, Belgium, Greece, Yugoslavia, Poland, Mauritius, Brazil and Mexico among others. The US forces even included Japanese soldiers – the Nisei or Japanese-Americans who had been born in the United States – while Italy, at first described as a co-belligerent partner, later joined the Allies. Alexander had over twenty nationalities under his command,* many with differing political and strategic objectives; holding together such an alliance demanded the wisdom and tact of Solomon and Alexander was one of the very few with the gifts of personality to carry out the task. They also provided a supply problem since the standard ration issue for

---

* In his *Despatch* he notes that there were twenty-six different nations in the Allied forces in Italy.

a British soldier could not be used for a Muslim or Hindu. But this was something that the British Army was used to and with which it coped even in difficult circumstances; so, too, did the French Corps, which also included many Muslims in its ranks.

A regular criticism of Alexander is that he was not an intelligent commander, that he lacked that little extra ounce of intellect that would have made him a military genius. While he may not have been a military genius, his critics tend to ignore Alexander's natural ability, an ability that meant he never appeared to exert himself in the same manner as Montgomery or Patton or Clark. The calm courage that he demonstrated so clearly during the Great War, at Dunkirk and in the retreat from Burma showed that he was cool and collected in any circumstances; his deeply felt sense of duty would never have allowed him to show any signs of stress or uncertainty.

However, Alexander possessed a quality that challenges the comments of those who questioned his intelligence; he was an excellent judge of men. His choice of staff officers was inspired and he knew how to delegate responsibility and allow subordinates to carry out their tasks. This, surely, is one of the hallmarks of a great commander. While Alexander's diplomatic skills were an important asset in the Italian campaign his ability to select good staff officers was probably of equal importance. The classic example must be John Harding, his Chief of Staff, who, as we have seen, was the mastermind behind the deception plan that allowed Operation DIADEM to be launched without the enemy realizing that it was about to happen. Alexander gave much of the responsibility for the planning of DIADEM to Harding and was confident that his subordinate would not let him down. Earlier, in the Middle East, he had also recognized the qualities of Richard McCreery, whose intervention at Eighth Army headquarters was crucial to the success of Operation SUPERCHARGE.

Two days after the fall of Rome the Allies landed in Normandy and the liberation of northwest Europe had begun. The Americans had never shared the British enthusiasm for operations in the Mediterranean, seeing them as indicating a British desire to protect the empire – which the Americans wanted to see dismantled – more than a strategy driven by military necessity; Brooke believed that the Allies should tighten the ring on Germany before moving in for the main assault and one of the regions in which that ring could be tightened was the Mediterranean. Now the US planners turned their attention from Italy to southern France. Operation ANVIL, an invasion of southern France, had been intended to coincide with D-Day in Normandy but, under British pressure, the Americans had agreed to a postponement. The British had assumed that the plan would be dropped completely but it was revived as Operation DRAGOON, a landing by Seventh US Army on the French Mediterranean coast; D-Day for DRAGOON was to be 15 August. This was to have serious consequences for Alexander's armies in Italy.

The fall of Rome was followed by a parallel pursuit by the two Allied armies that was stopped by the Germans at Lake Trasimene; this allowed the Germans to carry out a fighting retreat to their next major defensive line, the Gothic line. However, Alexander was planning a major offensive that would smash the Gothic line, allow Fifth and Eighth Armies to burst into the plain of Lombardy and bring the war in Italy to an end in the autumn of 1944. It might also allow an invasion of Austria through the Lubljana Gap, but this was unlikely to have succeeded.

Alexander's armies lost 100,000 men to Operation DRAGOON, thereby intensifying the manpower shortage in Italy, especially in Eighth Army. The latter had received no reinforcements from the United Kingdom since February and was told to find casualty replacements from within the Mediterranean area. This did not augur well for Alexander's planned offensive, Operation OLIVE. When the attack was launched in August it came tantalizingly close to success. While Fifth and Eighth Armies may not have broken through the Gothic line they had broken into it and the manpower lost to DRAGOON might have made all the difference, especially General Juin's French Expeditionary Corps with its mountain fighting skills. However, the attackers bogged down and Allied soldiers were condemned to another long, wet and cold Italian winter.

In April 1945 the Allied armies finally broke through the German defences into the plain of Lombardy. By now the army group was under Mark Clark's command, Alexander having been appointed Supreme Commander in the Mediterranean; he was now Field Marshal Alexander, having been raised to that rank in November 1944, although his promotion was backdated to June 1944 to maintain his seniority to Montgomery in the Army List. Eighth Army was commanded by Sir Richard McCreery and Fifth Army by Lucian Truscott, one of the best American generals of the war. Together their armies executed a superb operation that is still regarded as a masterpiece in its use of armour and infantry. Paradoxically, this took place under the overall command of a man who had been criticized for 'sadly mishandling' armour just a few years earlier. On 2 May 1945 Alexander accepted the surrender of all German forces in Italy and Austria; the long slog through the 'tough old gut' was over and victory in Italy came just days before the surrender of all German forces in Germany.

As Supreme Allied Commander in the Mediterranean, Alexander had been given many more responsibilities than the Italian campaign. One of these was Greece where a German withdrawal in late-1944 created a political vacuum that became civil war and threatened to take Greece into the communist bloc. Typically, Alex went to Greece to take command of the situation and his decisions and prompt actions, which included taking formations from Eighth Army in Italy, ensured that Greece did not become part of the Soviet empire in 1945.

In the New Year Honours' List of 1946, Alexander was created Viscount Alexander of Tunis and Errigal, combining his greatest military triumph with memories of boyhood holidays in County Donegal; he later became Earl Alexander. It had been expected that he would become CIGS but, instead, he was appointed Governor-

General of Canada, a post in which he proved extremely popular. He enjoyed working with Canadians and, although the question of French-Canadian separatism had not yet become acute, Alexander showed a sensitivity that made him as popular in Quebec as in Ontario. He improved his French with lessons from a nun, Mother St Thomas, in Ottawa and his speeches in Quebec were made in French.

In 1952 Sir Winston Churchill, who was again prime minister, appointed Alexander to his cabinet as Minister of Defence. The most important concern for the defence ministry was the Korean War and Alexander travelled to visit Commonwealth troops in the front line. However, as he was no politician, he became very unhappy in the post and, in the autumn of 1953, told Churchill that he would prefer to leave the cabinet for personal reasons. In the October cabinet reshuffle his place as Minister of Defence was taken by another former guardsman, Harold Macmillan. Thus ended the brief political career, and the public life, of Churchill's favourite general.

Basil Liddell Hart, one of the twentieth century's leading military commentators, wrote of Alexander that he was

> a born leader, not a made one. He won men's confidence at first sight. He was good looking in every sense, yet self-effacing to the point of handicapping his own powers.

And Lord Louis Mountbatten summed him up in these words:

> He was essentially kindhearted in every way. He was such a gentleman he put up with insubordination. I never did. I fired senior officers or governors if they crossed me and I was convinced they were in the wrong ... I was far less popular than Alex for that very reason ... Alex was beloved by everyone because he had never harmed anybody.

~ 4 ~

Dill

Arlington National Cemetery in Virginia, just outside Washington DC, once the family estate of General Robert E. Lee, the Confederate army's famous Civil War commander, is the resting place of some of America's greatest heroes and a focus for the nation's remembrance of its sons and daughters who died on active service. But among these American heroes lies a field marshal of the British Army, an Irishman who was so respected by his American colleagues that, when he died in the United States in 1944, he was given the privilege of burial in Arlington. As Winston Churchill wrote:

> He was accorded the unique honour of a resting place in Arlington Cemetery, the Valhalla hitherto reserved exclusively for American warriors.

The man of whom Churchill wrote was Field Marshal Sir John Dill, the vital link in Washington in the Anglo-American alliance from January 1942 until his untimely death on 4 November 1944. Dill represented Churchill as Minister of Defence, and was recognized by the Americans as an outstanding individual who did much to cement the alliance and make it work effectively in spite of the many differences on both sides that might have damaged seriously the Allied war effort. Churchill's posthumous tribute to Dill stands in stark contrast to his earlier attitude to him; when Dill was CIGS, Churchill had called him 'Dilly-Dally' and then removed him from that post.

For a man who rose to the British Army's highest rank, John Greer Dill came from an unusual background. Born the son of a banker in Lurgan, County Armagh, on Christmas Day 1881, he was only twelve when his father died. Months later, his mother also died. Both John and his sister were then cared for by an uncle, the Reverend Joseph Grundy Burton, a parish clergyman and ardent anti-home rule campaigner. Perhaps Dill was remembering something of his uncle's attitudes when he later recalled the Lurgan of his boyhood days as somewhere

> the Pope was not very well spoken of. In my youth I have seen Orangemen on sidecars driving down what they called Papish streets spoiling for a fight and getting it.

Part of his early education – from 1887 to 1889 – was in Belfast's Methodist College, which his sister Nicolina Frances also attended. John then went to school in Cheltenham in Gloucestershire before entering Sandhurst. His decision to enter the Army seemed unusual and may have been as a result of influences at Cheltenham College, as there was no military tradition in the Dill family. In those dying years of the nineteenth century, the sons of bank managers were not considered the normal stuff from which Army officers were made.

Dill's conduct at the Royal Military College was described as exemplary but there were no indications of the outstanding intelligence for which he would later be noted and his marks were described as mediocre. From Sandhurst he was commissioned into an Irish infantry regiment, of which there were then eight,* joining the Prince of Wales's Leinster Regiment in 1901. He later recalled that it was 'a serious thing for a black northerner like me to be thrown among a lot of gossoons from King's County' but they mixed and learned to like and respect each other. The mixing took place amid the turmoil of war as Dill joined 1st Leinsters in South Africa in the final stages of the South African, or Boer, War. After the war, Lieutenant Dill became the battalion's adjutant and quickly demonstrated an aptitude for staff duties; the ponderous schoolboy was developing into a sharp-minded soldier. In 1913 he attended Staff College where he studied under Sir William 'Wully' Robertson, later Field Marshal Lord Robertson and CIGS, the first man to have risen through all the ranks from private soldier to field marshal. Staff College certainly made Dill; his talents for planning and problem solving were discovered and honed during his year at Camberley and were soon to be put to the toughest test of all – war.

On the outbreak of the Great War, on 4 August 1914, Captain John Dill was serving on the staff of Eastern Command in England but by the end of the year he was brigade major of an infantry brigade in France. The conflict was then settling into the pattern of trench warfare that would last until March 1918 while the majority of the old Regular Army that had constituted the British Expeditionary Force had been killed or wounded in France and Flanders. Promotion was rapid for those who survived the early battles and especially for those with ability. Dill was one such and in January 1916 he was appointed as a divisional staff officer. This involved him in the Somme battles that raged from July to November that year but, as the Somme campaign drew to a close, Dill was moved to the Canadian Corps where his experience was valued highly. Perhaps his new comrades also appreciated the fact that Major Dill's regiment, the Leinsters, bore the secondary title 'Royal Canadians'.† However, his time with the Canadians was short; he was promoted to lieutenant-colonel in January 1917 and posted to 37th Division as its GSO1, or senior staff officer.

---

* These were the Royal Irish Regiment, Royal Inniskilling Fusiliers, Royal Irish Rifles, Princess Victoria's (Royal Irish Fusiliers), Connaught Rangers, Leinster Regiment (Royal Canadians), Royal Munster Fusiliers and Royal Dublin Fusiliers. The Irish Guards were formed in 1900 during the South African War; Guards regiments are not included in the Infantry of the Line.
† The Regiment had been raised by the Canadian government for service in the Indian Mutiny and was then handed over to the War Office. It was given the territorial title Leinster in the Childers reforms of 1881, although it had already had many Irish soldiers in its ranks.

In December 1917 Lieutenant-Colonel Dill was transferred to general headquarters in France to take charge of training, although he later became responsible for operational planning. When he moved to GHQ the German high command was planning a major offensive against the Allies, which was due to take place on the western front in March 1918. The October revolution had precipitated Russia's departure from the war and the Germans were able to move armies from the eastern front in readiness for Operation MICHAEL, the spring offensive of 1918. This was an attempt to knock the British and French out of the war or, at the least, bring them to the negotiating table, before significant numbers of American troops could arrive. Operation MICHAEL failed in its objective. It did not break the British armies that took the brunt of the offensive and, although casualties were high, British and Allied planners began preparations for their own offensive. One of the principal brains in that planning was that of Brigadier-General John Dill.

The Allied offensive was launched in August, with British troops playing the major role. Soon the Germans were forced onto the retreat. War on the western front had once again become one of movement as German armies were forced back along the front. In November the Germans asked for an armistice and the fighting ended at 11.00am on 11 November 1918. More recent historians of the Great War have used the operations of those final months of war as proof of the ability of Field Marshal Earl Haig, who commanded the Allied armies. This is a valid argument but the British Official History of the war identifies clearly John Dill as 'the real operations brain in GHQ'.

Bernard Montgomery was one among many critics of the staff in the Great War and from their comments it might be assumed that Dill had a relatively comfortable war, well away from the fighting and the danger. This is far from true as Dill spent much time in the lines rather than back at a rear headquarters. He earned the soubriquet 'Devil Dill' for his courage in action; that courage was also recognized by the award of the DSO. Dill was wounded in action and received no fewer than eight Mentions in Despatches. By the end of the war he was a highly decorated soldier with an unequalled reputation as a planner; his ability also earned him the Order of St Michael and St George. Thus the cadet who had not excelled intellectually at Sandhurst two decades earlier had achieved recognition as one of the finest brains in the Army. The bank manager's son had come a long way.

It was hardly surprising that Dill should find himself posted to the Staff College as an instructor after the war and in 1919 he was imparting his knowledge to students, all of whom were officers who had ended the war with a high reputation and had been recommended specially for attendance. This was the selection procedure for the first two post-war Camberley courses and both depended more on active participation in discussion seminars than in lecturing to orderly rows of students. By 1926 Dill had moved on to the new Imperial Defence College, established to bring senior officers from all three services closer together and to identify men who could control those services as a single entity. That Dill was involved in the foundation of such a development was entirely logical and illustrated further his abilities.

In spite of his undoubted abilities, Dill was subject, as were all his fellows, to a basic reality of inter-war Army life: promotion was slow. This was the era of the 'drunkard's bob' when a long service subaltern received an extra shilling – 'bob' in common parlance – that was allegedly invariably spent on drink to ward off boredom. Not until January 1931 was Dill finally promoted to major-general and appointed to command the Staff College. During his three-year tenure at Camberley he influenced many top commanders of the Second World War, who passed through the college as students or instructors. He also changed the way in which the College worked, developing the syndicate system that continues to this day and has been adopted by many other colleges. One of his students, Brian Horrocks, described him as 'a man of the greatest integrity, great charm and with a first class brain'.

There could be no doubt that someone with Dill's analytical mind would be a candidate for some of the Army's most senior staff appointments and, after his time at Camberley, he was appointed Director, Military Operations and Intelligence at the War Office. Those around him were coming to the view that Dill was more than a good staff officer; he was also the outstanding military thinker of his generation. To civilian ears the term 'staff officer' has a mundane sound. More than that, it can even arouse a feeling close to contempt, based on the longstanding allegations that Great War staff officers had soft and safe jobs well away from the front line and that such men were apt to spill the blood of the fighting soldier for no apparent reason. But staff officers are the keystone of any army; it is they who plan battles, campaigns and wars, who ensure that soldiers in the field are supplied with all that they need to live on and fight with and to treat them should they be wounded. Bad staff officers can lose battles. Good staff officers win wars. And John Greer Dill was now being seen as one of the best staff officers ever to grace the British Army.

From the War Office, Lieutenant-General Dill was posted to Palestine to command the small British garrison that was being reinforced following the Arab Rebellion that erupted in April 1936. After the Great War, Britain had been given a mandate by the League of Nations to govern Palestine but, by the mid-30s, the situation in that country was causing international concern. Palestine had a small Jewish community that was expanding with the influx of refugees from Germany. At this point Britain was assisting Jewish refugees to settle but Palestine's Arabs saw this as a threat; this caused tensions to rise and led to rebellion. Arab guerrillas attacked Jews and sabotaged roads, railways, telegraph wires and the oil pipeline to Haifa while a body known as the Arab High Commission organized a general strike in an attempt to force the British administration to stop Jewish immigration. Thus, when Dill arrived in Palestine, the garrison was changing its role from one of guarding installations and communications to the more active and effective one of carrying out offensive operations against Arab guerrillas.

Dill's sojourn in Palestine lasted a year until he was recalled to Britain to become GOC Home Command at Aldershot. Although this was one of the Army's top jobs it was almost a consolation prize for Dill, who ought to have been in an even higher position. In 1937 the Secretary of State for War, Leslie Hore-Belisha, interviewed Dill for the post of CIGS. According to Liddell Hart, Dill was the best candidate for the post 'on his record and strategic grasp' but the appointment went to Lord Gort of Limerick vc. Although an outstandingly courageous man, Gort proved a lacklustre CIGS and a personality clash developed between him and Hore-Belisha. This was exacerbated to the extent that the pair were barely on speaking terms, which, with war looming in Europe, did not augur well for Britain.

The appointment of GOC Home Command carried with it the understanding that the incumbent would command any future expeditionary force. At this stage the government had no plans for such a force, but military analysts realized that one would be essential. The cabinet finally decided to create a British Expeditionary Force when Hitler tore up the Munich Agreement in the spring of 1939. But Dill was to be denied the appointment, losing out again to Gort. In spite of their differences, or perhaps because of them, Hore-Belisha appointed Gort to command the BEF and Dill was not even appointed to Gort's former post of CIGS, which went to General Sir Edmund Ironside. Instead, he was given command of I Corps in the BEF. He had been disappointed in 1937 and now, in 1939, he was twice disappointed. But he was philosophical enough to realize that all was not yet lost, writing that

> I have no real complaint. I have lived long enough to know that these things have a way of righting themselves if one leaves them alone

He may well have been considering the fact that appointment as CIGS in the approach to a major war might not have been the most desirable thing for anyone. As the historians of the British Chiefs of Staff comment:

> Sadly it never pays to be a British Chief at the outbreak of a major war. The Chiefs in office when war is declared become scapegoats, who must carry on their backs into the wilderness not only the sins of past governments, but also the peacetime misjudgements of their predecessors.

'These things', as he described them, left Dill with a fundamental distrust of politicians; he saw Hore-Belisha as the source of many of the Army's woes through his muddled lack of knowledge of military affairs. In fairness to Hore-Belisha, however, he had tried to achieve a greater slice of the defence budget for the Army, a campaign that he and Gort had cooperated on, despite their personal rancour.

When the BEF embarked for France in late-1939 Dill took his I Corps headquarters across the channel but he had not been long in France when 'things righted themselves'. In April 1940 he was recalled to London and appointed Vice-Chief of the Imperial General Staff. His arrival brought a sense of purpose and authority into the War Office, which had behaved like a rudderless ship beforehand. But his first impressions of the War Office were far from positive.

The War Office is, as far as I can see, in complete chaos and the situation in Norway as bad as I expected ... I'm not sure that Winston isn't the greatest menace. No one seems able to control him. He is full of ideas, many brilliant but most of them impracticable. He has such drive and personality that no one seems able to stand up to him.

'Winston' was, of course, Winston Churchill, then First Lord of the Admiralty and soon to be prime minister. Dill was clearly not impressed by what he saw as Churchill's meddling and, as a Great War veteran, recalled Churchill's part in the tragedy of Gallipoli. The pair were soon to be thrown together even closer in the weeks and months that lay ahead. On 10 May 1940 German forces invaded the Low Countries and, on that same day, Churchill became Prime Minister; the architect of Gallipoli now became the fulcrum of British strategic planning. However, it would be both unfair and untrue to say that Churchill had no military knowledge. He had served in the Army and had seen active service in the Sudan, India and South Africa. After Gallipoli he had resigned from the cabinet and returned to the Army, commanding a battalion of Royal Scots Fusiliers on the western front. In addition to this practical experience of soldiering and, at battalion level, of command he also had a considerable amount of theoretical knowledge, much of it gained from his study of military history. He had written a book, *The World Crisis*, about the Great War and had also produced a study of his ancestor John Churchill, first Duke of Marlborough, which remains a classic of its genre.

His study of Marlborough had been acclaimed so highly as a thorough analysis of Marlborough the strategic commander that Churchill appears to have begun to think of himself as a similar strategic genius. Although there is no doubt that Churchill did possess great strategic vision, this particular conceit of his was to have serious consequences for many of his generals as the war progressed. While Churchill saw himself as a military man and wore uniform as often as possible,* the Army saw him solely as a politician and, all too often, as a nuisance. Dill was the first to come into close contact with the new premier on a daily basis and quickly recognized that he had to stand up to Churchill. General Sir Hastings 'Pug' Ismay, later Lord Ismay, Churchill's personal staff officer as Minister of Defence, referred to what he termed the 'one thing that was necessary, and indeed that Winston preferred – someone to stand up to him'.

Ismay and others have claimed that Dill did not stand up to Churchill but this is not true. It is an assertion that took root in the post-war years and is largely due to comments Churchill made about Dill in his history of the war, *The Second World War*, which is as much, if not more, an autobiography as it is a history. Those of the prime minister's entourage, including Ismay, who later produced their own accounts of the war years seemed to be mesmerized by the Churchillian version and reproduced his criticisms of Dill as though these were their own considered opinions.

---

* He was entitled to do so through honorary ranks in both the Army and RAF.

Napoleon's comment that history is 'the agreed lie' finds justification in the treatment of men such as Dill and Auchinleck.

By the end of May 1940 Dill had succeeded Ironside as CIGS and, as the Army's chief, fought his corner against Churchill when necessary. However, he was completely unprepared for the prime minister's behaviour. Churchill had been so long in parliament that parliamentary manners were now second nature to him. In common with most politicians he did not give a single thought to insulting an opponent across the floor of the house and then having a drink with him in the bar. However, to a soldier such behaviour was alien and few of Churchill's military associates were ever able fully to come to terms with it.

One December evening in 1940 Dill returned to his Whitehall office after a long and tiring meeting with Churchill and Anthony Eden, the Secretary of State for War. Clearly agitated, he told one of his staff:

> I cannot tell you how angry the Prime Minister has made me. What he said about the Army tonight I can never forgive. He complained he could get nothing done ... He wished he had Papagos [the Greek general] to run it. He asked me to wait and have a drink with him after the meeting, but I refused and left Eden there by himself.

Dill had become CIGS at a time of great turmoil for the Army and the country. The BEF was being evacuated from France and the French government appeared to have lost its will to continue resisting the Germans. Among Dill's first tasks, as VCIGS, had been to accompany Churchill to France to meet the French government and persuade them to remain in the war. Churchill even offered an indissoluble union of Britain and France if only they would continue the struggle. His offer was in vain, but Dill impressed the French with his grasp of the strategic situation, an assessment with which those British politicians present agreed. But he was an inherently shy man and not the type of individual who tries to project his own image; such behaviour would have been anathema to most Army officers of his generation. Churchill, mistaking Dill's gentlemanly manner, modesty and shyness for indecisiveness, began to call his CIGS 'Dilly-Dally'.

Dill's early days as CIGS witnessed the evacuation of the BEF and the fall of France. For neither of these calamities could he be held in any way responsible and thus there was a honeymoon period in his relationship with Churchill. In December 1940 the success of Operation COMPASS in North Africa, and the destruction of Tenth Italian Army, allowed the Army to shine in a more favourable light in Churchill's eyes. But the premier himself was to throw away all that had been gained in North Africa and then blame his generals, including Dill, for the subsequent disasters.

In February 1941 Churchill decided that Greece needed British assistance in its war with Italy and sent Anthony Eden and Dill to meet Lieutenant-General Sir Archibald Wavell, C-in-C, Middle East, to discuss how best this might be done. Dill was not keen on any British intervention, as he believed that this would only lead to the Germans coming to Italy's support. The Greeks, sharing Dill's view, refused offers of British support. But Churchill was persistent; he envisaged an alliance of Greece, Turkey and Yugoslavia opposing the Germans with British support. Eventually Dill and Eden were persuaded to accept the prime minister's idea of British intervention in Greece to support an anti-Nazi Balkan bloc. The pair flew to Ankara and Athens to try to form the alliance that Churchill wanted and, in the meantime, the plan for British intervention in Greece was implemented. But no alliance materialized; Turkey remained neutral* and Yugoslavia attempted to appease both sides before splitting in two with a Nazi puppet state in Croatia and German troops occupying the rest of the country. When Bulgaria joined the Axis, German forces had free passage to Greece. Wavell was forced to withdraw British formations from the desert for Greece but the Greeks already had the upper hand against the Italians and the net result of the arrival of British troops was that the Germans came in to back the Italians, as Dill had predicted. The Allies then had to evacuate Greece and Crete with heavy losses.

The Germans had also intervened in North Africa, sending a small expeditionary force under Major-General Erwin Rommel to Libya. This force, Deutsches Afrika Korps, began disembarking in Tripoli in February 1941 and, in the following month, attacked the British in Libya. Before Easter all the gains of Operation COMPASS had been lost and one of Britain's finest generals, Richard O'Connor, had been made prisoner. At this black time for Britain, Churchill needed a scapegoat. He was unlikely to blame himself, although much of the blame lay at his door, and so Dill, as CIGS, suffered his wrath. This led to a further deterioration in their already strained relationship, which was aggravated even further in May when the pair clashed over Egypt's strategic importance.

Since North Africa was the only theatre where British† ground forces were still engaging the Germans, Churchill attached great importance to Egypt and was prepared to reduce Britain's home defences to reinforce the desert army; he was especially keen to send tanks to Egypt. Dill disagreed and on 6 May 1941 presented Churchill with a rationally argued paper that ran to about a thousand words on the relative importance of Egypt vis-à-vis the United Kingdom. In his paper, 'The Relation of the Middle East to the United Kingdom', Dill began by discussing the possibility of a German invasion of Britain:

> The probability of invasion may seem to have receded for the moment, but the German land and air forces could be concentrated for invasion within six to eight weeks of their release from the Balkan theatre. As American aid grows the enemy must be closely watching for a favourable opportunity to launch the campaign which might win him the war.

* Turkey finally declared war on Germany in 1945.
† Many of the British formations in Middle East Command were from the Commonwealth and the Empire; these included Australian, New Zealand, South African and Indian divisions.

Outlining the state of British defences on land, at sea and in the air, Dill then considered the difficulties that would face the Germans in any invasion:

> It is dangerous to discount the possibility of heavy armoured attack on the grounds that Germany has not command of the sea; that our air force would destroy the expedition before it sailed and on the beaches, or would sweep its supporting air force out of the sky; or that the technical difficulties of landing on such a scale would be insuperable. It would take five to seven days for us to concentrate adequate naval forces in home waters. Our bombers cannot deal with more than six invasion ports effectively and then only if the weather is favourable. Air attack cannot be relied on to break up a disembarkation, any more than it did our embarkation at Dunkirk. Our fighters will not neutralise completely the enemy's bombers if he is ready to face the heavy losses which he will certainly incur ... As for technical difficulties of landing the Germans have given many proofs of their skill and thoroughness in planning and in the preparation of special equipment; and they have had time to perfect their arrangements ... We underestimated the Germans in Norway and in Belgium, and recent events in Libya and the Balkans have taught us once more their capacity for overcoming the most formidable obstacles.

But what of Egypt?

> The loss of Egypt would be a calamity which I do not regard as likely, and one which we would not accept without a most desperate fight; but it would not end the war. A successful invasion alone spells our final defeat. It is the United Kingdom therefore and not Egypt that is vital, and the defence of the United Kingdom must take first place. Egypt is not even second in order of priority, for it has been an accepted principle in our strategy that in the last resort the security of Singapore comes before that of Egypt. Yet the defences of Singapore are still considerably below standard.
>
> Risks must of course be taken in war, but they must be calculated risks. We must not fall in to the error of whittling away the security of vital points. If need be, we must cut our losses in places that are not vital before it is too late.

The paper made Churchill, very angry. He accused Dill of defeatism and replied that, while he accepted some of Dill's points, he could not accept all of them. Mischievously, he accused Dill of being prepared to throw away the army in Egypt, accept the loss of that country and the surrender of some half-million servicemen rather than lose Singapore. Churchill wrote that he did not take that view and did not believe the alternative was likely to present itself. Of course, he had misinterpreted deliberately what Dill had written, for the CIGS had stated clearly that Egypt would not be given up without a fight; he had also noted that he did not think it likely to happen.

On the basis of this exchange it would be difficult to accuse Dill of failing to stand up to Churchill. However, his opposition was far from effective as he was still unable to adapt to Churchill's idiosyncratic behaviour. Not only did he have to deal with the prime minister's parliamentary mannerisms, but also had to suffer his wild mood swings, the result of Churchill's battle with depression. Perhaps had Dill stood in the prime minister's office and argued violently with him Churchill may have listened more closely to his views but such was not Dill's style. Moreover, the frequent calls to dinner with Churchill, the talking into the small hours, the weekends spent at Chequers all proved extremely wearing for Dill. This may even have been a manifestation of the health problems that would lead to his death in November 1944. Churchill's confidence in Dill was evaporating throughout 1941 and, by the autumn, he had decided to replace him as CIGS. His successor was another Irishman, General Sir Alan Brooke, who would remain as CIGS for the rest of the war. Brooke did stand up to Churchill, although he also found the prime minister's behaviour wearing, and his being seen to do so was vital to all three services. But it can be argued that Dill had paved the way for Brooke. On 18 November 1941 Dill stood down from his duties as CIGS although he was officially in post until his birthday, 25 December.

Following his retirement, Dill was to become Governor of Bombay, a ceremonial post with few responsibilities but with 'a bodyguard of lancers'. However, on 7 December 1941, the Imperial Japanese Navy attacked the US Pacific Fleet at Pearl Harbor in Hawaii and America was in the war. Four days later, Germany and Italy also declared war on the USA and before long Churchill was crossing the Atlantic to confer with Roosevelt, taking with him a group of military advisers. Among those advisers, at the behest of Brooke, who had to take over at the War Office, was General Sir John Dill.

Earlier in 1941 Dill had met his American counterpart, General George Marshall, and the two men had got on well. Recognizing this mutual respect, Churchill decided to appoint Dill to lead the British Joint Staff Mission in Washington DC and be the senior British representative on the Combined Chiefs of Staff Committee. He was also promoted to field marshal, the highest rank in the Army. Dill was the ideal choice for this appointment for not only did he enjoy Marshall's respect and friendship but he was also respected and liked by senior American servicemen who saw him as a man devoid of the pomposity, snobbery and patronizing manner that they associated with senior British officers. As a result of this mutual respect, Dill was able to make progress with plans and proposals in Washington. Correlli Barnett described him as

> a man with exactly the qualities of high professional ability, personal integrity and tact needed to create a fruitful working relationship with the leaders of the American fighting services. As the personal representative of Churchill in

his capacity of Minister of Defence, Dill also enjoyed direct access to President Roosevelt.

Churchill had emphasized Dill's role as his plenipotentiary with the US President and others in a private note in which he told the former that he would, from time to time, receive guidance from the prime minister that would allow him to represent Churchill's views. Dill was also authorized to correspond directly with Churchill when necessary.

There was a certain humorous irony in this situation that Dill recognized and on which he commented in a letter to Wavell soon after his appointment to Washington.

> It is odd that Winston should want me to represent him here when he was clearly glad to get me out of the CIGS job. We disagreed too often ... among other things, on what we should do for the Far East.

Dill now enjoyed an almost independent authority in his liaison with US officials. In addition to his friendship with Marshall, he also established close links with Harry Hopkins, Roosevelt's personal adviser. But it was the friendship with Marshall that would prove crucial to the Allied war effort for the pair worked as a team and their efforts were not marred by chauvinism. This was especially important since Marshall did not like Brooke, Dill's successor as CIGS, whom he regarded as being too cold and calculating, an unfortunate misjudgement shared by a number of other senior Americans. In addition, Marshall was wary of Churchill who, in turn, believed the Chiefs of both nations were apt to combine against him. In contrast, Marshall reposed complete trust in Dill, calling him the 'finest soldier and greatest gentleman I have ever known'. Dill and Marshall shared information on a regular basis, preparing together privately for Combined Chiefs' meetings and Dill was often able to give Marshall advance notice of Roosevelt's intentions. This he was able to do since Churchill would have informed Dill of those intentions. Marshall would then pass on the information to the US Chiefs with the warning that, until they had received notification from the White House, they did 'not officially have' the information provided by Dill.

For his part Dill had an equally high opinion of Marshall. He wrote that

> Marshall improves greatly on further acquaintance. His difficulties are immense, but he is straight, clearheaded and undoubtedly dominates the conferences on the American side.

For the American Chiefs, however, Dill was more than simply the senior British service representative in Washington; he was also a guarantor of British behaviour, a man to be trusted in all respects since he was incapable of duplicity. Lord Moran, Churchill's doctor, wrote of watching Dill and Marshall in conversation and of how Dill appeared to hang on Marshall's every word. According to Moran, Dill's openness and trustworthiness were obvious. And these were the two men who made the concept of the Combined Chiefs of Staff work effectively, and as one American commentator observed

> Not as a mere collecting point for individual rivalries between services and nations but as an executive committee for the prosecution of global war.

Stating that Dill was crucial to the smooth working of the Anglo-American alliance would not be an exaggeration since, through his work with the Combined Chiefs, Britain had, as Dill himself noted,

> the constitutional right to discuss her needs on equal terms instead of receiving gratefully such crumbs as may be left from the rich man's table.

Unfortunately, Dill's health was deteriorating. He suffered from an incurable form of anaemia and the pressures of his position could only have exacerbated the deterioration. However, he continued to work at reinforcing the Anglo-American relationship and being the pivot of military cooperation between the two allied nations. It is significant that the first major Allied dispute over strategy in the Mediterranean in 1944 occurred when Sir John Dill was in hospital and unable to mediate. The American Chiefs went ahead with their plans for Operation DRAGOON, an invasion of southern France, which the British saw as being strategically wasteful since it deprived Allied forces in Italy of manpower that might have brought the Italian campaign to an end in 1944.[*]

Sir John Dill died in the United States on 4 November 1944. A memorial service was held in the National Cathedral in Washington at which General Marshall read the lesson. The funeral cortege then wound its way along a route lined by thousands of soldiers to Arlington National Cemetery where the coffin was transferred to a gun carriage drawn by six grey horses. The US Joint Chiefs acted as honorary pallbearers as the coffin, draped with the Union flag, was carried to the graveside. Salutes were fired over the grave, Last Post and Reveille sounded and official America mourned a British field marshal. One American present described the scene vividly, 'I have never seen so many men so visibly stricken by grief. Marshall's face was truly stricken'. Sir John Dill had made a remarkable impression on his American colleagues and friends and some may have considered it highly appropriate that this gentleman general be laid to rest on what had been the land of another gentleman general, the Virginian Robert E. Lee.

---

[*] Originally planned as Operation ANVIL to coincide with Operation OVERLORD, the invasion of Normandy, this was postponed from its planned date but the Americans went ahead with it on 15 August in order to open shipping lines through the Mediterranean to a southern French port. This proved valuable to the armies on the continent with the failure to open the Scheldt estuary.

The US Joint Chiefs sent a unique message to their British counterparts conveying their condolences at

> The loss to our combined war effort resulting from the death of Field Marshal
> Sir John Dill. His character and wisdom, his selfless devotion to the Allied
> cause, made his contribution to the combined British-American war effort of
> outstanding importance. It is not too much to say that probably no other indi-
> vidual was more responsible for the achievement of complete co-operation in
> the work of the Combined Chiefs of Staff ... We mourn with you the passing
> of a great and wise soldier and a great gentleman. His task in this war has
> been well done.

Could any greater tribute have been paid to a truly outstanding general?

~ 5 ~

O'Connor

Early on the morning of 9 December 1940 the British Western Desert Force launched a surprise attack on Tenth Italian Army's positions at Sidi Barrani in Egypt. Operation COMPASS led to the rout of Tenth Army and a telegram from Churchill to General Sir Archibald Wavell, C-in-C, Middle East, congratulating him on winning the battle of Sidi Barrani. Churchill told Wavell that the 'Army of the Nile'* had given 'glorious service' to the Empire and to the Allied cause and that Britain was already reaping rewards 'in every quarter'.

The victory passed into legend in Britain as the success of 'Wavell's thirty thousand' but while Churchill congratulated Wavell and asked him also to convey congratulations to Air Vice Marshal Longmore, commanding the Royal Air Force in the Middle East, he did not congratulate the man who commanded Western Desert Force and was the chief architect of victory. That man, Lieutenant-General Richard O'Connor, was also overlooked by the press at home, although he was recognized by King George VI who made him a Knight Commander of the Bath.

Richard O'Connor was born in Srinigar in Kashmir, one of the most beautiful places on earth but which is still disputed and fought over by India and Pakistan, on 21 August 1889. The O'Connor family home was in Ballybrock, County Offaly, then Queen's County, but his father, Major Maurice O'Connor, was serving in India with his regiment, Princess Victoria's (Royal Irish Fusiliers). Some time later, Major O'Connor was forced to return to Britain following injuries sustained in an accident and, in 1894, retired on half pay. The family returned to Ballybrock but when Maurice died in 1903 his widow moved to join her family in Scotland; she was Lilian Morris, daughter of Sir John Morris KCSI,† erstwhile governor of India's Central Provinces. Richard was educated at Wellington College before entering Sandhurst in 1908. When he passed out from Sandhurst he had done well enough to be commissioned into a Scottish regiment, which were then considered elite. His chosen regiment was the Cameronians, the Second Battalion of which always preferred to be

---

* The Army of the Nile did not exist but was a term used romantically by Churchill to describe the ground forces in Egypt which were barely of corps strength.
† Knight Commander of the Star of India.

known as The Scottish Rifles; and it was to 2nd Cameronians that Second-Lieutenant O'Connor was posted. That he was commissioned into a Scottish regiment and had a Scottish mother, coupled with the early death of his father, has often obscured the fact that Richard O'Connor was Irish. Had his father not died so young, his son may well have followed him into the Royal Irish Fusiliers.*

In September 1911 the Scottish Rifles became part of the Malta garrison. By then O'Connor had achieved a reputation as a very capable signals officer which enabled him to transfer from the battalion in August 1914 to become signals officer of a brigade in 7th Division, part of the BEF in France. Soon he was showing himself to be an extremely courageous officer. Wounded in the fighting at Ypres in Belgium, in February 1915 he was one of the first officers decorated with the newly instituted gallantry decoration, the Military Cross. Throughout 1915 he was on active service, seeing action at Neuve Chapelle, Frommelles, Givenchy and Loos before being promoted to command 7th Division Signals Company. Although the divisional history praises O'Connor's ability, his organizational skills and his success in ensuring his company's efficiency, he himself was anxious to return to the infantry and command a rifle company.

His efforts to return to the Scottish Rifles were unsuccessful and O'Connor continued to command 7th Division Signal Company through the opening weeks of the Somme campaign in 1916. It seemed that he might never achieve his wish of returning to the infantry, especially when he was promoted to be brigade major of one of 7th Division's brigades, the first of two such staff appointments. Then, in early June 1917, he received two pieces of good news, the first being the award of the DSO. Much more important to O'Connor, however, was the second piece of news: he was being promoted to lieutenant-colonel commanding a battalion of the Honourable Artillery Company in 7th Division. Despite its title, the Honourable Artillery Company (HAC)† included infantry in its order of battle and thus O'Connor had at last achieved his desire.

When he joined 2nd Infantry Battalion, HAC, O'Connor was 'faced with problems which would have appalled an older and more experienced officer'. His battalion had fewer than 300 men and was short of specialist soldiers, having just come through an action at Bullecourt in which it had been reduced to four officers and ninety-four men. O'Connor's arrival transformed the battalion. He imposed strict discipline but raised morale to a very high level and gained his soldiers' respect. One of them, Sergeant-Major W.J. Bradley DCM MM, later described the impression their new commanding officer created:

---

* From 1881 until 1922 the official title of the regiment was Princess Victoria's (Royal Irish Fusiliers). However, it was rarely known by the official title to those who served in its First Battalion, who continued to call their regiment the Royal Irish Fusiliers.
† The Honourable Artillery Company is the senior regiment of the Territorial Army and is, in fact, older than any regiment in the Regular Army, making it Britain's oldest regiment.

Since the arrival of the new CO, food improved considerably and we had a good wet and dry canteen,* but a new nightmare was introduced – Colonel's inspection. Every time we were in reserve it happened and it was unbelievably thorough, even to the number of studs on the soles of our boots. All men on details had to parade with platoons which was a terrible shock for most of them, not having been inspected since they arrived in France. Although we did not like it at the time, it was a very good thing for morale and discipline. Colonel O'Connor made a great impact on the battalion from which we all benefited and made us into a battalion to be proud of.

Morale and discipline were crucial concerns, especially as the battalion spent the next few months in and out of the front line. O'Connor had also introduced a carefully planned training programme to raise operational efficiency.

By October 1917 the Passchendaele battles were underway and O'Connor's battalion was in action at Reutel. They suffered very heavy losses while advancing in a frontal attack; eight officers and forty-nine men were killed, while 189 were wounded and another forty-nine reported missing; almost all of the latter were subsequently confirmed as dead. The attack was successful but O'Connor's abiding memory was of those who had died and, thereafter, he always sought opportunities to attack an enemy from the flank rather than head-on, or to achieve surprise, as at Sidi Barrani in 1940.

The Reutel action – an attack on the Reutel–Broodseinde track – was 2nd HAC's last battle in France before 7th Division moved to the Italian front in November 1917. The battalion entered the line in January 1918 but was not committed to battle until October when it was ordered to take part in an attack on an island, Grave di Papadopoli, in the Piave river. Although the island was occupied by Austrian troops, their strength was not known. Intelligence estimates were flawed badly; it transpired that the garrison was five times stronger than believed. As a result, O'Connor's men were involved in a very bloody battle against a determined foe with no intention of surrendering. Not until two additional battalions were sent to support 2nd HAC were the Austrians finally defeated and the island fell to the Allies. The capture of Grave di Papadopoli permitted the launch of a successful Allied offensive on the Italian front. In turn that offensive led to Austria's surrender on 3 November 1918.

For his achievements at Grave di Papadopoli, O'Connor was applauded by both British and Italian high commands, receiving a Bar to his DSO from the former while the Italian government honoured him with the Silver Medal for Valour. In addition to these, and his earlier DSO and MC, he had also received nine Mentions in Despatches in the course of the war. He had survived four years of almost continuous active service but, apart from that early injury at Ypres, emerged from the conflict almost unscathed. While there is no doubt that he had been lucky, it must be

---

* A 'wet' canteen was one where alcoholic refreshments were available whereas a 'dry' canteen served no alcoholic drinks. Drunkenness had been a severe problem in the nineteenth-century army and the dry canteens were part of an effort to curb the problem.

remembered that luck plays an important part in the life of a soldier; Napoleon's dictum that he wanted lucky generals underlines that point.

With peace came a reversion to the rank of major for O'Connor; his lieutenant-colonelcy had been a temporary wartime rank. Of course, he was not alone in this and, with the slow rate of promotion in the post-war Army, it would be the mid-1930s before O'Connor again became a lieutenant-colonel. Before that he attended Staff College as a student and served there as an instructor, while he was also a company commander at Sandhurst. For a two-year period he held a staff post at the War Office under the Director of Staff Duties. This was among the most desirable postings in the Army for a middle-ranking officer who wished to achieve promotion. His duties were principally concerned with the Staff College, including the placing of successful students in appropriate appointments at the end of each course. From the War Office, O'Connor went to the Imperial Defence College before being appointed to command the Peshawar Brigade in India's North-West Frontier Province.

O'Connor worked hard at this prestigious command during his two-year tenure. He obviously made a favourable impression as he was then promoted major-general commanding 7th Infantry Division in Palestine. He took up his new command after the Arab rebellion had begun; there had been serious loss of life following Arab attacks on Jews, civil authority was almost non-existent in many areas and Jerusalem was virtually besieged. On 16 October, O'Connor arrived in Jerusalem and, next day, Arab rebels announced that they now controlled Old Jerusalem. To deal with this situation, O'Connor was appointed military governor of Jerusalem on the 18th with authority over the police and the civil administration as well as his own soldiers. He was determined not to lose any time and decided that the first task would be re-occupying the old city. Planning began immediately for this and O'Connor carried out a personal reconnaissance, looking at Old Jerusalem 'from various points of vantage' and noting that it consisted of a 'tangle of very narrow streets' surrounded by a high wall with a number of turrets overlooking all parts of the old city.

O'Connor's plan involved soldiers operating from the city's flat roofs, a concept with which some commanding officers were unhappy since they considered that their battalions might sustain heavy casualties. In spite of these fears the operation was 'highly successful and went off strictly in accordance with the plan' with but a single casualty. Following the operation in Jerusalem, O'Connor went on to execute similar sweeps in Ramallah, Jericho and Haifa; all were free from rebels by the end of November. At much the same time, Major-General Bernard Montgomery arrived to command 8th Division in northern Palestine. It was not long before Montgomery was telling everyone how to put things right, although he was quick to adopt O'Connor's methods. He even sent a report to the War Office in December in which he detailed his operations against the Arab rebels and wrote:

> I started off with this policy in the north and Dick O'Connor is doing much the same thing in the south. He and I are great personal friends and we are keeping in the closest touch.

It was typical of Montgomery that he should claim the credit for all successful operations in Palestine but there is no doubt that it was he who was following O'Connor's example and not vice versa as he inferred. However, O'Connor was much too modest to boast about his own achievements, a fact of which Montgomery undoubtedly was aware.

Palestine was not the only troubled spot in the world in the late-1930s and, in fact, the unrest there was partially an echo of what was happening in Europe with the Nazi regime in Germany persecuting Jews, many of whom sought refuge in Palestine. Europe was moving inexorably towards war as German aggression increased and so the British government began withdrawing troops from the Holy Land to strengthen defences elsewhere. Montgomery returned to the United Kingdom to command a division of the BEF while O'Connor remained in Jerusalem. In August 1939, as Germany prepared to invade Poland, O'Connor's divisional headquarters moved to Cairo and, following the declaration of war on 3 September, began moving into the Western Desert. A new headquarters was established in the seaside resort of Mersa Matruh, which was to be the main base for desert operations.

When Italy declared war on Britain and France in June 1940, O'Connor was appointed Commander, Western Desert Force with the rank of lieutenant-general. However, as he later recalled, he was given little direction on policy, a situation to which he had no real objection as 'I don't mind being left on my own'. He established a new headquarters for Western Desert Force at Ma'ateen Baggush, east of Mersa Matruh. Patrols from the force were already crossing the frontier into Libya to harass the Italians and gather information on their strength and dispositions.

Mussolini, the Italian dictator, had declared war on Britain against the advice of most of his senior officers. *Il Duce* saw the possibility of expanding the Italian empire in Africa. Italy already possessed Libya, Abyssinia, conquered just a few years earlier, and Italian Somaliland. Taking Egypt, the Sudan and the British territories along the Red Sea would give Italy control of all north-eastern Africa. Although Mussolini believed that Britain was beaten, with its morale broken, his generals did not share his confidence. They argued that Italian military equipment was so inferior to British equipment that it would be 1943, at the earliest, before they could guarantee a successful campaign against the British in Egypt. However, arguing with dictators is usually a pointless exercise and Mussolini overruled his generals' objections. In September 1940 General Rudolpho Graziani attacked across the border from Libya into Egypt. It was not an advance in blitzkrieg style; Graziani's army lumbered less than fifty miles into Egypt until, following opposition from a single British infantry battalion, Tenth Army dug in around the village of Sidi Barrani. Italian propaganda declared to the world that the trams were running normally in Sidi Barrani. The village did not even have a railway. Expecting Graziani to attack Mersa Matruh, O'Connor had positioned 7th Armoured Division to the south of the Italian line of advance, ready to thrust north for the coast and cut off Italian supply and communication lines. However, with Italian civilian labour being brought in to dig defences around Barrani, it became clear that Graziani intended moving no farther. Noting that it was 'all rather a disappointment', O'Connor withdrew his tanks.

In Britain Churchill was demanding action in the desert. While O'Connor was determined that there would be action, he had first to establish the strength of the opposition. When this had been done it appeared as if Western Desert Force faced an impossible task; O'Connor had two divisions at his disposal whereas the Italians had almost ten between Sidi Barrani and Tobruk. The *Regia Aeronautica*, the Italian air force, outnumbered the RAF by five-to-one while there were over 80,000 Italian soldiers in Egypt against O'Connor's 36,000. However, the quality of much of the British equipment was superior; the Matilda Infantry – or I – tanks, although slow, were virtually impervious to Italian anti-tank weapons while even the British cruiser and light tanks were better than most Italian tanks. The Italians were unaware of the availability of Matilda I-tanks to Western Desert Force; fifty were being held in the Nile delta but could be called forward by O'Connor. However, the Italians still enjoyed numerical superiority; to beat them O'Connor needed to give his soldiers two decided advantages: surprise and exact planning.

O'Connor began planning for an operation that would provide the maximum possible surprise. In these preparations, the RAF played a major role by achieving air superiority over the Italians whose aircraft were unable to observe the build-up of Western Desert Force, the movement of equipment and supplies from the Nile delta and the concealed dumps being built to hold those supplies. The mastery later achieved by Montgomery's Eighth Army in concealing such preparations before El Alamein in October 1942 had its genesis in the work carried out before the attack at Sidi Barrani. Plans for the attack were drawn up by O'Connor and a triumvirate of brigadiers, John Harding, Eric Dorman-Smith and Sandy Galloway, who had the advantage of a study demanded by Wavell before Graziani's attack. General Wavell's call for a study had been based on a possible British attack into Libya in late-1940 or early-1941; he had asked for an innovative approach, avoiding what he described as the 'slow ponderosity which is apt to characterise British operations'. By so doing, averred Wavell, it should be possible to 'take a certain degree of risk' especially as the Italians were likely to be dispirited. Wavell's suggestions were almost unnecessary with the team of O'Connor, Harding, Dorman-Smith and Galloway; these were men prepared to take risks and to whom slow, ponderous movement was anathema. The quartet drafted plans and oversaw exercises until they were confident that they had a scheme that would guarantee the element of surprise and play to British strengths while exploiting Italian weaknesses. Their plan, Operation COMPASS, received Wavell's full approval. The degree to which it departed from British orthodoxy is illustrated by the comment of one historian that 'any student who had produced such a solution at a Staff College exercise in peace would have been ridiculed by his fellows and very roughly handled by the directing staff'. However, attaining surprise required unorthodox thinking that left the foe unsettled from the first contact. And Wavell, probably the most intellectual of British commanders of the war, encouraged unorthodox thinking.

Operation COMPASS was planned as a five-day raid to destroy the enemy's bridgehead in Egypt but the overall plan allowed for exploiting the initial success to the greatest possible degree. The degree to which such exploitation proved possible may even have surprised the planning team but did not inhibit their resolution to take advantage of Italian disorganization. Once Wavell gave his approval, preparations began although, to maintain security, only a small group of officers knew the full extent of the plan; very little was committed to paper. The first movements of troops to assembly areas were disguised as exercises, which Churchill described in eloquent fashion in *The Second World War*. On 6 December the first forward movement was made by what Churchill termed a 'lean, bronzed, desert-hardened and completely mechanised' army leaping forward some forty miles to lie up all through the next day in the desert without being detected by the Italian air force. They 'swept forward' again on the 8th and that evening learned that this was no exercise but the preliminary moves of an offensive. The battle of Sidi Barrani opened at dawn on 9 December.

Reconnaissance had identified a gap in the Italian defences, which was to be exploited in the opening phase of COMPASS. Before dawn on the 9th infantry and armour moved forward. In Nibeiwa camp, Italian cooks were preparing breakfast; they and the sentries were probably the only men fully awake. As the sun came up over the horizon a salvo of British shells came down on the eastern edge of the camp. Naturally all eyes turned towards there, for in that direction lay the British lines. Nobody in Nibeiwa expected the British to come in from behind; but that is exactly what was happening.

The heavy Matildas were attacking Nibeiwa from the northwest. They crashed through roadblocks and gates and fanned out to overrun the camp. Although Italian gunners reacted quickly their guns were facing the wrong way and they had first to swing them round to face the British armoured attack. But their shells made no impact on the Matildas' heavy carapaces, bouncing off without impeding the tanks' advance. No one could doubt the courage of the Italian gunners for they remained at their guns as the tanks drove over them, destroying the weapons as if they were toys. Many gunners perished. Close behind the Matildas came the soldiers of 11 Indian Infantry Brigade but most Italian soldiers were so shocked that they put up little resistance and, within two hours, the camp had fallen with some 4,000 prisoners taken. Attacks were made on two further camps and, although the element of surprise had gone and resistance stiffened noticeably, only one section of Tummar East camp was still holding out at dusk; its defenders surrendered next morning.

Sidi Barrani and Maktila were surrounded while an armoured brigade cut the road from Sollum to Barrani, along which Italian reinforcements would have to come. By dusk on the 10th, O'Connor's greatest problem was feeding and accommodating almost 40,000 prisoners before moving them back to the Nile delta. But he also wanted to continue his advance since it was now clear that he could exploit his initial success and push Graziani's army out of Egypt; he might even be able to strike into Libya. Before that, however, Western Desert Force would have to clear up Italian garrisons at Sofafi and Rabia while the armoured brigades would have to capture Buq Buq and Sollum, on the coastal road to Libya. As he was preparing for these operations, O'Connor received an order to send 4th Indian Division back to the delta; it was to move from there to the Sudan to participate in the invasion of Italy's east African empire. This order, as unexpected as it was unwelcome, was a tremendous blow to O'Connor who had 'had no previous intimation of it and it came like a bolt from the blue'. The Indians were to be replaced by 6th Australian Division who, although tough, fit and enthusiastic, were not yet trained for desert warfare; some of their soldiers were only recently out of basic training but made up for lack of experience by a determination to get to grips with the enemy and continue the reputation earned by their fathers in the Great War. Undeterred, O'Connor went ahead with his plans; 4th Indian Division completed the capture of Sidi Barrani before being withdrawn from action to return to the Nile delta.

On 12 December Churchill made an announcement to the house of commons of the initial success of COMPASS. Although he said that it was uncertain how many Italians had been captured in the battle, he expected that the best part of three divisions, including numerous Blackshirt formations, would have been taken prisoner or destroyed. Western Desert Force, he continued, was pursuing the enemy to the west 'with the greatest vigour' and, although it was too early to measure the full scale of the operations, it was clear that this was a major British victory that reflected the highest credit upon the commanders and staff officers who had planned the operation.

Churchill named the commanders as Wavell and Sir Henry Maitland Wilson, commander of British Troops, Egypt. O'Connor was not named but was one of the 'staff officers'. However, at this stage, Churchill was probably unaware of the full extent of O'Connor's role in COMPASS. For his part, O'Connor would not have sought any public recognition but would have been pleased with the prime minister's complimentary remarks about the soldiers of Western Desert Force who, Churchill said, had performed 'remarkable feats of endurance and daring'.

As we have seen, the operation had been intended to last for five days, but with the possibility of further exploitation. Those five days were fast coming to an end, Western Desert Force was running short of ammunition and, of course, 4th Indian Division had been withdrawn. Graziani's command was falling back on Bardia on the western littoral of the gulf of Sollum and there were many fresh Italian formations in Libya. Mussolini was determined that Bardia should be held and sent a message to its commander to that effect:

> I have given you a difficult task, but one well suited to your courage and experience as an old and intrepid soldier – the task of defending Bardia to the last.

The 'old and intrepid soldier' was General Berganzoli, better known to Italian soldiers as 'Barba Elettrica' – Electric Whiskers – because of his flamboyant and bushy facial hair. Replying to Mussolini, Berganzoli assured him that he would obey his exhortation, which he considered an honour, and which he had passed on to his soldiers, telling them that 'In Bardia we are and here we stay'. This stirring message was the type of encouragement that Churchill might have liked British generals to use but, although Berganzoli's order to his troops appears romantic, the reality was that the situation favoured the Italians. Berganzoli had strong defensive positions and his command, with some 400 guns and over 45,000 men, outnumbered the British; it was also well supplied. In O'Connor's position, many generals would have hesitated but he decided to go on. One brigade commander later commented that O'Connor told him he was determined to go, even though his command had been reduced to 7th Armoured Division and 16 Australian Infantry Brigade.* The soldiers of 6th Australian Division, the first Australians to see action in this war, carried out aggressive patrolling, harrying the garrison, while RAF aircraft bombed the area at night.

In late-December Western Desert Force cleared the area before Bardia and on 2 January 1941, 6th Australian Division attacked. By the evening of the 3rd the defences had been cut in two and, on the morning of 5 January, Berganzoli's soldiers began surrendering. All opposition had ceased by the afternoon of the 6th. As this battle raged, 7th Armoured Division and 19 Australian Brigade were advancing to cut off the port of Tobruk, which surrendered to Western Desert Force on 22 January; few could have realized at the time that Tobruk would achieve legendary status before the year was out. Even as Tobruk's garrison was abandoning the struggle, 7th Armoured Division was probing west towards Derna and Mechili.

All Italian opposition in the northern sector of the Cyrenaican bulge had ended by early-February. O'Connor's five-day raid had turned into a major offensive with over 100,000 prisoners taken, together with thousand of guns, tanks and lorries. However, O'Connor, now the victim of his own success, faced a major problem: his next major objective was the port of Benghazi, on the gulf of Sirte, but Benghazi was on the far side of the Cyrenaican bulge. Western Desert Force had two possible lines of approach to Benghazi, either by crossing the bulge across the Jebel Akhdar, or Green Mountain, or by staying to the coast and using the Italian-built coast road, the Via Balbia. By crossing the Jebel Akhdar, Western Desert Force might be able to cut off the retreating Italians as well as attacking Benghazi. But there were no proper roads across the Jebel and O'Connor's tanks were already suffering from worn tracks. Sending them across the Jebel would be a tremendous risk.

O'Connor took that risk and, while 6th Australian Division cut across the Jebel from Derna towards Benghazi, 7th Armoured took a line farther south to intercept the Italians at Beda Fomm. Combeforce, the leading element of O'Connor's armour, had established a position blocking the main road south from Benghazi on 5 February. This had been a remarkable feat with the armour and motorized infantry covering 150 miles across appalling, unmapped country in just thirty hours. Not long after Combeforce reached the road the first column of retreating Italians appeared.

---

* The other two brigades of the division had yet to arrive as there was insufficient transport to bring them forward.

Once again the Italians were taken completely by surprise. The battle of Beda Fomm had begun. It lasted until the morning of 7 February when the Italians surrendered.

Among those captured at Beda Fomm was General 'Electric Whiskers' Berganzoli, who had abandoned his soldiers successively at Bardia, Tobruk and Benghazi. He lamented to a British officer that 'You were here too soon, that is all. But we gave battle at once … and, as always, here as everywhere else, we were grossly outnumbered'. The truth, of course, was that the Italians had always had the advantage of numbers. Less than two months after the launch of COMPASS as a five-day raid, O'Connor's command had advanced over 500 miles, destroyed Tenth Italian Army and taken more than 130,000 prisoners. And all this from a contingency plan to exploit initial success.

In the days following the battle of Beda Fomm, elements of XIII Corps, the new title given to Western Desert Force, advanced to El Agheila, on the border between Cyrenaica and Tripolitania, with armoured cars of 11th Hussars, the *Cherrypickers*, patrolling into Tripolitania. Mussolini's empire in northern Africa appeared doomed. The degree to which the British plan had succeeded was due largely to Richard O'Connor. Although Wavell may have had the original idea and been prepared to support O'Connor's unorthodox planning, it cannot be disputed that the planning and, especially, the execution were O'Connor's work. One historian commented that O'Connor had made a decision that very few military commanders would have made. Having done so, O'Connor proved the soundness of his judgement of the capabilities of his foe in the implementation of his plan. In this he may have been helped by his having fought alongside Italians in the Great War but, whatever the reason, his calculations of risk proved always to be correct. Invariably, he had avoided frontal attacks, preferring to use flanking movements that caught the Italians off balance and exploited the element of surprise.

In the difficult and hostile terrain of the desert and the jebel, O'Connor had also displayed another mastery: of logistics and communications, prerequisites for any successful commander. His force now stood poised to take all Libya, thereby dealing Italy a devastating psychological blow. Although XIII Corps' men were tired, thirsty and hungry with their vehicles in need of repair and maintenance, all were eager to go on and O'Connor despatched Brigadier Eric Dorman-Smith to Cairo to let Wavell know that XIII Corps was ready and willing to advance into Tripolitania and to seek the necessary equipment and supplies. Dorman-Smith was shocked to enter Wavell's office and see that the maps of North Africa had gone from the walls to be replaced by a map of Greece. Behind that exchange of maps was Winston Churchill who, as noted in Chapter 4, had decided to deploy a British force to Greece. In a long letter to the Chiefs of Staff on 6 January, Churchill had written that the further westward advance of O'Connor's force, which he continued to call 'the Army of the Nile' might be seriously cramped after Tobruk and that it was his view that, having secured Egypt's western flank, priority should be given to supporting Greece. The problem was that Egypt's western flank could only be given guaranteed security if the Italians were forced to surrender in Libya. But Churchill did not recognize that; he considered that flank secure.

XIII Corps would advance no farther. Not only that, but it would also be stripped of troops for the Greek expedition. This time it was the turn of the Australians; 6th Division was withdrawn from Libya to move to Greece where it would be destroyed in the subsequent disastrous campaign. The remnants of XIII Corps, now restyled Cyrenaica Command, sat in defensive positions on the El Agheila line. O'Connor was in hospital in Cairo, suffering from a stomach ailment that had probably been exacerbated by his time in the desert and the strain of command. And now the Germans had arrived in North Africa to assist their Italian allies. Adolf Hitler had despatched a small force under Major-General Erwin Rommel to Libya. This force, *Deutsches Afrika Korps*, had been formed in Tripoli as the battle at Beda Fomm raged and Rommel reached Tripoli the following week. By the end of March, contrary to orders, he had ordered Afrika Korps forward on the offensive. The Germans probed the British line, found it to be held only lightly, pressed on and within a week had driven deep into the Cyrenaican bulge, spreading confusion among British troops.

On 2 April Wavell visited the front, realized that disaster was imminent and sent for O'Connor to come immediately to help General Neame, the commander of XIII Corps. O'Connor arrived next day but demurred at Wavell's suggestion that he relieve Neame, offering instead to assist the latter. Three days later, O'Connor and Neame were travelling together behind British lines when they ran into a small force that Rommel had sent out in front of Afrika Korps. The luck that had stayed with O'Connor throughout the Great War now deserted him; both generals were captured in a

> tragic incident [that] robbed the British of the greatest of all their desert generals and inflicted on the eager, ardent little commander the gnawing frustration of the prison camp. The most fascinating of all desert encounters, O'Connor versus Rommel, would never take place.

Since North Africa was an Italian theatre, O'Connor was sent to a PoW camp in Italy where he spent almost three years in captivity. A suggestion by Wavell that any six Italian generals in British hands should be exchanged for O'Connor was rejected in London as it might set a precedent. O'Connor was not treated badly, as the Italians were generally evenhanded with officer prisoners but there was little food. However, this did not affect his health dramatically since he had never had a large appetite; Red Cross parcels also helped. In December 1943, after the Italian armistice, O'Connor at last succeeded in escaping to join the Allied forces that had invaded Italy in September. On his return to Britain O'Connor was appointed to command VIII Corps of Second Army, the British Liberation Army, for the invasion of France.

VIII Corps crossed to France in the week after D-Day and, thereafter, was involved in much of the heavy fighting for Normandy. In this campaign there was much less opportunity to exercise independent and original thinking than in the desert. O'Connor had to conform to plans laid down by Second Army and by Montgomery, 21 Army Group's commander, who tended to act as if he were still an army commander. Soon after its arrival in Normandy, VIII Corps was designated for a breakout operation, codenamed DREADNOUGHT, that was to take the corps across the Orne and out of the congested bridgehead. However, O'Connor was unhappy with the concept and told Montgomery of the difficulties that would be involved. The operation was cancelled. As a result the corps' first experience of battle came in Operation EPSOM at the end of June. This was intended to place VIII Corps on high ground dominating the exits south from the city of Caen. O'Connor had asked for strong air support but weather conditions precluded most of this; the operation was also postponed and when it did go ahead the failure of XXX Corps, on the right flank, to take the Rauray spur meant that enemy forces overlooked the line of advance of O'Connor's force. Against doughty opposition, foul weather and determined counter-attacks, EPSOM ground to a halt. The corps had suffered heavy casualties; one division lost a quarter of all its casualties from D-Day to VE Day in the five days of EPSOM.*

After Operations WINDSOR and JUPITER, VIII Corps was assigned to Operation GOODWOOD, a massed armoured assault intended to strike through Caen and 'write down' the German armour in battle. O'Connor was to command Guards, 7th and 11th Armoured Divisions, with about 800 tanks. The plan was flawed deeply and, once again, demonstrated Montgomery's lack of appreciation of armoured warfare. Both O'Connor and Major-General Pip Roberts, commanding 11th Armoured, were concerned about the lack of infantry and the need to keep infantry units close to the armour. They proposed, therefore, to use improvized armoured personnel carriers and O'Connor ordered

> That a number of the self-propelled gun carriers of the artillery be turned over to the infantry for use as armoured personnel carriers. There were predictable howls of outrage at this temerity to violate the hidebound organizational structure of the army, and the order was soon countermanded by Dempsey, who was not convinced of its merit. O'Connor's protests to Dempsey fell on deaf ears ...

However, O'Connor continued to push for the APC concept, writing to an old friend from the Cameronians who was now a special adviser to the Ministry of Supply to press for the development of specialized APCs. GOODWOOD was also doomed to be stopped by adverse weather and strong opposition. Casualties were again heavy with tremendous loss in tanks; both Montgomery and Dempsey seem to have believed that tanks could be lost in battle without serious loss in manpower.

---

* This was 15th (Scottish) Division.

Following the breakout from Normandy, VIII Corps drove towards the Maas river where O'Connor commanded it in Operation CONSTELLATION. This was the fourth major assault in which he had led his corps in northwest Europe and, Pip Roberts, commander of 11th Armoured Division, later wrote, his role in this operation was 'the best he had shown in the campaign'. Roberts had been critical of O'Connor's earlier handling of his corps but it must be remembered that the latter had yet to regain his confidence, adjust to the situation in Europe and absorb new tactical and operational lessons. Much had changed in the years of his imprisonment and, as his good friend Field Marshal Lord Harding commented, 'no man can be a prisoner for nearly three years and remain unaffected in some way'.

O'Connor's biographer, John Baynes, suggests that he may have lost some of that original fire and confidence of desert days, pointing out that O'Connor reached his fifty-fifth birthday in August 1944 and that his time as a prisoner may have given him the mental approach of a man of sixty. But he overcame this and by the time of CONSTELLATION in October 1944 was showing all the flair and vigour of earlier days in the desert.

At the end of November 1944 O'Connor was told that he was to be posted to India, a decision about which he was not very happy.

> I was greatly distressed leaving VIII Corps, the more so as I was given such a proof of their confidence and affection when I went round to say goodbye to the various units of the corps. It was no doubt a young man's war, and perhaps I was getting too old for the job.

Although his active war was over, he played an important role in India where he was appointed to command Eastern Army, a non-operational command; he was also promoted to full general in April 1945. Auchinleck, the C-in-C, then transferred him to take over Northern Command, which covered the area that would become modern Pakistan. In the difficult times before Indian independence and the partition of the sub-continent, he and Auchinleck worked together well, with the Auk looking to O'Connor for advice and guidance. However, O'Connor was not to be in India when the country gained its independence. In May 1946 he was appointed Adjutant General and left for Britain to take up his final appointment.

Once again O'Connor applied all his energy to the post, making visits to all the many outposts in which British troops were stationed to explain what was being done to arrange the repatriation of those with several years' service overseas. He had also to oversee the reduction of the infantry with most regiments, including the Cameronians, losing a battalion. But O'Connor was serving under Montgomery as CIGS and when American lawyers approached Monty in America about the dismissal of Major-General Lindsay Silvester of 7th US Armored Division in 1944 it appears that Montgomery blamed O'Connor for the approach. Certainly, O'Connor had opposed the removal of Silvester, who was then under his command; but Monty had engineered the American's dismissal with Eisenhower. With the ghost of Silvester haunting their working relationship, O'Connor decided to resign, although Montgomery tried to make it appear that he was being dismissed. Finally, however, he was allowed to resign and Sir Richard O'Connor retired from the Army in 1948. In Correlli Barnett's words he had been Britain's greatest desert general but the misfortune of being captured had robbed the Army of an outstanding commander as well as robbing O'Connor of the opportunity to reach the very top of the military tree.

Historians ought not to speculate but that does not prevent them from doing so from time to time and it is intriguing to think what might have happened had O'Connor not met the Germans in April 1941. Remembering that he and Montgomery were contemporaries, there is very possibility that O'Connor might also have become a field marshal. It is also intriguing to wonder what might have happened in the desert had O'Connor and Rommel faced each other. They had much in common, but I believe that O'Connor was the better commander, since he had a much greater appreciation of the importance of logistics than Rommel. Of course, the most interesting speculation of all is what would have happened had O'Connor been allowed to continue his advance into Libya. The North African war could have ended in early-1941 – the Italians were defeated in east Africa at this time – and Richard O'Connor might have become the hero he deserved to be – and would we ever have heard of Montgomery?

Lord Harding, one of O'Connor's greatest friends and admirers, gave the address at O'Connor's memorial service in 1981.

> Dick O'Connor was my ideal of a commander in battle; always approachable and ready to listen, yet firm and decisive and always fair in his judgement of people and events; modest to a degree, shunning the limelight and embarrassed by praise; calmly resolute and courageously determined.

~ 6 ~

Pile

In Chapter Four (p. 66), we noted the comment of the historians of the British chiefs of staff that it never pays to be a British chief at the outbreak of war since incumbents usually become scapegoats for the politicians' mistakes. The same is true of those who hold high command; they frequently pay the price of perceived failure in their command. As with every rule, however, there is an exception, and during the Second World War that was General Sir Frederick Pile, who was GOC, Anti-Aircraft Command when war broke out and who held that post throughout the war.

Pile's greatest hour probably came with the V1 flying-bomb offensive, launched against Britain on 13 June 1944. The V1 was the first of Hitler's 'vengeance weapons' and, until spring 1945, would cause thousands of deaths in Britain. No effort was spared to combat V1s but the most effective weapons used against them were Anti-Aircraft Command's guns, which brought down so many that the full effect of this vengeance weapon was never realized. Churchill wrote to Pile saying that the 'flying-bomb battle was a great triumph' for Anti-Aircraft Command, the men, and women, of which were in action from the first day of the war until the last. Theirs was the longest land campaign of the Second World War, all conducted under the sure leadership of General Sir Frederick Pile, better known as 'Tim'.

Born in 1884, Tim Pile was a Dubliner, whose earliest memories of 'the great world' included 'the death of Parnell, followed, some years later, by that of Gladstone'. His father, a Protestant home rule supporter, a nationalist, and member of Dublin Corporation, later became the city's Lord Mayor. In that capacity, he welcomed Queen Victoria to Dublin in 1900 to pay tribute to the gallantry of her Irish soldiers in the South African, or Boer, War. Proposing a civic reception for the Queen, with Dublin decorated in her honour, Pile met opposition in the Corporation but his proposal was carried by a narrow margin. His opponents told him that he was finished politically, but when he offered himself for re-election he 'got in by the biggest majority he had ever had'.

Tim's decision to join the Army led to intense study for the entrance examination to the Royal Military Academy, Woolwich, the 'Shop', which trained officers for the Royal Regiment of Artillery and Corps of Royal Engineers. Although he failed the examination he scraped in after another attempt when a number of candidates failed their medicals. This prompted him to comment in his memoirs that 'The only exam I ever passed with flying colours was that medical'. Pile entered Woolwich as the bottom man of his term and passed out twenty-sixth to be commissioned into the Royal Field Artillery. He served in Britain, South Africa and India, where he achieved the ambition of every young gunner subaltern and was transferred to the Royal Horse Artillery, thereby receiving his 'jacket' – the hussar-style jacket worn by the RHA. This was one of the highest distinctions a young gunner officer could gain, since the Royal Horse Artillery, on parade with its guns, takes precedence over all other regiments and corps of the Army, including the Household Cavalry. As a result the RHA is referred to as 'the right of the line and the pride of the British Army'.

Tim Pile returned to Britain as a horse artillery officer and when the BEF sailed for France in 1914, Captain Pile was ADC (aide-de-camp) to the Commander Royal Horse Artillery. He survived four years on the western front, mostly at regimental level. In his memoirs he virtually dismisses his wartime service, describing it only briefly and then without referring to his earning the DSO, the MC and three Mentions in Despatches. However, he did note his impressions of war:

> I cannot say that I think war is an amusing practice. The man who described it as long periods of gloom enlivened by stretches of acute fear was near the truth, but there was a bit more to that campaign than boredom and fear. The war was not fought by machines like the last [Second] war, but by flesh and blood, and the horse played a tremendous part in it. Anyone who loves horses would not wish them ever again to take part in a war.

Such was the ebb and flow of the Great War that Pile ended the conflict within a mile of where he had seen his first Germans in 1914. After the war he was posted to a staff job in Germany but applied to return to the United Kingdom and became brigade major at Shoreham. However, his brigade was due for disbandment and Pile found himself back in Germany as adjutant to a field artillery brigade* in Cologne. In 1922 he entered Staff College as a student.

Pile applied himself diligently to his studies but discovered that the more effort he put into researching papers the less favourably they were received. He also found that papers based on little research but backed by the knowledge he already possessed were commended. This led to the realization that the directing staff wanted students to demonstrate that they knew how to think for themselves. Following this, Pile began producing original ideas that were not always received well, but did produce an unanticipated result – an invitation to join the Tank Corps, which was then being re-formed. The invitation came from a Staff College member, Colonel 'Boney' Fuller, Britain's leading armour expert. Pile agreed quickly and, six weeks later, transferred to the Tank Corps, going on to command a tank battalion.[†]

---

* Until 1938 there were no 'regiments' in the Royal Artillery. Instead, pairs of batteries were brigaded and the battery itself was the accounting unit. In 1938 regiments, usually of three batteries, were created with the regiment as the accounting unit. However, individual gunners' loyalties remained, as ever, with their batteries.
† Until after the Second World War, the British Army used infantry nomenclature for its tank units rather than the cavalry nomenclature which has been used since.

During exercises on Salisbury Plain, Pile upset the directing staff when he moved his armour, which was operating in an advance guard role, into 'enemy' positions before the 'enemy' had even reached them. He had adopted the simple tactic of leaving armoured cars at each reporting line to relay reports to the attackers' main body and had carried on with the rest of his unit. Present at the exercises was the *Daily Telegraph*'s military correspondent and world-renowned military critic, Captain Basil Liddell Hart, who was most impressed with Pile's tactical thinking. So, also, was Pile's divisional commander who commented that such 'methods would certainly be used in the next war – especially if there were people like Colonel Pile to lead the armoured forces'.

From battalion command, Pile went to the War Office where he spent four years before taking up another active command, this time of the Suez Canal Brigade in Egypt, in 1932. Normally, this was considered an infantry officer's appointment but the C-in-C, Egypt – General Jock Burnett-Stuart, Pile's divisional commander on those Salisbury Plain manoeuvres – had asked for the Irishman. Burnett-Stuart was not disappointed as Pile again showed his capacity for original thought. He decided that his troops should practise battalion-scale night attacks, although conventional military wisdom was that such attacks were foolish. Company-level attacks were known to be possible but, historically, anything above that level had ended in disaster. However, Pile believed that such disasters had occurred because soldiers had never been trained adequately for such attacks and so he endeavoured to remedy the situation.

Two of his battalion commanders opposed Pile's thinking and tried to sabotage a night exercise. These were fellow Irishmen, Lieutenant-Colonels Bernard Montgomery and Harold Franklyn. Such was the dressing down that both received from Pile that they mended their ways and resolved to give his ideas a thorough testing. In one night exercise, Montgomery's Royal Warwicks carried out a seven-mile approach march to attack positions held by a Guards battalion. All the defending soldiers were captured. Pile later wondered if when Montgomery 'was planning the great Battle of El Alamein [whether] that bloodless triumph remained in his mind'. Montgomery's biographer, Nigel Hamilton, does not accept that Pile was the man responsible for this, suggesting that Montgomery was the brain behind the night training. If this were the case, then one wonders why Montgomery tried to sabotage Pile's exercise.

There were many innovative soldiers in Egypt at that time whose thinking played a major part in reshaping British tactics during the war that lay ahead. Sir Francis de Guingand wrote that

> We were lucky enough to have 'Tim' Pile as our Brigade Commander. It surprised none of us that later he was given the important post of Commander-in-Chief AA Command of Great Britain.

However, Pile's performance as commander of the Canal Brigade did not guarantee him a future posting and when his tenure ended in 1936 he was promoted to major-general and 'promptly put on half-pay'. This was a most disappointing development, which might have led to retirement.

> This system of half-pay which obtained before the War was extremely hard on many officers. Half-pay was actually less than retired pay, and unless one had a private income or one got some temporary job, it was very difficult. In fact, many people preferred to retire at once and get a job in civil life. I was fortunate, as during my year on half-pay, I was given one or two jobs which kept the wolf from the door.

Pile's time on the half-pay list came to an end when Hore-Belisha, the Secretary of State for War, offered him command of 1st Anti-Aircraft Division, an appointment that would take him back to the Royal Artillery. There had also been the possibility of his staying with armour as there had been talk of raising an armoured division and he had been considered for command. But Britain, in the throes of re-armament, was undecided as to whether it could afford simultaneously both armoured and anti-aircraft divisions.

Pile told Hore-Belisha that he 'knew little or nothing about anti-aircraft' but was assured by the secretary of state that this was the Army's most important command and 'so I told him that I would take it on and do my best'. The task that faced Pile was difficult. Expecting to find a formed and equipped formation, he was surprised and disillusioned when he first visited 1st AA Division's headquarters, located alongside the RAF at Uxbridge and 'housed in the most dismal huts'. There was virtually no equipment and the division was composed of Territorial Army soldiers; this was the sole AA division in the Army. The few Regulars served on the divisional commander's staff or as regimental adjutants and instructors. Pile's first priority was to recruit new personnel to bring the division up to strength and he and his staff spent much time on recruiting. The equipment shortage had also to be overcome; this was no easy task. Since equipment was so scarce the division had to carry out its early training on obsolescent guns and equipment. Although new weapons and equipment were on order their delivery was still some way off; when they did appear there would be many more ack-ack units in the queue for them.

The Munich crisis in the autumn of 1938 led to the mobilization of the AA defences and galvanized government into improving the lot of the AA units. By this time the UK's AA defences had been increased from one division to a corps of two divisions plus two independent brigades; the AA Corps was commanded by Lieutenant-General Alan Brooke. Further expansion of the gun and searchlight defences to seven divisions led to the creation of Anti-Aircraft Command, of which Brooke became first GOC. In July 1939, Tim Pile succeeded Brooke as GOC-in-C, Anti-Aircraft Command. Pile's command came under the overall control of an organization known as the Air Defence of Great Britain (ADGB), which was responsible for co-ordinating all aspects of defence against air attack; this included the RAF's Fighter and Balloon Commands as well as AA Command. Pile's headquarters was established at 'Glenthorn', a house in the grounds of Fighter Command's headquarters at Stanmore in Middlesex; anti-aircraft gunners in the UK would serve under the operational control of Fighter Command.

When war was declared in September 1939, AA Command was still woefully short of resources while the standards of many gunners and searchlight operators were far from those required for operations. Aware of these shortcomings, Pile knew that his Command had much leeway to make up in a very short time. However, the heavy air attacks anticipated in the early days of the war did not materialize, although there were occasions when anti-aircraft gunners were called on to fire in anger with mixed results. On 6 September, three days into the war, guns at Sheerness fired on several aircraft, one of which was shot down. Tragically, the aircraft were British and, furthermore, had given the correct recognition signal; other British aircraft were fired on elsewhere that day but without causing any damage. In mid-October heavy guns in the river Forth area fired on German bombers attacking warships in the river. Two enemy aircraft were damaged by ack-ack fire in the course of a two-hour engagement; one was among three later shot down by RAF aircraft. RAF fighter pilots reported that shellbursts from AA guns were a great help in locating the raiders. No bombs fell on land, or in the dockyard area, although there were some casualties on, and slight damage to, ships. On this occasion the gunners had performed well; in fact, they were later credited with destroying one of the bombers.

However, there were other occasions on which the gunners either did not, or could not, do so well, as on 16 March 1940 when the Luftwaffe made a surprise raid on the Royal Navy anchorage at Scapa Flow in the Orkneys, just as darkness was falling. Dive-bombers attacked the Home Fleet while high-level bombers gave their attention to the airfield. Although Scapa was well defended in terms of the number of guns, many had only been emplaced and of fifty-two guns that could fire only forty-four did so. The heavies were unable to engage dive-bombers and this task was left to the light guns, which failed abysmally: many guns jammed and most others found that flashes from their own discharges were so bright in the gloaming that detachments were unable to observe their targets. Only thirty of the 108 searchlights were in action and the radar station had failed to detect the attackers until it was too late to be of value to either guns or fighters; those aircraft that got off the ground were too late to intercept the bombers, which escaped with neither damage nor casualties.

In spring 1940 Anti-Aircraft Command was still critically deficient in guns and equipment. The initial planning for the Command had called for an establishment of nearly 1,300 heavy guns, 2,000 light guns and almost 5,000 searchlights. However, the first winter of war saw demands for AA protection soar; the Admiralty wanted guns to defend anchorages and dockyards; the RAF to defend airfields; industry to defend centres of production. Thus the numbers of equipment considered necessary increased to 3,744 heavies, 4,410 light guns, 8,000 single- or double-barrelled AA rocket projectors, 160 multi-barrelled rocket projectors, and 8,500 searchlights. A similar increase was necessary in the equipment for gun control, such as predictors. To add to Pile's worries there were demands for anti-aircraft guns for the Norwegian expedition in early 1940 and for the French channel ports.

However the Command had had a comparative respite during that first winter and was, therefore, able to concentrate on creating defences, getting guns and ancillary equipment in position and training soldiers. Manpower presented another problem since AA Command was seen as a source of men for other duties and was raided for that purpose, while the conscripts being sent to man the anti-aircraft guns 'were the leavings of the Army intake after every other branch of the Services had had their pick'. The first intake to reach Anti-Aircraft Command at Christmas 1939

> had had extensive medical examination, but many ... were quite unsuited for any military duty, let alone the highly technical duties of AA. Out of twenty-five who arrived at a fairly representative battery, one had a withered arm, one was mentally deficient, one had a glass eye which fell out whenever he doubled to the guns, and two were in the advanced and more obvious stages of venereal disease.

This was no isolated example chosen by Pile. In one brigade, from an intake of some 1,000 recruits, fifty had to be discharged immediately on medical grounds from conditions that included deafness, arthritis and congenital abnormalities; another twenty were considered mentally deficient while nearly as many again were below medical category B2.

As he tackled the problems of equipment and manpower shortages, Pile was also working to improve the effectiveness of his guns. To all three questions he applied his analytical mind while his ability to establish a rapport with almost anyone became one of AA Command's finest and most important assets. Pile established relationships with politicians and with other senior servicemen that would ease the problems faced by his command while his appreciation of the importance of scientists would revolutionize anti-aircraft gunnery.

> I have never faltered in the opinion that AA Command was the most highly technical army that ever wore khaki ... All its problems ... were taken to the scientists, and never once did they fail me. If the Command finished the war in a blaze of glory that glory was the result of the five years' unremitting work of our scientists.

The first major test for the Command came in summer 1940. Following the fall of France a German invasion of Britain was expected. However, before German forces could cross the channel, the Royal Air Force had to be neutralized and, as a result, Luftwaffe operations intensified over Britain in July 1940. Thus began the campaign that Winston Churchill described as the battle of Britain. In the first phase the

Luftwaffe attacked shipping in the channel and struck at airfields and ports. Although bombers caused considerable damage to several ports the guns shot down a number of raiders; those at Dover accounted for half of the first twenty-six Luftwaffe planes destroyed over Britain. However, these were mostly daylight attacks in which gun detachments had the advantage of being able to see their targets. Less success was enjoyed at night since the searchlights were unable to provide full support unless the weather was clear, and the first gun-laying (GL) radar sets were experiencing teething troubles.*

The Luftwaffe attacks in July gave the gun defences the unexpected bonus of stimulating the gunners and boosting their confidence in their ability to deal with raiders. There was much less intensity in German operations at this stage than would later be the case; Hitler still believed that he might be able to persuade Britain to negotiate a peace settlement. Had the Luftwaffe's operations in July been delivered with the intensity that came later, the end result might have been very different. On 12 August, a fine summer day, German bombers attacked airfields and ports in the first really big raids. These took place at dawn with airfields at Manston, Hawkinge and Lympne the targets. At the end of the day almost every airfield in south and southeast England had been hit while the Luftwaffe had struck at shipping off the Isle of Wight and in Portsmouth harbour. Some airfields had been hit more than once and Manston was out of operation for a time in the afternoon, following its second raid of the day. A pattern had been set that would be followed in the ensuing days of battle during which the gunners would come under intense pressure with little opportunity for rest.

A careful study was made of Luftwaffe tactics: Pile was at Hawkinge one day when the airfield was raided and 'literally, until the bombs began to fall no one had any knowledge that enemy aircraft were in the neighbourhood'. Aware of the British early-warning system of radar stations, the raiders had flown low, using the cover of valleys until nearing Hawkinge and then popping above the trees to drop their bombs before using a similar low-level homeward route. To counter such tactics, lookouts were posted on high towers overlooking possible approach routes and the Royal Observer Corps was strengthened. This began to pay dividends and both guns and fighter aircraft were able to inflict damage on the attackers. From that first August day the guns were taking their toll of the Luftwaffe; they shot down eight on 12 August and damaged another so seriously that it was unlikely to reach home. On succeeding days, as raids continued with similar intensity, Pile's guns brought down more attackers, with fourteen falling on the 14th and five damaged. Dowding, who commanded Fighter Command, rang Pile to congratulate him on his gunners' achievements.

However, these successes did not blind Pile to the fact that there were still many deficiencies in the gun defences. Pre-war training had been based largely on the presumption that bombers would fly at constant speeds and heights; and this the

---

* At this time radar was still known as RDF, radio direction finding.

Luftwaffe had not done, choosing instead to use a variety of tactics that included dive-bombing and low-level approaches. Thus the gunners virtually had to relearn their trade as the battle developed. With the fire-control equipment available in 1939 it would have been difficult to have trained any other way. Even with that presumption, Pile had realized that there was a problem before war began when he noted that gunners tended to fire behind and below the target-towing aircraft against which they had practised; these had all been flying straight and level. As a result Pile and his scientists were now devoting considerable time and effort to resolving the problems of fire control. Thus the quest for better fire control, which meant eliminating as far as possible the human factor, was already underway as the battle of Britain began.

Throughout the long days of the battle of Britain anti-aircraft guns continued playing their part, although then, and ever since, the focus of public attention was on the pilots of RAF Fighter Command – Churchill's 'Few' – while the role of the guns was overlooked. What was worse was that the gunners were criticized by members of the public and by some MPs. Tim Pile had to become used to this phenomenon as the battle was being waged in full view of the British public; his guns were also operating under that same gaze with some of them very close to Westminster and the houses of parliament. Pile took a realistic view of the credit given to the RAF.

> There is no doubt that the RAF played the predominant part ... nor is there any doubt of the heroic fighting qualities of the pilots who took part in that battle. It is, therefore, not unreasonable to expect that the lesser role played by the ground defences should, first of all, fade into the background, and then into complete obscurity. Yet without the ground defences the Battle of Britain could not have been won by the fighter pilots, any more than the Battle of El Alamein could have been won by the infantry and tanks without the gunners.

Nor was this view held solely by Pile. At the height of the battle Dowding demanded more anti-aircraft guns and searchlights, thus indicating the importance the head of Fighter Command attributed to the ground defences.

In spite of this, Anti-Aircraft Command continued to suffer shortages, especially of the Bofors 40mm light guns and their Kerrison predictors, which were critical in combating low-level attackers. Pile described these as 'the most efficient killing-weapons' in his armoury. He was doing everything possible to make good the shortages; his knack of being able to make friends and gain their confidence paid dividends as he now numbered among those friends and confidants Lord Beaverbrook, minister for aircraft production.* Beaverbrook promised to do all he could to increase production of Bofors guns and their fire-control equipment.† So impressed was Beaverbrook with Pile's performance at AA Command that he later

---

* Beaverbrook later became minister of supply.
† Although a Swedish design, the Bofors was built under licence in Britain. It was also used by other Allied forces and by the Germans.

1 Second-Lieutenant Harold Alexander with his platoon of Irish Guards at Wellington Barracks, London in 1914. (Irish Guards) 2 Major Richard McCreery, XIIth Royal Lancers. A portrait photo taken between the wars, it shows the future general as an already well-decorated officer. (McCreery family)

3 Egypt, 1940. Lieutenant-General Richard O'Connor, left, confers with General Sir Henry Maitland 'Jumbo' Wilson, centre, and Brigadier A.R. Selby, who commanded Selby Force, drawn from the garrison of Mersa Matruh. (Imperial War Museum photograph E 971) 4 Field Marshal Sir John Dill, Chief of the Imperial General Staff (CIGS), photographed during a visit to the Middle East in February 1941. (IWM, E 2384) 5 General Sir Frederick 'Tim' Pile, Commander-in-Chief, Anti-Aircraft Command, at his desk in AA Command Headquarters at Stanmore in Middlesex. (IWM, H 4004)

6 General Sir Claude Auchinleck, left, and General Sir Archibald Wavell discuss the Middle Eastern situation as Auchinleck prepares to take over from Wavell as Commander-in-Chief, Middle East in June 1941. (IWM, E 5448)

7 The GOC, Northern Ireland, Lieutenant-General Harold Franklyn, a Cork man, on a visit to the Battle School at Poyntzpass, County Down, carries out an inspection accompanied by the commandant, Lieutenant-Colonel Pat Scott, Royal Irish Fusiliers. (IWM, H 19203)

8 President Roosevelt and Prime Minister Churchill, seated centre, during an Allied conference attended by the Chiefs of Staff of Britain and the United States. Seated front right is Field Marshal Sir John Dill, Churchill's representative in Washington DC, while on his right is Field Marshal Sir Alan Brooke, Dill's successor as CIGS. (US National Archives; ARC 292267) 9 Egypt, June 1942 and General Sir Claude Auchinleck studies a map as Eighth Army withdraws to the El Alamein-Qattara Depression line, where it will stop Rommel's Panzer Armee Afrika in its attempt to reach the Nile Delta. (IWM, E 13873)

10 Although Eighth Army fought Rommel to a standstill in July 1942, Churchill was unimpressed and travelled to Egypt where he sacked Auchinleck. Among the other casualties of the Auk's departure was Major-General Eric Dorman-Smith, or 'Chink', seen here with Churchill in the Western Desert. (IWM, E15313) 11 General Eric Dorman-Smith with Field Marshal Sir Alan Brooke, the CIGS, who had long disliked and distrusted 'Chink'. (IWM, E 15298)

12 Following Eighth Army's victory at El Alamein, Allied forces pursued the Germans and Italians out of Egypt, through Libya and into Tunisia. On 23 January 1943, Eighth Army captured Tripoli, the capital of Libya and a vital port. Anti-aircraft defence for Tripoli was provided by 9th (Londonderry) HAA Regiment, which received an early visit from Lieutenant-General Bernard Montgomery, Eighth Army's commander. Photographed here with gunners of 24 HAA Battery, Monty, wearing his trademark black beret with two badges, told the soldiers that he, too, was 'a Derryman'. (Author's collection)   13 General Sir Harold Alexander was the new C-in-C, Middle East. Here he is seen with HM King George VI during a visit by the King to Middle East Forces. (Irish Guards)

14 Christmas Day 1942 and General Alexander joined Eighth Army in the front line. He is seen taking part in the Christmas Service at Army Headquarters. (IWM, E20727)   15 Following the battle of El Alamein, Allied forces landed in French Northwest Africa in Operation TORCH. Included in those forces was the Irish Brigade, commanded by Brigadier Nelson Russell from Lisburn. (IWM, NA 3336)   16 A crayon and charcoal portrait of Nelson Russell as commander of the Irish Brigade by Frank McKelvey. (Lisburn Museum/Robert McKelvey)

17 Field Marshal Sir John Dill was awarded an honorary degree of doctor of laws by Princeton University, New Jersey. He is seen, centre, with Dr Harold W. Dodds, president of Princeton, walking to the university chapel where the degree was conferred. Behind Dill is Major-General Frederick H. Osburn, US Army. (IWM, NYP 24632) 18 In Britain, Anti-Aircraft Command continued to fight its war against enemy aircraft. The loss of personnel to other arms was offset to some degree by the re-roling of units of the Home Guard to anti-aircraft duties. Tim Pile visits a Middlesex Home Guard AA unit and talks to a captain of that unit. Note the AA Command archer badge and the numerals 101 denoting a Home Guard AA unit on the captain's uniform. His medal ribbons indicate that he had served in the Great War. (IWM, H 39594)

19 During the Tunisian campaign, Lieutenant-Colonel Adrian Gore distinguished himself as the commanding officer of a battalion. He was subsequently promoted to Brigadier and commanded 61 (Rifle) Brigade in Italy. (Royal Green Jackets Museum)   20 In Burma, Major-General Orde Wingate's Chindits launched their second long-range operation behind Japanese lines in 1944. Shortly after the beginning of operations, Wingate was killed in a plane crash and was succeeded as commander of Special Force by Major-General 'Joe' Lentaigne. (IWM, IND 3426)   21 Major-General Gerald Templer, GOC 56th (London) Division meets General Sir Bernard Paget, who succeeded Alexander as C-in-C, Middle East. Also in the photograph is Brigadier J. Scott-Elliott, commander of 167 Brigade. (IWM, E 28727)

22 Montgomery, in a typical pose, stands on a DUKW while speaking to Canadian soldiers of Eighth Army during the campaign in Sicily. (Frank Royal/National Archives of Canada/PA-130249) 23 Major-General Gerald Templer with General Mark Clark, commander of Fifth (US) Army, in which 56th (London) Division was serving in the early months of the Italian campaign. (IWM, NA 8676)

24 Lieutenant-General Richard McCreery commanded X (British) Corps in Fifth (US) Army in the invasion of Italy at Salerno and in the subsequent battles though the winter of 1943–4. The badge on his left sleeve below the shoulder is that of X Corps. (IWM, NA 19063)   25 General Sir Harold Alexander, commanding Allied Armies Italy, celebrates St Patrick's Day 1944 with the traditional shamrock. He marked the occasion at Sorrento with the survivors of 1st Irish Guards who had been evacuated from the Anzio beachhead. This was Alex's fifteenth St Patrick's Day on parade with the regiment and his fifth on active operations. (Irish Guards)   26 In the invasion of northwest Europe, which began on 6 June 1944, one of the major British formations was XXX Corps. From late August this was commanded by Lieutenant-General Brian Horrocks who had been wounded badly in Tunisia. Horrocks is seen here in a staff car shortly after his arrival in France. (IWM, BU 376)

27 Montgomery, with his usual casual attitude to dress regulations, is pictured with three of his commanders. On the left is Major-General Allan Adair, GOC of Guards Armoured Division, who maintains Guards' standards even in the field. On Monty's left is Horrocks while the officer on the right is Major-General 'Pip' Roberts, GOC of 11th Armoured Division. (IWM, B 9973)   28 On 25 July 1944, King George VI knighted Lieutenant-General Sir Richard McCreery in Italy. The King, who had travelled to Italy under the pseudonym General Collingwood to visit the troops of Eighth and Fifth Armies, is seen congratulating Sir Richard after dubbing him with the accolade of knighthood. (IWM, NA 17165)

29 Major-General Allan Adair acknowledges the greetings of the citizens of Brussels as their city was liberated by Guards Armoured Division on 3 September 1944. (IWM, BU 479)   30 On 7 October 1944, the massed pipe bands of 15th (Scottish) Division played in the grounds of Helmond castle in The Netherlands for the people of the town of Helmond. Lieutenant-General Sir Richard O'Connor, commanding VIII Corps, was present and is seen talking with Major Ferguson, a visitor from 51st (Highland) Division. (IWM, B 10600)

31 In October 1944, Eighth Army in Italy saw much re-organization with command passing from Sir Oliver Leese to Sir Richard McCreery. In this photograph, General McCreery is seen talking to Brigadier David Dawnay, commander of 21 Tank Brigade. Dawnay had commanded the North Irish Horse and continued to wear that regiment's shoulder title. (IWM, NA 19238) 32 Brigadier J.O.E. Vandeleur, who had commanded 3rd Irish Guards and the Irish Guards Group from Normandy to the Low Countries, was appointed to command 129 Brigade in 43rd (Wessex) Division from 15 November 1944. (Irish Guards)

33 As commander of 129 Brigade, Joe Vandeleur was awarded a Bar to the DSO he had earned as a battalion commander. He was invested with the ribbon of the DSO by Field Marshal Sir Bernard Montgomery. (IWM, B 12493) 34 Major-General Frederick Loftus Tottenham commanded 81st (West African) Division in its highly successful campaign in the Kaladan valley in Burma in late-1944 and January 1945. This campaign was fought largely on foot in the manner of the much acclaimed Chindit campaigns but, although Loftus Tottenham's command achieved more than the Chindits, less has been written about them. Loftus Tottenham was an inspiring and self-effacing commander, as can be seen from this photograph, taken on active service. (IWM, IND 4388)

35 Field Marshal Sir John Dill died in Washington DC on 4 November 1944. Such was the respect that he commanded in the United States that he was given a funeral service in the National Cathedral followed by interment in Arlington National Cemetery in Virginia. His grave is marked by this equestrian statue of Dill which was unveiled by President Truman. (Author's photograph) 36 In Italy, the Irish Brigade, now commanded by Brigadier Pat Scott, celebrated St Patrick's Day 1945 in Forli. Since the Brigade had been in the line on the 17th, the Saint's day was marked on 29 March. Shamrock was distributed at a parade and church services were held. Pat Scott addresses the Brigade and guests at the parade. (Author's collection)

suggested that Pile succeed Dill as CIGS. Another friend and confidant in Pile's circle was Churchill himself, who took a close interest in the activities of AA Command; his daughter Mary later served in an anti-aircraft battery while his son-in-law Duncan Sandys was a liaison officer with the Command. However, friendship did not stop Churchill from taking the occasional sideswipe at Pile, commenting in one note to the latter's chief of staff that the low expenditure of Bofors ammunition suggested that such guns could be replaced by rockets; the low ammunition expenditure was due, however, to the shortage of such weapons.

Meanwhile the scientists continued their efforts to improve radar so that it might be used to control the guns and, thereby, reduce the number of rounds needed to shoot down an aircraft. The urgent need for this was emphasized in the aftermath of the battle of Britain when the Luftwaffe switched to night raids on the United Kingdom. The 'blitz' brought devastation to cities throughout the UK and Anti-Aircraft Command became the first line of defence since fighter pilots were blind during the hours of darkness. Airborne-interception (AI) radar was in its infancy and the first aircraft to which it was fitted, the Bristol Blenheim, was not fast enough to catch the bombers. Hurricane fighters, controlled by ground radar stations, provided a stop-gap air defence alongside Blenheims until the much faster Bristol Beaufighter could be available in sufficient numbers to provide an effective nightfighter force.

Anti-Aircraft Command's gun-laying radar sets were too few in number and lacked the sophistication needed to allow radar control of the gun defences, forcing Pile and his staff to fall back on a method developed during the Great War – the barrage. The underlying principle of the barrage was to put a curtain of shellbursts in front of any attacking aircraft, thereby forcing attackers to turn away, take avoiding action that would put them off their aim, or be shot down. The system used large amounts of ammunition which brought a caustic note from Churchill in which he commented that 260,000 rounds for September was a heavy expenditure and demanding a weekly return.

The guns were firing in the dark, both literally and metaphorically, and Pile considered the London defence a 'policy of despair' rather than a barrage, with every gun ordered to fire every available round on an approximate bearing and elevation. This policy was intended to boost civilian morale as much as deter the Luftwaffe and it certainly succeeded in its morale effect. Fortunately, progress was being made with gun-laying (GL) radar; the new GL II set was being used experimentally at the Burnt Farm gun-site where Cossor's, the manufacturers, had a facility. This link-up between Cossor's and the guns, although entirely unofficial, produced such good results that Pile was convinced that had forty GL II sets been available in the winter of 1940–41 the skies over London would have become a death-trap for the Luftwaffe. Such co-operation between equipment manufacturers and users symbolized the way in which Anti-Aircraft Command and its GOC dealt with producers.

> I doubt if there has been a Command in war which had so much influence on the type of equipment it was eventually armed with. The producers heard

once a month ... what we required and why. I am also in no doubt that a similar committee ... would have resulted in far better tanks and anti-tank guns than we possessed ... If Sir Robin Sinclair had done nothing else in the war, and he did a lot, his work as DGAR [Director General of Army Research] would have been sufficient to earn him a place in history.

The blitz ended in the spring of 1941as the nights became too short for bombers to operate in safety over Britain. Preparations were also being made for their transfer to the east and in June 1941 the Germans invaded Russia. There was no quick victory and German bombers did not return to France to renew the night offensive against Britain that autumn. They were not to come back in large numbers for almost three years, although, in between, there would be tip-and-run raids by fast fighter-bombers and attacks by small formations of aircraft.

For the gunners and for the people of London there was relief; between 23 August 1940 and 1 January 1941 the capital had had only eight bombing-free nights. It was hardly surprising that morale had begun to sag; the unfortunate Londoners were apt to vent their frustration on the gunners. Pile received letters demonstrating that frustration, with one correspondent telling him that the 'anti-aircraft defence of London [is] the biggest scandal since Nero', while another expressed the view that Pile did not 'understand the meaning of the word barrage'. But the 'policy of despair' barrage had turned away up to forty-eight per cent of the raiders although, as Pile conceded, that brought no consolation to those who suffered from the fifty-two per cent that did not turn away.

Well-planned and carefully calculated barrages could, and did, achieve much better rates of success. Of course, these also needed an appropriate density of guns, as at Scapa Flow where the barrage system saved the Fleet on at least one occasion. Professor A V Hill was highly critical of the system, arguing that, since a cubic mile of space contained five-and-a-half-thousand-million cubic yards and the lethal zone of a bursting 3.7-inch shell was only a few thousand cubic yards, and then only for about one-fiftieth of a second, it was nonsense to talk about a barrage. To have a one-fiftieth chance of downing a bomber travelling at 250mph through a ten-mile-wide, four-mile-high vertical rectangle would require 3,000 shells per second. Mathematically, Hill may have been correct but, as with many scientists, he failed to appreciate the human factor; a pilot seeing ack-ack shells explode in front of him does not begin to compute the mathematical probability of a hit but sees something that he knows can kill him or bring down his aircraft and, as a result, will take avoiding action or even drop his bombs in the wrong place. One former pilot once told me about seeing an ack-ack barrage that was so thick that 'it looked like you could have got out and walked on it' while Luftwaffe pilots flying over Tripoli in early-1943 described the ack-ack defences of the city as a '*wand aus stahl*', or wall of steel. Pile and his gunners were aware fully of this human factor, even if Professor Hill was not.

Not every complaint received in Pile's Headquarters was from a critic of the barrage system; some came from people who did not want AA guns close to their homes. Among the latter was a letter from a London borough whose residents were concerned that blasts from ack-ack guns were cracking lavatory pans in their homes and would General Pile mind moving his barrage elsewhere? Needless to say, such a request could not be countenanced. For many complaints, Pile's policy was to invite the complainant to visit a gun-site and see the work of an AA battery. These visitors were asked not to divulge any information of an operational nature and none ever did. The policy proved very successful and gained Pile many supporters in public positions; of course, the general's own affable nature had much to do with that.

Lack of resources continued to plague the Command into 1941. This had been exacerbated during the blitz by calls for additional guns for Coventry, the western ports and Northern Ireland but the shortage of guns meant that those requests could not be met immediately. Both Belfast and Coventry suffered particularly heavy attacks with serious losses. German bombers inflicted the highest single night's casualties on any UK city outside London when they targeted Belfast on Easter Tuesday night in 1941; not until the autumn of that year did Belfast have its full complement of guns. Fortunately, there was also good news as the scientists had discovered a method of improving the effectiveness of GL radar by surrounding the site with a 'mat' of wire netting to overcome signal distortion from uneven ground. Implementing this scheme required all the wire netting in Britain plus some 3,500 miles of stay wiring to support the 'mats'. By the end of January 1941 about one in ten GL sites had been treated; in the same month the number of rounds needed to shoot down each unseen aircraft had reduced to 4,087, over 2,000 less than the previous average. However, it was considered that this had more to do with improvements in gunner efficiency than with the radar 'mats'.

When the blitz ended, AA Command had the opportunity to improve both levels of defences and training in anticipation of Luftwaffe bombers returning the following winter. But, as we have seen, the invasion of Russia took the bulk of those bombers eastwards and the blitz was not renewed in the winter of 1941–2. As equipment continued improving and GL II radar became available in large numbers while development work moved on to the next version, GL III, other demands were made on the Command. Some were for manpower and others for guns, either for overseas' use or for the Admiralty. With reduced pressure at home, the Command was seen as a large pool of manpower and other resources, a problem that taxed Pile considerably.

Tip-and-run raiders, 'Baedeker' raids – where the Luftwaffe attacked towns and cities of historic interest, as listed in the Baedeker guides – 'scalded cat' raids and the 'little blitz' of early 1944 all helped keep the ack-ack gunners on their mettle and to prepare them for their greatest test, and their greatest triumph: the V1, or flying-bomb, attacks that began on 13 June 1944, a week after the D-Day invasion of France. A simple, unmanned aircraft, powered by a pulsejet engine and with a warhead of about a ton, the V1 wreaked considerable damage and destruction in

Britain. Its flight was described by the Americans as 'cruising' and it thus gave its name to its modern successor, the cruise missile.

These attacks had been expected, although Lord Cherwell, one of the government's scientific advisers, thought the V-weapons to be a hoax. In a speech at the Mansion House in November 1943, Churchill had hinted at the expected use of new weaponry and, the following month, Anti-Aircraft Command had been told to expect the arrival of pilotless aircraft at a rate of some 200 an hour. Within a week plans had been made to defend key targets, including London and this at a time when the Command was committed heavily to protecting the forces assembling for Operation OVERLORD, the invasion of France, and the vessels to carry them. To everyone's surprise the Luftwaffe made only token attacks on these prime targets.

The first flying-bombs ushered in an onslaught that would last over nine months and leave thousands dead. Flying straight and level, the V1 was, in theory, an ideal target for anti-aircraft guns; however, it flew just too high for effective engagement by light guns and too low to be an easy target for the heavies. The Germans had planned well. Pile was not disheartened for he saw a bright ray of hope from a new American GL radar, SCR 584, that he believed would give his guns a better chance of defeating the V1s. He sought Churchill's assistance to obtain this new radar for the Command. With a new predictor and remote power control for traversing and elevating the guns, SCR 584 provided a 'robot defence against a robot weapon'. Churchill was also instrumental in giving the guns a much greater role in the battle against the V1s by approving Pile's plan to establish a gun belt along the south coast as the first line of defence. That line was to include static 3.7-inch guns that could traverse more smoothly than their mobile counterparts at the higher traverse speeds needed in this battle. However, static guns had always been just that, fixed to concrete platforms that took time to construct. Once again Pile's technical staff solved the problem. His Deputy Director Mechanical Engineering (DEME), Brigadier Burls, designed a latticework platform of steel rails and railway sleepers. Such 'Pile Platforms' could be moved from site to site and, when filled with ballast, were as steady a gun platform as solid concrete. Hundreds of static guns, with their fire-control equipment and stores, were moved to the south coast into what was called 'Diver Belt'; the V1s were codenamed 'Divers'. This massive redeployment began on 14 July and the heavies were in position by dawn on the 17th; the light guns were ready for action on the 19th.

The move of guns and equipment was an outstanding operation but what followed was even better. First priority against the V1s was now given to the guns; in their first week of operations they destroyed seventeen per cent of all targets entering the gun area; this improved steadily until, in their fifth week, the guns were accounting for fifty-five per cent of V1s. Gun detachments were being worked harder than at probably any other time of the war, with days when detachments were called on to man their weapons for the full twenty-four hours. In spite of that the kill rate continued to rise, reaching sixty per cent by 23 August and increasing to seventy-four per cent by 1 September when the first phase of the V1 campaign ended. On one night the guns accounted for eighty-two per cent of targets. The searchlights also played their part, helping fighters to engage those V1s that escaped the guns.

The first wave of V1 attacks came to an end when the Allies overran the launch sites in the Pas de Calais. By then the guns had accounted for over 1,550 V1s while searchlights had helped fighters down another 142. Churchill sent a message to Pile conveying his congratulations on the 'brilliant work of the anti-aircraft batteries'. But the public believed that the RAF was doing all the destruction; no news bulletin ever explained that ack-ack guns had shot down even a single V1 in the first phase. The official view was that disclosing the effectiveness of the guns to the public would have provided information 'valuable to the enemy'.

On 6 September the second phase of the V1 campaign began with bombs coming in from the east coast; these included some launched from bombers over the sea. Again the defences had to be uprooted. The guns from Diver Belt were moved into Diver Strip, stretching from the Diver Box around the Thames estuary up to Yarmouth and Lowestoft. Once in position the guns enjoyed even more success than before and, by 30 November, were accounting for eighty-two per cent of all targets. For this phase the average kill rate was sixty-five per cent and each V1 shot down needed only 156 rounds of ammunition, thanks to the new VT fuses. Also known as proximity fuses, these had been developed in the United States from a British invention, a valve small enough to fit into a fuse.

This success was achieved against a background of further demands for manpower from the Command: 50,000 men transferred to reinforce 21 Army Group on the continent; 23,000 ATS women also transferred;* and a number of regiments sent to Belgium to defend Antwerp against V1s. Other areas of the UK had to be stripped of guns to maintain the Diver defences, which were extended further when Diver Fringe was established from Skegness north to Whitby. The latter was created only in skeletal form and by then the V1 menace was almost over. In November and December 1944, Pile was asked to give up another 40,000 men for Europe but by then the battle of the V1 was almost over and Anti-Aircraft Command had been the most important element in winning it.

The final German weapon was the V2 rocket, which arrived with no warning since it was supersonic and followed a ballistic trajectory. By then, Pile and his scientists were so confident that they believed that a system could be developed to combat the rockets. This scheme involved predicting the point of fall of the rockets and firing guns to burst shells in their paths. Only two seconds were available in which to make the gun predictions, since firing had to start when the rocket was over thirty miles from its point of impact. Creating plans for this scheme involved 'more than 25,000 complicated mathematical calculations' and radar was vital; in trials for the scheme, radar sets were found to be detecting meteorites that produced a signal

---

* Auxiliary Territorial Service, many of whose members served in AA Command in a range of duties including operating fire-control equipment.

similar to a V2. However, the threat of the V2 ended before the scheme could become operational.

Whether that scheme would have worked is another story. The first apparently successful defence against missiles came with the American Patriot air defence system against Iraqi Scud missiles in the 1991 Gulf War but doubt has been cast on that success in the intervening years and the UK plan to purchase Patriots for heavy air defence units has never been implemented.

The enthusiasm shown by the scientists and gunners involved in planning defences against the V2 is a clear indication of how successful Tim Pile was in conducting his Command in liaison with the scientific establishment. It also indicates the level of morale that Pile built up in AA Command throughout the war. The ack-ack gunners could hardly have asked for a better chief.

In March 1945 the Luftwaffe carried out Operation GISELA, the last major raid by enemy aircraft on Britain. RAF bombers returning from raids on Germany were infiltrated by enemy fighter-bombers that escaped gunfire for fear of RAF machines being hit and went on to attack bombers as they landed, shooting down twenty-four, as well as hitting at airfields, roads and other targets; some even struck at London. Pile noted that it 'was almost impossible to distinguish friend from foe in the confusion'. The following night there were further attacks but on a reduced scale and, although some small raids took place later in the month, these were the last significant attacks on Britain. On 29 March the last V1 exploded in a sewage works near Hatfield in Hertfordshire.

Anti-Aircraft Command had done its job well and deserved much more credit and praise than it has ever received. So, too, did its GOC-in-C who retired from the Army in April after a distinguished career that saw him take a makeshift defensive organization and turn it into one of the most effective weapons of the Second World War. One of Tim Pile's greatest regrets was that his gunners were never recognized by the award of a clasp to the 1939–45 Medal; nor were any decorated for courage. The War Office seemed to believe that they were not engaged in frontline warfare, as were AA gunners in the field. By contrast the Royal Navy took a different attitude and when Leading Seaman Jack Mantle died at his AA gun on board HMS *Foylebank* at Portland on 4 July 1940 he was recommended posthumously, and successfully, for the Victoria Cross. Thus a naval AA gunner could receive the country's highest award for gallantry while his Army counterparts, performing the same duty, were considered ineligible. Pile and his Gunners deserved better.

~ 7 ~

Brooke

Following VE Day, a general election in Britain resulted in a Labour government. Winston Churchill received many messages of sympathy on his loss of office. One came from the wartime Chairman of the Chiefs of Staff, Field Marshal Brooke, to whom Churchill replied saying that he was deeply grateful for all that Brooke had done for the country and how much Brooke's charming letter had touched him. He reminded Brooke that he valued his friendship as he did his memories of other members of the Brooke family in earlier times and concluded by writing that 'Our story in this war is a good one, and this will be recognised as time goes on'.

Brooke had probably been closer to Churchill than anyone else during the war and Churchill's comment that their story was a good one was no hollow claim, since their partnership had been one of the keys to Allied victory in the Second World War.

Born in July 1883, Alan Francis Brooke was the ninth child of Sir Victor Brooke Bt, of Colebrooke, County Fermanagh, and Lady Brooke, formerly Alice Bellingham; Sir Victor died when Alan was only eight. Alan was born not in Colebrooke but at Bagnerres-de-Bigorre near Pau in the French Pyrenees where the Brookes had a home. One of Ulster's best-known families, the Brookes came to Ireland during the Elizabethan era when they were granted land in County Donegal. During the 1641 rebellion Henry Brooke held Donegal castle against the rebels and was rewarded the following year with 30,000 acres in County Fermanagh, forfeited from the executed Concobhar Rua Maguire.

Over the centuries the Brookes became a prominent British military family. While they undoubtedly felt that they had to protect their lands in Ireland against future rebellion, they also played a significant part in the British Army's many overseas campaigns. A Brooke commanded the expedition that burned the executive mansion, home of the President of the United States, during the war of 1812. Refurbishment included painting white the building's scorched walls and, in this way, the mansion became the White House. Perhaps the best summary of the family's contribution to British military history is shown in the numbers who served in the twentieth century's two world wars: twenty-six Brookes served in the first, twenty-seven in the second. Twelve died in those wars and many decorations were earned, including a Victoria Cross.

With such a family background it was natural that young Alan would enter the Army, but before doing so he had to become a naturalized British subject since by birth he was French. In fact, he spoke French before he spoke English – he was also fluent in German – and never quite mastered the nuances of English grammar and syntax. In common with Tim Pile, Brooke was not a Sandhurst man, opting instead for the Royal Military Academy, Woolwich, which he entered in 1900, hoping for a commission in the Royal Engineers. However, since only fifteen engineer commissions were granted in the year he passed out, he went instead to the Royal Artillery. His high placing at Woolwich allowed him to select his own branch of the gunners and he chose the field artillery. In the years before the Great War Brooke served in Ireland and India and was awarded his 'jacket' when he was selected for the Royal Horse Artillery.

In September 1914 Brooke's battery, N Battery, also known as the Eagle Troop, Royal Horse Artillery, was posted from India to join the BEF. N Battery did not arrive in France until after the German offensive had been checked and the Allied counter-offensive had also come to a halt, causing the war to settle into a pattern of trench warfare that would last until spring 1918. This stalemate emphasized the importance of artillery, which came to dominate the battlefield. In the British Army almost one man in six served in the Royal Artillery and high quality gunner officers became some of the most sought-after men of the war. Brooke was one such and his rise was rapid. In January 1915 he became the Royal Artillery staff captain of an Indian division and by June 1918 Lieutenant-Colonel Brooke was the senior gunner staff officer in First Army. The intervening years saw him discharge most of the duties of an artillery officer in war. With the Indian division his task was selecting observation posts, OPs, from which gunner officers could direct artillery support for the infantry. When OPs were established he had to ensure that the officers did their jobs effectively, which meant visiting them often. This was a dangerous job that left a lasting impression on Brooke; he later wrote about some of what he had witnessed on the front line, as at the battle of Festubert in May 1915. Commenting that he would never forget the 'ghastly sights' he described how the ground between the trench lines was covered in dead and dying men. Wounded soldiers lay in agony under a scorching sun and without water throughout the day. When darkness fell some could be brought in, but no rescue efforts were possible in daylight. He considered Festubert 'one of the worst shambles in no man's land that I have ever seen'.

During 1916 Brooke was the Royal Artillery Brigade Major of 18th Division, one of the best-trained British formations in France. That was due to the divisional commander, Major-General Ivor Maxse, an outstanding trainer and thorough planner with whom Brooke got on well; both were perfectionists. It was Brooke who was largely responsible for 18th Division's artillery plan for the Somme offensive; for this he adapted a French concept, the creeping bombardment, designed to keep pace with advancing infantry, thereby providing them with the maximum support. The gunners were given maps showing the exact timings of each bombardment and the 'lifts' onto the next bombardment.* Brooke also decided to use trench mortars rather than shrapnel to cut barbed-wire entanglements in no man's land; this technique proved extremely effective whereas shrapnel failed to cut the wire, either bursting too soon and dispersing in the air, or too late and bursting underground. It was no coincidence that 18th Division had the most successful advance of any British division on 1 July 1916. The first objective was taken in twenty minutes and the division captured and held some of its principal objectives. As the campaign continued, Brooke's system was refined until he was able to report that 'the map procedure was working like magic and being copied on all sides'. Brooke's work in the Somme offensive was rewarded with the DSO.

In spite of this success, Brooke believed that there was still progress to be made; he later wrote that:

> We had made great progress in the co-ordinated control of artillery. We were, however, still obsessed with the idea that the total destruction of all enemy defences must be achieved before the attack. We were, therefore, still wedded to lengthy preliminary bombardments which sacrificed all the advantages of surprise.

Brooke's next posting allowed him even more opportunity to develop his thinking and refine his tactics. He was posted to the Canadian Corps whose artillery commander knew little about the tactical handling of artillery and thus left Brooke to write all orders and plans. In April 1917 the Canadians assaulted Vimy Ridge supported by one of the greatest artillery fireplans of the war. The plan had been drafted by Brooke and drew praise from a Canadian gunner officer who commented that Brooke made 'his greatest and initial reputation as a gunner staff officer in the 1st Canadian Corps in the artillery plans he drew up for and executed in the capture of Vimy Ridge by the corps in April 1917'.

Although a staff officer, Brooke was not one to remain in a safe rear headquarters: he visited the front regularly and also took to flying over it to see for himself conditions in the line and no man's land. When the war came to an end he was at First Army HQ as GSO 1 (General Staff Officer), Royal Artillery. Although he had broadened his experience over the four years of conflict the war left an indelible impression on him. Following a visit to the ruins of Lens in October 1918 he wrote:

> I climbed onto a heap of stones where the church once stood, and I looked down on the wreckage. One could spend days there just looking down picturing to oneself the tragedies that have occurred in every corner of this place. If the stones could talk and could repeat what they have witnessed, and the thoughts they had read on dying men's faces, I wonder if there would ever be any wars.

---

* Although there is a tendency to describe artillery fire as 'barrages' the term 'barrage' refers strictly only to fire in a defensive situation, such as anti-aircraft fire, while offensive fire against enemy positions is properly called bombardment.

The Great War was almost over. German forces were on the retreat and in early November Germany sought an armistice. At 11.00am on 11 November, the guns fell silent for the last time. The killing on the western front had ended and the survivors would soon be demobilized, leaving only regular soldiers in the armies. Alan Brooke was one of those regulars and, having ended the war with a superb reputation as an artillery officer, was invited to be a student on the first postwar Staff College course. During that course, he impressed both staff and fellow students with his mental ability, breadth of knowledge and eloquence.

In the interwar years Brooke served on the staff at Camberley as well as being both a student and staff member at the Imperial Defence College. As a brigadier he commanded the School of Artillery and subsequently, as a major-general, became an inspector of artillery. In addition to gunner appointments he commanded infantry formations and in 1936 was appointed Director of Military Training. By then Britain was re-arming in preparation for war with Germany and attention was being turned to the country's anti-aircraft defences. In 1938 an Anti-Aircraft Corps was created and Brook was appointed to command it. He handed over command of what had by then become Anti-Aircraft Command to Tim Pile in August 1939; Pile would command the ack-ack defences for the entire war. General Brooke took over Southern Command before becoming commander of the BEF's II Corps in late-1939.

In France Brooke was not impressed with the attitude of the BEF commander, Lord Gort of Limerick vc, nor with that of the War Office. Gort gave the impression that he considered the Germans to be overrated since they had only defeated the Poles who, Gort averred, had a second-rate army. In February 1940 Brooke confided to his diary that 'all indications show that the War Office now look upon this front as one of stalemate. They will have a rude awakening'. That 'rude awakening' came in May 1940 with the German invasion of the Low Countries. Immediately, orders were issued to the BEF to advance into Belgium to meet the German attack, abandoning the defences prepared in France. But, as the Belgian army collapsed and the French wavered, the BEF was forced to withdraw. That advance into Belgium had almost led to the loss of the BEF; only the ability of men such as Brooke saved it from destruction.

Throughout the brief campaign Brooke's ability as a commander was clear: with the Belgian collapse, the left wing of II Corps was 'in the air' and exposed, but Brooke's cool genius prevented the situation from becoming disastrous. He redeployed his troops, with Montgomery's 3rd Division making its famous night march from the south of the corps line to the north. Everyone who saw Brooke in action was impressed by his performance; he chose to praise the abilities of two of his generals, Alexander and Montgomery. In the final days of the campaign, Brooke was recalled to England and handed command of II Corps over to Montgomery. On his return to Britain he was amazed at his new orders: 'return to France and form a new BEF'. That order, from Sir John Dill, the new CIGS, was intended to bolster the French army and ensure that France remained in the war. Although Brooke felt that the plan had almost no chance of success, he realized that Winston Churchill, the new prime minister, was determined that it should go ahead and so Brooke returned to France.

Brooke's new BEF was to be made up of formations that had not been evacuated from Dunkirk and, with the French army, was to hold a line around Brittany, thus turning that province into a redoubt. However, on the day that Brooke landed in France, one of the formations still in the country, and intended to be part of the new BEF, surrendered. Although there were promises of more troops, including the Canadians who had arrived in Britain, Brooke regarded Whitehall as being wildly optimistic. Anthony Eden, the Secretary of State for War, recorded that 'Brooke left me in no doubt as to what he thought of the situation, but had a happy knack of strong criticism without rancour'.

Across the channel Brooke discovered that the French army had almost ceased to exist, thus making the plan for the Brittany redoubt an impossibility. Defending Brittany would have required at least fifteen divisions but only four British divisions were available. The French collapse saddened Brooke, especially because of the empathy he felt with the land of his birth and his admiration for the French in the Great War. But he had seen the low level of French morale in November 1939 when he had attended a ceremony at a French army headquarters. During the march past he was aghast at the soldiers' slovenly appearance; they were unshaven, dirty and lacking pride. However, what most shook him was

> the look on the men's faces, disgruntled and insubordinate looks, and although ordered to give 'eyes left' hardly a man bothered to do so.

Combined with visits to the Maginot line, he had no illusions about the French army. He made clear his views on the impracticability of the Brittany redoubt in June 1940 and, as a result, the BEF was again evacuated.

After his return to Britain Brooke was appointed C-in-C, Home Forces with the immediate priority of preparing to meet a German invasion. However, that invasion never materialized and, following the German attack on the Soviet Union in June 1941, troops in Britain were able to train for more flexible forms of warfare, including the future invasion of Europe. Brooke remained C-in-C, Home Forces until December 1941 when he was appointed to succeed his friend Sir John Dill as CIGS. Among the many congratulatory messages he received was one from the elderly former rector of Colebrooke in County Fermanagh.

> I do hope I may live to see you when you have finished with Hitler. It will beat the night that Colonel Ronnie came back after the South African War. Brookeborough was full of lighted tar barrels and Orangemen and Nationalists were all shaking hands with one another. Half the crowd did not get home until next day ...

With America now in the war, following the Japanese attack on Pearl Harbor and Hitler's and Mussolini's declarations of war four days later, Churchill was en route to Washington to meet Roosevelt, a meeting that established Allied strategy for the remainder of the war. Churchill had left Brooke in England so that he could settle into his new post and had taken Sir John Dill to Washington – after much persuasion by Brooke. Since Dill subsequently headed the British Military Mission in Washington, Brooke always considered this to be one of his most important achievements.

> Thank Heaven I succeeded in persuading Winston, as few men did more in furthering our cause to final victory than Dill. From the very start he built up a deep friendship with Marshall and proved to be an invaluable link between the British and American chiefs of staff ... I look upon that ... as one of my most important achievements during the war or at any rate among those that bore most fruit.

When Brooke prevailed upon Churchill to take Dill to Washington, he had not at that stage succeeded to the post of CIGS, as Dill did not stand down officially until Christmas Day 1941. It is interesting to note that Churchill had tried to block Brooke's appointment; when he heard who was to be the Army's new professional head, he had said:

> When I thump the table and push my face towards him what does he do? Thumps the table harder and glares back at me – I know these Brookes, stiff-necked Ulstermen, and there's no one worse to deal with than that.

However, the relationship between this particular 'stiff-necked Ulsterman' and Britain's wartime premier was to be one of history's most important and it was Brooke's ability and willingness to 'thump the table harder' that made that partnership so strong. Churchill might complain of Brooke's obstinacy but he himself gave Brooke much cause for complaint. The prime minister could be scathingly critical of his commanders and once commented that his generals seemed willing to expend more energy fighting each other than in combating the enemy; his most famous criticism was the comment: 'Put the bravest soldier, sailor and airman together in one room and what do you get? The sum of all their fears.'

When Churchill and Roosevelt forged their agreement in December 1941, the defeat of Germany was the first priority. To the Americans this meant the earliest possible invasion of mainland Europe from Britain, an interpretation that would lead to friction between the Allies, especially between the heads of their armed forces. As 1941 turned into 1942, the Germans were being engaged actively in North Africa by British forces and in eastern Europe by the Russians. The British view was that an invasion of France would be impossible in 1942 and might not even be possible in 1943 but American forces could join the campaign in North Africa; this was agreed finally. US troops took part in Operation TORCH, the invasion of French Northwest Africa in November 1942 and fought in the subsequent Tunisian campaign. When that campaign ended in May 1943 it raised the question of what to do with the Allied troops in Africa.

The Americans argued for an invasion of France, which would have meant transferring the forces in North Africa to Britain, while the British favoured a Mediterranean strategy, using those forces to dominate the Mediterranean and knock Italy out of the war. Brooke argued that by invading Sicily and then Italy to force an Italian surrender, every Italian formation in the Balkans, on the Russian front and in Italy would have to be replaced by German troops. The Americans eventually agreed to this British strategy of 'closing the ring', although it went against American military philosophy, which was to use the maximum concentration of power on the main front. Both American service chiefs and politicians were also suspicious of what they perceived as British obsession with the Mediterranean, which they attributed to Britain's desire to protect the Empire's sea lanes, whereas they wanted to see the Empire dismantled. As a result the Americans agreed initially only that Sicily should be invaded; further Mediterranean operations would be considered once Sicily had been conquered.

The US Chiefs, still anxious to invade France, considered British caution a symptom of an unwillingness to accept the need to tackle the largest part of the German armies in western Europe. However, the British had been planning for such an invasion ever since they had been forced to quit France in 1940. They had even begun preparation for the Mulberry harbours that would prove so useful in 1944 as well as designing a range of landing craft and landing ships that would make the invasion possible. What the British appreciated more than the Americans was the strength needed to invade France, and to maintain the invasion force there. Landing an army on the continent was not the biggest problem; reinforcing it, supplying and maintaining it was. In British eyes that would not be possible until 1943, since the ring around German needed further tightening, more attrition of German forces and Germany's ability to wage war, and ascendancy over the Kriegsmarine's U-boats. These were the arguments presented by Brooke to his American counterparts but, while they appreciated his ability, he was not popular with them, due to his style of presenting facts, his ability to recall information without notes, and the speed at which he did all this. That fluency noted by his contemporaries at Camberley seemed to the Americans to be a superiority complex in operation; they suspected that Brooke regarded them as being less capable than himself. However, while he had doubts about them to begin with, and never considered Marshall to have strategic flair, he came to appreciate their many strengths and abilities as the war progressed. The role of Sir John Dill was critical in this respect, since Dill was able to let Brooke know the direction in which American thinking was going; as a result Brooke was prepared.

Brooke's problems were not restricted to his relationships with the Americans. His greatest problems lay at home. In March 1942 he succeeded Admiral Sir Dudley Pound as Chairman of the Chiefs of Staff Committee, thereby assuming the role of representing the service chiefs to Churchill. He often had to argue long and hard to make Churchill see the services' point of view. Essentially a parliamentarian, Churchill saw himself, with some justification, as a grand strategist but did not tackle matters of strategy with the same calm, reasoned arguments used by the service chiefs. Instead, he acted as a devil's advocate, arguing and shouting against proposals from his service chiefs. In this respect, Brooke scored over his predecessor, Sir John Dill, since he was ready and able not only to thump the table harder than the premier but also to shout louder as well. The most frequent result of such heated discussion was that Churchill would accept Brooke's point of view, and then present it as his own. However, as with Dill, Brooke was being worn down by this combative relationship with Churchill and by the long evening hours spent listening to the premier. But Brooke was younger than Dill and had the safety valve of his diary, which he wrote every night, and in which he vented his exasperation with Churchill; this diary was really a series of letters to his second wife. A typical entry, after a few days away from Churchill read:

> The PM is starting off in his usual style! We had a staff meeting with him at 5.20pm for two hours and a Defence Committee from 10.20pm for another two hours. And we accomplished nothing! I don't think I can stand much more of it.

Brooke was given one opportunity to get away from the CIGS's job. In August 1942, when Auchinleck was relieved as C-in-C, Middle East, Churchill offered the post to Brooke. Although it was a tempting offer, with the opportunity of an active command well away from Whitehall and Churchill, Brooke turned it down because he realized the importance of his role as Chairman of the Chiefs of Staff; he also considered the really significant job in the region to be Eighth Army commander rather than that of C-in-C.

With a genius for grand strategy, Brooke also recognized Churchill's deep appreciation of the strategic realities of the war. After all, it was Churchill who had drafted the papers on which Allied strategy was based, but the premier's weakness was his desire to interfere in the details of operations and Brooke often had to protect field commanders from prime ministerial interference. Such was his objective in appointing Alexander and Montgomery in the Middle East in August 1942. Brooke considered Montgomery the ideal commander for Eighth Army. He also appreciated that Churchill admired Alexander more than any other general and reasoned, therefore, that Alex would be able to protect Montgomery from Downing Street pressure. Needless to say, Brooke would also be acting as a buffer between Churchill and Alexander's headquarters in Cairo.

The highly emotional Churchill was occasionally prone to wild ideas and Brooke had to ensure that these did not materialize into real plans. One of Churchill's recurring obsessions was the idea of invading Norway to strike Germany from the flank. Brooke had to dissuade him from this on more than one occasion. By a remarkable coincidence, Adolf Hitler was also obsessed with the possibility of an Allied invasion of Norway. On another occasion, as the Allies were preparing for Operation OVER-LORD, Churchill demanded to know why they were not planning to land in Portugal instead of France. Although neutral, Portugal was Britain's oldest ally and there would be an unopposed landing, following which the armies could march across Spain – also neutral, but sympathetic to Germany – to invade France. Here were shades of Wellington's Peninsular War. Brooke's planners were ordered to work through the night to prepare a paper on a campaign in the Iberian peninsula. The first that Brooke knew of it was when it was presented to the Chiefs the following morning. He described the concept as nonsense. Even so, when the Chiefs met Churchill, Brooke spent fully fifteen minutes outlining the details and facts provided by his staff before spending another five minutes bluntly telling Churchill his views on this idiotic idea. Thus ended the peninsular campaign of 1944.

Churchill was not the only opponent faced by Brooke in Britain; there were occasions when he had problems with the other service chiefs and especially with Portal, Chief of the Air Staff, who wanted priority for the strategic bomber offensive. Portal was an advocate of the theory that Germany's industrial power could be destroyed by bombing, thus making an invasion a much simpler task, and, possibly, even unnecessary. The airmen also argued that the bomber offensive and land operations against mainland Europe should not be executed at the same time: they held that bombing was a much more economical form of waging war and, therefore, made more military sense. Brooke disagreed with this theory. Neither he, nor the other members of the committee, were convinced of the value of strategic bombing and, while he supported the principle of intensifying the bomber offensive, he argued that Britain should:

> exert pressure on the German military and economic machine from every quarter and should take full advantage of the sea and air bases in North Africa to exert a heavy pressure on Italy with a view to turning her into a serious liability for Germany.

Although this argument was based on the 'closing the ring' strategy, Brooke remained convinced that the Allies would have to invade Europe to bring about the final destruction of German forces. He also considered that arguments such as those espoused by Portal could only provide ammunition to Americans who believed that Britain was shying away from land operations in mainland Europe. It is, however, interesting to note that the Portal theory was not restricted to British airmen but was adhered to by American airmen as well; it was a natural outworking of the Trenchard–Mitchell–Duohet doctrine of winning war through strategic bombing.*

Brooke had argued against an Allied invasion in 1942, telling the Americans that it would be impossible to sustain such a venture. The tragic failure of Operation

---

* This trio of apostles of strategic bombing were British (Trenchard), American (Mitchell) and Italian (Duohet).

JUBILEE, the Dieppe raid, in August 1942, emphasized his argument. (It also taught many valuable lessons that helped ensure the ultimate success of Operation OVER-LORD in 1944.)* Brooke was non-committal about an invasion in 1943, arguing that the Germans would have to sustain heavier losses before such an operation could be successful. Such losses were occurring on the eastern front and, by 1944, were so severe that the size of forces that Germany could deploy into France was reduced significantly. The Italian campaign was also drawing German forces away from France while another critical factor was the battle of the Atlantic. In 1943, sustaining an invasion would have been very difficult when the supply lines to the United States were threatened so seriously by U-boats, whereas the Germans had the advantage of internal lines of communication on the continent and would, therefore, be able to reinforce more speedily than the Allies. Although the U-boat menace was curbed from May 1943 onwards, it had been at its height as late as March 1943 and the change in tactics ordered by the Kriegsmarine from late-May would not have been obvious to the Allies for some weeks, leaving the opportunity for an invasion to July or August; in turn, that meant that the chances of breaking out of the beachhead before winter were much reduced and the success of any invasion depended on such a breakout before winter set in.

Brooke continued supporting the principle of tightening the ring around Germany until it was possible to invade France and represented British views on this to both the Americans and Soviets. Such views were not always popular while some of Churchill's wilder ideas caused dismay and suspicion among the other allies. In the end, Brooke was justified, although he had to persuade Churchill, almost at the last minute, that the invasion of France should be undertaken, only to find the prime minister so overenthusiastic about the venture that he made a 'bloody nuisance' of himself, even wanting to sail with the invasion fleet. Before D-Day Churchill's 'black dog' of depression had caused him to reflect on the possible failure of OVERLORD with the loss of life that would be involved in such failure. Haunted by the ghosts of the Somme and, more particularly, Gallipoli, Churchill feared the worst but Brooke assured him that the invasion had to go ahead, and it did.

On 12 June Brooke, Churchill and Field Marshal Smuts visited the beachhead in France, being met on the beach by Montgomery with a 'team of jeeps'. For Brooke it was 'a wonderful moment to find myself reentering France almost exactly 4 years after being thrown out for the second time, at St Nazaire'. But there must also have been a tinge of regret since Churchill had once promised Brooke overall command of the Allied Expeditionary Force before, in late-1943, telling him in casual fashion that the appointment would go to an American, General Dwight Eisenhower. By then, of course, the United States was the senior ally and entitled to the supreme commander's appointment. Eisenhower was a good choice for a multi-national command since he had the right touch of diplomacy necessary to encourage people to work well

---

* These included avoiding landing at a port, the need for a much heavier naval bombardment than that provided by destroyers at Dieppe and the requirement for specialized armoured vehicles to overcome anti-invasion obstacles on the beaches.

together. Brooke would have made a much better commander in the strategic and operational conduct of the northwest European campaign but would not have been able to handle the personalities with quite the same flair as Eisenhower.

There was still much of the war to come with, of course, Japan still to be defeated. And it was Far Eastern strategy that caused probably the greatest disagreement between Churchill and his service chiefs. Since the Americans provided the bulk of Allied forces in Southeast Asia and the Pacific, the Chiefs of Staff believed that British operations in Southeast Asia should be minor and that British support should be given to the Americans in the Pacific. Brooke wrote to Dill, telling him that 'strategically it is right for us to use all our forces in close co-operation from Australia across the Pacific in the general direction of Formosa'. Churchill disagreed with this strategy, arguing instead that British forces should carry out a British offensive in a British theatre as liberators of territory occupied by the Japanese.

Much bitter wrangling ensued over this issue before a compromise 'middle strategy' was developed but this was never put into effect due to American suspicions of British intent: the US Joint Chiefs had no wish to see a British task force in the Pacific. American opinion was that Britain should concentrate on a land campaign in Burma that would help keep China in the war against Japan. Such a campaign also satisfied Churchill's desire for a British campaign with British forces operating from a British base – India – in a British theatre of operations. The US also agreed that a British fleet should support the US fleet in the Pacific but that there should be no British task force.* Disagreements between Churchill and the Chiefs became so acrimonious that Brooke and his fellow chiefs even considered mass resignation. Such a move would have been pointless anyway since Churchill was removed from office in the general election following VE Day and Japan's subsequent collapse came so suddenly that it owed nothing to British strategy, either in collaboration with the Americans, as the Chiefs wanted, or independently, as Churchill wanted.

Until the end of the war, Brooke fought the corner of the professional heads of the forces against their political masters. Always suspicious of politicians, he noted on one occasion that the arguments put forward by four cabinet ministers were so puerile that it made him ashamed to think that they were ministers.

In January 1944 Brooke was promoted to field marshal and, after the war, was created Viscount Brookeborough of Colebrooke. Although today his role in achieving Allied victory may not be as widely acknowledged as it deserves to be, his contemporaries, during and in the aftermath of war, had no doubts. Admiral Ramsay,[†] who masterminded the Dunkirk evacuation, said that 'no one will ever know what the country owes to Alan Brooke. His worth is quite incalculable'. Stalin

---

* The British Pacific Fleet was the largest such fleet ever sent to sea by the Royal Navy but it still constituted only a small part of the Allied naval forces in the Pacific, most of which were American.
† Ramsay was killed in January 1945 when his plane crashed on take-off from a snow-covered airfield in France.

described him as a 'very clever military leader' while Portal, with whom he argued over the bombing strategy, wrote to tell Brooke that;

> I have an unbounded admiration for the way you handled our COS affairs and for the forcefulness and complete sincerity and the clearsightedness and soundness with which you always dealt with ministers on our behalf – no one could ever hold a candle to your record in that respect and it was about the biggest factor in getting results.

Montgomery, his successor as CIGS, later described Brooke as 'the greatest soldier – sailor, soldier or airman – produced by any country taking part in the last war'. Of all the Allied military leaders of that war, Brooke was the only one whom Montgomery regarded with genuine respect and approval. As for Brooke himself, he had a definite respect for Churchill, once commenting that he wondered what Britain would have done without him as prime minister. After the war Brooke wrote of their partnership:

> I shall always look back on the years I worked with him as some of the most difficult and trying ones in my life. For all that, I thank God that I was given an opportunity of working alongside such a man.

Churchill certainly needed someone of Brooke's calibre to channel his energies and his genius in the most effective manner and this was Brooke's greatest contribution to the war. His biographer, Sir David Fraser, wrote of him that his destiny was

> to come to authority at exactly the right hour; an hour when the country was in fearful peril, and was mercifully sustained but sometimes endangered by the mercurial genius of Churchill. Alanbrooke was the perfect complement to that genius.

Perhaps the finest summary of Brooke's achievements came from an Australian, Robert Casey, later Lord Casey.

> Alan Brooke is a man of unusual quality and intensity. I know of no service leader who contributed more to the winning of the Second World War than he did, by his military capacity, by his judgement and by his complete honesty of thought and expression.

~ 8 ~

Templer

Following the Second World War many countries fell under communist domination, either through conquest by the Soviets, or through the activities of communist-inspired wartime resistance movements that used the equipment and experience of wartime days to impose their writ on their countries. One country targeted for communist takeover was Malaya. That it did not fall into the communist bloc was very largely due to one man, who also has the distinction of winning a guerrilla war. He was Sir Gerald Templer who, soon after his appointment as High Commissioner and Director of Operations in Malaya in 1952, declared that:

> Malays, Chinese, Indians, Eurasians, British, we are all in this together. The educated have a particularly heavy responsibility to help in reaching the hearts and minds of the people.

The term 'hearts and minds' is more often associated with American policy in Vietnam but it was over a decade later before the Americans adopted Templer's words and attempted to repeat his achievements in Malaya. Succeeding in gaining the hearts and minds of the Malayan people was, Templer believed, seventy-five per cent of winning the campaign against communism. By the time that Gerald Templer left Malaya in 1954 that campaign was almost won while his name continues to be respected in Malaya today as the man who saved the country from communism.

Gerald Templer was born in the garrison town of Colchester, Essex in September 1898, the son of an officer in Princess Victoria's (Royal Irish Fusiliers). Walter Templer, Gerald's father, was from Loughgall in County Armagh while his mother was descended from a west of Ireland family, a fact of which he was very proud. In spite of that family connection with Armagh, and his spending much of his boyhood there, Gerald never liked to be described as an 'Ulster field marshal', considering this description to be born of a sectarianism that he loathed. Schooled in England, young Gerald then went to Sandhurst. The Army was a natural career choice for him and he followed his father into the Royal Irish Fusiliers, being commissioned in July 1916 at the height of the Great War. In later life he would comment that he had not been a particularly good cadet but that no one failed at that time because of the war. That comment indicates Templer's ability to poke fun at himself, an ability that he never lost.

Since Gerald Templer was not yet eighteen, he was posted to Buncrana in County Donegal to serve with 3rd Royal Irish Fusiliers. Not until late-1917 did he reach France to join a battalion. There was little more than a year of the war left but Templer considered himself fortunate to survive. Had it not been for an attack of diphtheria that hospitalized him in March 1918, he might not have survived; while he was in hospital the Germans launched Operation MICHAEL, the spring offensive of 1918, during which, in the battle of St Quentin, his battalion suffered over 750 casualties. For Templer, as with so many other survivors, the abiding memory of the Great War was of the terrible loss of life and, in common with many other commanders of the Second World War, he was determined to avoid sending men into the type of action that cost so much for so little apparent gain in France and Flanders.

The interwar years brought a variety of service to Gerald Templer, including active service in Persia, now Iran, in 1919 as part of an international force to prevent the spread of bolshevism into that country. Later, following service in Egypt with the Royal Irish Fusiliers, Lieutenant Templer returned to Britain to attend Staff College. By then, he enjoyed a high reputation in his regiment, being regarded as an authority on its history and traditions. Templer was the youngest – and most junior – student at Camberley but he excelled at his studies and impressed the staff, including the future Field Marshal Montgomery.

Following Staff College, Templer was forced to transfer out of the Royal Irish Fusiliers to gain promotion. His regiment had been reduced to a single battalion in 1922, when most Irish regiments were disbanded,* and so promotion was restricted even more than elsewhere in the contemporary Army. Gerald Templer went to The Loyal Regiment (North Lancashire) with whom he served in Palestine during the Arab rebellion in 1936. There he became known as an outstanding company commander, especially for his handling of sniper attacks on convoys along the Nablus–Jenin road. Convoys had come under regular sniper fire from high ground and a number of elaborate schemes to counter this threat had been devised but none had succeeded.

> Major Templer decided on a simpler plan. He trained a small force of soldiers in advance and then on this day he had [a convoy brought] through the pass.

---

* The initial proposal was to disband all the Irish infantry regiments but this was amended to include only those whose recruiting areas were in the new Irish Free State. However, the Royal Irish Fusiliers had only one of their four recruiting counties – Armagh; the remainder were Cavan, Louth and Monaghan – in Northern Ireland and so faced the axe. Pressure from supporters, including the regiment's Colonel-in-Chief, King George V, and a proposal from the Colonel of the Royal Inniskilling Fusiliers that his regiment lose a battalion to save the Faughs, resulted in a reprieve with the loss of the Second Battalion. The Inniskillings' Colonel's proposal had been based on the War Office decision that only four battalions from Northern Ireland would continue; he suggested that these be chosen on the basis of their pre-1881 seniority and thus both battalions of Royal Ulster Rifles survived but only one each of Inniskillings and Faughs. (The pre-1881 seniority was: 27th, 83rd, 86th, 87th, 89th and 108th; the last two were the 2nd Royal Irish Fusiliers and 2nd Royal Inniskilling Fusiliers respectively.)

As usual the snipers from their hill sangars opened fire. The convoy stopped. Out jumped the soldiers in gym shoes, armed with fixed bayonets. They dashed straight up the hills on both sides. The snipers were completely taken by surprise. One or two were killed and the rest captured.

This operation demonstrated another Templer characteristic, the ability to distil a problem to its simplest form. During the Second World War he showed this quality many times; it was particularly obvious in conferences when he explained plans for operations. With his clear and analytical mind such conferences were masterpieces of detailed but uncomplicated presentation.

The Palestine experience left a marked impression on Templer.

I've felt terribly strongly all my life, from my youth, on racial and religious clashes – ever since my boyhood in Ireland. That was a feeling that was strengthened by my service in Palestine in 1935–6, the Jew-Arab problems: I felt them bitterly in my heart.

This statement explains why Templer did not like the description 'Ulster field marshal': he could not abide the intolerance that existed in the province.

For his service in Palestine Templer was awarded the DSO and a Mention in Despatches. Moving to a staff post in England he again impressed those who met him. In 1937 the C-in-C, Western Command asked him to give a talk on intelligence to a group of his officers. One described Major Templer's talk as

The most brilliant speech I had ever heard. It was not just his subject matter, but his presentation: he really gripped his audience and had them eating out of his hand. It made an enormous impression on me.

His next post, also a staff job, was in military intelligence at the War Office where he was still working when war broke out in September 1939. It was to Templer's efforts that the British Army owed the successful creation and functioning of the Intelligence Corps, a debt acknowledged in the title of the Corps' depot – Templer Barracks – at Ashford in Kent. When the Germans launched their offensive in May 1940, Templer, still involved in intelligence, was in France and became one of the principal members of Macforce, a formation organized hastily to protect the BEF's flank. That role was performed well.

It reconnoitred, it carried out considerable demolition programmes on canal and river lines, it was an organised force, it directed stragglers, it kept its finger to the best of its ability on the pulse of the French formations on its right. It did what it could to direct the terrible refugee traffic, it shot down a considerable number of dive-bombers. It fought some small actions, it fed itself without worrying superior authority, it controlled looting.

Following the evacuation of France, Templer was recognized as one of the Army's most promising officers and was promoted to command a brigade. Montgomery specifically requested that he be posted to his corps and, although the pair had very different personalities, they got on well together, with Monty developing considerable respect for the younger Irishman. One of Brigadier Templer's company commanders described him as

> One of the most inspiring and efficient officers I had come across. Eyewash served no purpose with Templer, and we liked him the better for it. The questions he asked were always to the point. He had a rather disconcerting way of whipping round on you and demanding information but he did not ask the futile questions that other senior officers sometimes did.

By March 1942 Templer was a major-general commanding a division, but he almost lost his life when RAF aircraft accidentally opened fire on spectators at a firepower demonstration at Imber Down in Wiltshire. He was fortunate to escape with only slight injury but twenty-seven were killed and a further sixty-eight wounded in the tragedy.

In September 1942 Gerald Templer was promoted to lieutenant-general, the youngest in the Army, commanding II Corps. But this command reduced his chances of seeing active service at a time when preparations were being made to send a new field army to North Africa; one of his divisions was taken from II Corps and posted to First Army. With the North African campaign nearing its end, following the battle of El Alamein, Allied troops, including the spearhead of First Army, landed in French Northwest Africa in Operation TORCH in November. Now commanding XI Corps and frustrated at not seeing active service, Templer offered to give up his new rank to command a division on active service. He was given 1st Division, the formation taken from II Corps for First Army, and joined them in Tunisia in August 1943. This was a prestigious appointment and he was pleased that the division included 1st Loyals, with whom he had served in Palestine, as well as 1st Irish Guards, the latter being in 24 Guards Brigade.

The fighting in North Africa was over but Templer, believing that 1st Division would soon be deployed to Italy, set about training his soldiers in mountain warfare with his customary attention to detail. Nothing escaped his attention and he inspired confidence wherever he went in the division. But he was not to command 1st Division in action. Shortly after the invasion of Italy, the commander of 56th (London) Division was seriously injured and Gerald Templer was chosen to succeed him. On 15 October, he reached his new command, which was involved in battle along the Volturno river, north of Naples.

It was a difficult time to take over, especially as 56th Division had suffered considerably in the Salerno landings and the operations to break out of the beachhead. When Gerald Templer assumed command the division had crossed the Volturno and was advancing on X (British) Corps' right flank.* Its objective was a

---

* X Corps was part of Fifth US Army and was commanded by Richard McCreery.

line from Rochetta across Route 6, the main Naples–Rome road, to Montanaro. These two villages lay on the slopes of Monte Maggiore, the former to the right of Route 6 and the latter to the left. Determined German rearguards did their utmost to impede 56th Division's advance and although Allied artillery helped that advance, the final decision came down to the infantry soldiers with Templer's men fighting several intensive actions. His brigade and battalion commanders quickly recognized their new commander's tactical skills: not only did he have a good eye for the location but he was also able to visualize how the land lay from a map, a most useful skill for a soldier. By 25 October, 201 Guards Brigade, temporarily under 56th Division's command, had cleared Monte Maggiore while 169 (Queen's) Brigade had secured Montanaro. Lieutenant-General Mark Clark, commanding Fifth Army, then switched X Corps to operate west of Route 6 to clear Monte Camino.

Monte Camino was part of the Bernhardt line, a forward element of the major German coast-to-coast winter fortifications, the Gustav line. The assault on Monte Camino led to a difficult and bloody battle on the slopes of the mountain, which were swept by German machine-gun fire and artillery. Eventually, 56th Division had to be withdrawn, even though 167 Brigade was close to one major enemy position. However, the division attacked Monte Camino again in early December, this time with much better logistical support, arranged by Templer, and with more effective artillery support. This fresh assault was launched on the night of 1 December and several days of bitter struggle followed before the Allies succeeded. By 9 December Monte Camino was in Allied hands; 56th Division received a message of congratulations from Lieutenant-General McCreery, commanding X Corps.

> This has been a fine achievement, and your division has shown great fighting spirit, determination to surmount difficulties and endurance. I congratulate all ranks, and I particularly admire the magnificent initial attacks ... which were so carefully planned and successfully executed in the most difficult mountain country.

Ahead of 56th Division lay the Garigliano river which was crossed in mid-January 1944 as part of an operation to break through the Gustav line. The Garigliano crossing was a complete success and 56th Division was able to advance, in spite of spirited German counter-attacks. However, only one other division – 5th – was across; efforts to cross by 36th (US) and 46th (British) Divisions failed. The Americans suffered very high casualties at the Rapido river, which flows into the Liri river to form the Garigliano. Another German counter-attack was launched against the British divisions in the bridgehead but, after three days of fighting, 5th and 56th Divisions remained in position.

By now the Allies had landed at Anzio, south of Rome, in Operation SHINGLE, which had been timed to coincide with the assault on the Garigliano. This operation had been intended to outflank the Gustav line, and force a German withdrawal. Although the landings achieved complete surprise, this was not exploited effectively by General Lucas, commander of VI US Corps, which had made the assault; this corps included a British division, Templer's former command, 1st Division. The Germans were able to move reinforcements to the area and begin a series of counter-attacks that threatened the bridgehead. VI Corps had to be reinforced and among the first fresh formations to land was 56th Division. Templer reached the beachhead on 12 February and his arrival lifted spirits among the British troops at Anzio as Raleigh Trevelyan, who served there, recorded.

> Some hopes were raised with the arrival of the commander of the British 56th Division, General Gerald Templer, an electric personality and an energizer, though perpetually looking dog-tired – he lived on his nerves, they said.

However, in the beachhead there was little that a divisional commander could do, other than boost morale. Actions were usually fought by companies and platoons, although, soon after its arrival, 56th Division was called upon to meet an enemy assault, launched on 16 February. During this engagement, 1st Division's commander was wounded by a shell splinter and Templer also assumed command of that division. For the next week he commanded all British troops in the beachhead and did his best to raise morale by visiting soldiers of 1st and 56th Divisions in their forward positions as the struggle developed into a kaleidoscope of small skirmishes. Even a brief visit by Templer had an electrifying effect on the soldiers but his own morale was not helped by the knowledge that the corps commander, Lucas, was suffering from inertia.

Templer reported his views on Lucas to both Mark Clark, commanding Fifth Army, and Sir Harold Alexander, the army group commander. This confirmed both in the belief that Lucas had to go; Clark decided to replace him with the much more capable Lucian Truscott, who would later command Fifth Army.

In spite of their losses – by early-March the division was reduced to about a quarter of its normal strength – morale remained high in 56th Division. This was confirmed by the nickname bestowed on them by their opponents: Hell's Kittens, which came from their British nickname, the Black Cats.* The Germans made their last major attack against VI Corps on 28 February and, although the principal effort was made against American troops, there were strong diversionary assaults on 56th Division. The Black Cats, however, inflicted severe casualties on their assailants. On the evening of 1 March, Field Marshal Albert Kesselring, the German commander in Italy, called an end to offensive operations against VI Corps and switched his forces to the defensive.

Less than two weeks after this battle, 56th Division was relieved at Anzio and with-drawn to Egypt to rest and re-organize. Gerald Templer was not to lead the Black Cats in battle again since, in late-July, he took command of 6th Armoured Division,

---

* As a London formation, 56th Division had chosen a black cat as its divisional symbol, the cat recalling Dick Whittington's companion.

then in action north of Rome. Having held the rank of lieutenant-general, Templer might have expected to be promoted to command a corps but he accepted that there were men, such as Charles Keightley, who had much more experience of active divisional commands. Keightley, who had just been promoted to command V Corps, had commanded both 6th Armoured and 78th Infantry Divisions. A successful period as commander of 6th Armoured would make Gerald Templer a leading candidate for the next available corps command. Meanwhile he set about making himself known to his soldiers, driving up to the front to visit advancing units and giving the men first-hand encouragement.

In early-August, 6th Armoured Division was advancing towards Florence and Templer, in his usual fashion, decided to visit his forward units, driving his own jeep on the journey. As he sped along the narrow road in the Arno valley he met a truck coming in the opposite direction. Recognizing the general, the truck driver pulled over to allow the jeep to pass. However, the roadside was mined and the truck struck a mine just as the two vehicles passed. A rear wheel from the truck was blown through the air and struck Templer in the back, crushing him against the steering wheel. His back was broken – and his war was over. Even such a serious injury could inspire Templer to humour and he joked that he had been hit by a piano, normal front-line impedimenta for a Guards' battalion. The lorry, which belonged to Headquarters, 1 Guards Brigade, had indeed been carrying a piano; ever afterwards, Templer insisted that the Grenadier Guards were responsible for his injury.

Templer's recovery was amazingly quick and he returned to duty in March 1945, although he was still not fit enough for an active command. He was appointed to the headquarters of Montgomery's 21 Army Group in Brussels which took him into the military government of post-war occupied Germany where he became Director of Civil Affairs and Military Government. Montgomery delegated all responsibilities in those spheres to Templer who, as one historian of British military government in northwest Europe in 1944–5 recorded, became

> virtually Prime Minister of the British Zone of Germany and more than any other man saved the zone from famine and anarchy through the desperate winter of 1945–6.

The problems facing Templer's administration were many. Not only did he have to establish some form of German civil authority as well as preventing famine but he also had to be careful of anything that might endanger the army of occupation, or involve that army in police actions. There was a desperate need for food while water supplies and sewerage systems had to be restored to prevent epidemics breaking out; housing was also needed for the German people. Each requirement created its own problems: roads, railways and canals had to be repaired to allow the distribution of food; electrical supplies had to be restored to allow water and sewerage systems to operate; and building materials were needed for houses. Labour was needed to tackle all these problems but a labour force needs food and the occupying armies were not prepared to cope with the prevailing famine conditions. Not only had the Allies expected the Germans to be able to feed themselves, they had also expected them to feed the occupying troops. As a result of the American Henry Morgenthau, the Allies had accepted Roosevelt's argument that

> The German people as a whole must have it driven home to them that the whole nation has been engaged in a lawless conspiracy against the decencies of modern civilisation.

Those words represented the politicians' viewpoint but the military men had planned a much more liberal regime, which had been overturned. Templer, therefore, had to work against the background of this much more vengeful political dispensation. Fortunately for everyone, commonsense prevailed and the Morgenthau Plan was allowed to fade away. Even as it faded, Gerald Templer was ignoring it. Recognizing the need for food and fuel in Germany he initiated operations to ensure adequate supplies in the British zone, releasing from prisoner-of-war camps any former German soldiers who had been miners to work in Operation COALSCUTTLE, while farmworkers were released in Operation BARLEYCORN. The latter started in May 1945 and by September over 1,250,000 German soldiers were back in civilian employment. Templer's analytical mind and planning skills had often been proved in battle but in the aftermath of war those same skills were employed for the relief of the German population – his former enemies. The prevention of famine and the restoration of coal supplies were great victories for Gerald Templer, but victories that were not marked by battle honours.

At all times, Gerald Templer worked himself hard and expected full commitment and support from his own staff and German members of the civil administration. In September 1945 he was dismayed with the state of the city of Cologne, which was in

> a terrible mess, no water, no drainage, no light, no food – nothing. It stank of corpses. The German municipal services had completely broken down. It required a very strong man to take charge.

Templer considered that the *Oberburgomeister* was unfit for the job. The seventy-year-old incumbent was Dr Konrad Adenauer, later to be Chancellor of Germany. Templer sacked him. By working himself and his staff to the limit Gerald Templer won the battle of the 1945–6 winter, thereby saving the German people from tragedy. To achieve this end he had initiated the revival of the German coal industry and begun to import wheat in advance of economic policy being framed, and while the hard-line Morgenthau Plan still held sway. Needless to say, these two decisions

> were not popular. They were taken in view of the existing circumstances but against what was known of government policies at the time. They were coura-

geous and statesmanlike decisions and were among the earliest, and by no means the least important, of the steps taken to preserve and consolidate the anti-communist bridgehead in Europe.

From Germany Templer returned to Whitehall and the War Office, where Montgomery was now in post as CIGS. Templer became Monty's Director of Military Intelligence before becoming Vice-Chief of the Imperial General Staff in February 1948. This proved to be a difficult post, since Montgomery was a difficult CIGS, who had antagonized the First Sea Lord and the Chief of the Air Staff to such a degree that the three were scarcely on speaking terms. As a result Montgomery frequently sent Templer to deputize for him at Chiefs of Staff meetings. Life became more tolerable for Templer when Bill Slim succeeded Montgomery as CIGS, especially as Slim shared Monty's high opinion of his deputy.

Templer left the War Office to take charge of Eastern Command, considered the Army's best home command and he was there when Prime Minister Sir Winston Churchill decided that he was the man needed for Malaya. Following the war, it had appeared as if Malaya might fall into the communist camp; a guerrilla war was being fought in the peninsula by communists, who chose to portray it as a nationalist struggle against the old imperial master. Churchill had decided that Malaya needed a capable and ruthless supremo and asked Montgomery for a recommendation. Monty nominated Templer immediately. However, Churchill did not accept this nomination, wanting someone better known. He approached Slim, who refused the post, as did Sir Brian Robertson. Then, in January 1952, Churchill attended a Commonwealth conference in Canada and took the opportunity to solicit the advice of Field Marshal Alexander, the Governor-General. Alex suggested Templer. That settled the matter for Churchill and Templer was appointed with full military and civil authority in Malaya. He was faced with a daunting and dangerous task: Sir Henry Gurney, the previous High Commissioner, had been murdered in October 1951. There was a stark reminder for Templer of Sir Henry's fate when he made his first journey in Malaya: the car in which he was transported was the vehicle in which Sir Henry had been murdered; it still bore the marks of the assassins' bullets.

To the problems of Malaya, Gerald Templer once again brought his clearsightedness. Although not impressed with some of the people with whom he had to work, he identified the problems quickly, noting that 'The shooting side of the business is only 25 per cent of the trouble and the other 75 per cent lies in getting the people of this country behind us. So we shall see who wins'. Not long afterwards he coined the 'hearts and minds' phrase. Determined to gain popular support for the war against the communist guerrillas, he also made it clear to officials that:

> Any idea that the business of normal government and the business of the Emergency are two separate entities must be killed off for good and all. The two activities are completely and utterly interrelated.

One of Templer's immediate initiatives was to convene regular meetings with the local rulers, the Mentri Besars. Although he found the Malayan system of government very cumbersome, he established a good rapport with most local rulers and gained their respect. While he had to be careful of personal security, there were times when he ignored this, even taking one of his colleagues on a drive around Kuala Lumpur in the evenings to see the city as its people saw it. On occasions they might even stop for a drink. This was Templer's old habit of visiting his soldiers in the front line transferred to a different setting and, with his background, he saw little danger in this activity. He made his first major speech to the Legislative Council in March 1952, in the course of which he told members that the emergency could not be resolved by military action alone. He outlined his plans for common citizenship, a well-trained police force and the formation of a Federation Regiment open to all races in Malaya. In addition, he proposed better health and education services, increased security of tenure for the Chinese in resettlement areas, which he renamed 'New Villages', and advocated a youth programme, local government reform and economic improvements that would benefit all Malayans. His speech proved to his listeners that Gerald Templer had grasped the essentials of the Malayan situation in a very short time.

However, he appreciated the communist hold in many areas and the fear that the communists created in those areas. Although he held extensive powers to deal with the threat, he was reluctant to use them. One such power was Regulation 17D, allowing the collective detention and deportation of communities. That sanction was used only once by Templer, in Tanjong Malim in late-March 1952. Guerrillas cut the town's water supply before ambushing the repair party that arrived to restore it, killing twelve men and injuring seriously several more. Templer went to Tanjong Malim, gathered the leading community members together and told them that he knew they were fully aware of what had happened and that it could not have taken place without their knowledge:

> None of this would have happened if the inhabitants of this part of the country had had any courage. You want everything done for you, but you are not prepared to assume the responsibility of citizenship. I want law and order, so that I can get on with many things which are good for this country. Why should it be impossible to do these good things? Because people like you are cowards? Do you think that under a communist regime you will be able to live a happy family life? Are there any of you communists in this room?

For two weeks a twenty-two-hour curfew was imposed, schools were closed, the town was sealed off from the outside world and the rice ration was halved. Although there was uproar in sections of the press, Templer had made his point and not only did he never use Regulation 17D again but he announced its abolition in 1953.

Following his iron fist demonstration, Gerald Templer still preferred the velvet glove, carrying out a series of reforms that included improving the police and local military services; he also continued discussions with Malayan politicians. The intelligence service was rationalized and liaison between police and military intelligence became routine. Since this was one of Templer's priorities, his past intelligence experience, including his time as Director of Military Intelligence, was of considerable benefit. Efforts to get guerrillas to surrender were made and, on occasion, these succeeded with many of those who surrendered being willing to enlist in the security forces. Their cooperation improved greatly the intelligence available to the authorities. Templer opposed capital punishment and persuaded the Sultan of Perak to commute the death penalty on Lee Meng, a leading female guerrilla. He believed that executions would only create martyrs, thereby exacerbating the situation. Perhaps, as an Irishman, he was mindful of the effects of the executions in Ireland following the 1916 rebellion.

While Templer was happy to leave operational details to the military commanders, he felt that tactical changes were necessary and therefore set up the Combined Emergency Planning Staff to implement such changes. One change was to replace large-scale jungle sweeps with small patrol operations; the former had proved of little value but the latter became highly successful. Another success came with the re-forming of the Special Air Service Regiment, initially as the Malayan Scouts (SAS). The regiment played a major role in jungle operations and gained the full and enthusiastic support of the High Commissioner. Templer also obtained helicopters to assist and support operations; these proved particularly valuable. Needless to say, he continued his practice of making morale-boosting visits to units under his command.

Based on his 'hearts and minds' theme, a major public relations exercise was begun to increase Chinese recruitment into the police and to improve relations between police and public. This was called Operation SERVICE, since the head of the police, Arthur Young, later to be the last Inspector General and first Chief Constable of the RUC, wanted his organization to be seen as a service. Speaking on radio about Operation SERVICE, Templer said that it would be 'a poor victory if, in rooting out terrorism, we were only to substitute one fear for another'. In less than a year the initiative had been wrested from the terrorists and there was a steady trickle of surrenders while police and military casualties reduced to almost none. His staff considered that Templer's own ability, and knack of identifying troublespots, was invaluable; one staff member commented that 'Gerald Templer had that knack of being able to put his finger into the place that was hurting'. His concern for the people of Malaya was also demonstrated in many ways. To improve health and welfare services he sought the help of many agencies across the world, including the Red Cross, the Methodist Church in America and the College of Propaganda in Rome. Receiving no reply from the latter, he wrote to a friend who could contact the Pope directly. Within two weeks teams of monks, nuns, doctors and nurses began to arrive from Rome. Some years later Gerald Templer was able to thank Pope Pius XII in person for his help.

By the time Templer's tour of duty in Malaya was over the communist threat had gone and the country was well on its way to independence. However, Templer's interest in Malaya never ended; he had supported the creation of a national museum because he believed that an independent nation should take a pride in its past. In his farewell speech he wished

> good luck to you all whoever you are and wherever you may be in the Federation of Malaya. May your future be happy and assured. May your children grow up in peace and prosperity.

Gerald Templer was invited back for Malaya's independence celebrations in 1957. By then he was CIGS. Sir Gerald held this appointment at one of the most difficult times in the Army's three-century history and, for him, it was a far from happy time. During his tenure, in the autumn of 1956, the Suez crisis occurred. Although military intervention by Britain and France, Operation MUSKETEER, was highly successful, the USA and USSR threatened both European nations with military and political sanctions if they did not withdraw from Egypt. This led to a distrust of the USA in British political circles, as a result of which an independent British nuclear deterrent was advocated strongly; this was later enshrined in the Sandys Defence White Paper of 1957. However, the rationale – and cost – of a nuclear deterrent also meant smaller conventional forces and so the Sandys proposals included reducing the size of the services with the Army suffering the largest manpower cuts.

Gerald Templer had a strong commitment to and enthusiasm for the history and traditions of the British Army and it was painful for him to have to preside over its reduction. However, he was determined to save the regimental system on which the Army had been based for centuries and which he considered its greatest strength. He wrote:

> That so many famous regiments and units should lose their separate identity is an unavoidable consequence of the present reorganisation of the armed forces. All have played a glorious part in our history. The British Army has been reorganised before now, but the honours and traditions of its regiments and corps have never been lost to the service, and once again they will be carried forward.

Templer won the battle to retain the regimental system rather than introduce a corps of infantry, although he had to oversee the disappearance, through amalgamation, of a number of regiments; the process thus begun would lead to the later absorption of his own Royal Irish Fusiliers into a new Irish infantry regiment, The Royal Irish Rangers, in 1968.*

There were other ways in which the post of CIGS was a difficult time for Templer. He neither liked nor trusted politicians. He disliked the Prime Minister, Harold

---

* In 1992, as part of the Options for Change defence review that followed the end of the Cold War, The Royal Irish Rangers amalgamated with The Ulster Defence Regiment to form another new regiment, The Royal Irish Regiment.

Macmillan, although the latter had a high regard for Templer, and had no time for Duncan Sandys, the Minister of Defence, who was determined to reduce the powers of the professional heads of all three services. Templer and his fellow chiefs fought a rearguard action but Sandys' philosophy prevailed with the creation of a unified Ministry of Defence and the new post of Chief of the Defence Staff.

When he retired as CIGS, Templer also retired from the Army and was able to give much more time to the two regiments of which he was colonel: The Royal Irish Fusiliers and The Blues, one of the two Household Cavalry regiments. Never one to take such duties lightly he paid close attention to the affairs of both regiments, but especially those of the Faughs, for they were his own regiment, to which he owed an intense loyalty. He had assumed this colonelcy in 1946 and Kendal Chavasse, whom he brought from a staff post to command the 2nd Battalion, recalled the regular letters he received from Templer encouraging him to ensure that the pre-war standards of the Irish Fusiliers were instilled into the new generation of officers and men. Those letters indicate his abiding enthusiasm for the Army's history and traditions, an enthusiasm that also led him to become the driving force behind the establishment of the National Army Museum on Royal Hospital Road in London's Chelsea.

Sir Gerald continued to lead an active life until just before his death in 1979. An outstanding soldier, he was thorough, efficient and effective, although not always popular, as well as being an outstanding administrator, as shown in Germany and Malaya. He remains the only man to have fought a successful war against guerrillas. Probably the best summing up of his character is provided by his biographer, John Cloake, who described him as

> this complicated, yet in some ways very simple, character – full of contradictions, fierce but kind, rude but cultured, tough but sentimental.

~ 9 ~

Russell

Winston Churchill's mercurial genius spawned many ideas during the Second World War, some impracticable but others worthy of development. Among those that deservedly came to fruition was an idea that occurred to Churchill in the autumn of 1941. On 9 October he penned a note to the CIGS, General Sir John Dill, that read: 'Pray, let me have your views, and if possible your plans, for the forming of an Irish Brigade.'

The margin of his note to Dill was annotated 'action this day' to indicate that the premier considered this a serious proposition. In fact, the previous day, Churchill had written to both the Secretaries of State for War and Air suggesting not only the creation of an Irish Brigade in the Army but also the formation of an Irish squadron or wing in the Royal Air Force, to be known as the Shamrock Wing, possibly commanded by the Irish fighter 'ace' Brendan, 'Paddy', Finucane. Only the Army's Irish Brigade came into being. Created formally in January 1942, by the end of the war it had the reputation of being the finest brigade in the British Army. Much of that reputation was due to its outstanding commanders, the first of whom was Brigadier The O'Donovan, who created the brigade and did much to establish its very special ethos.*

Churchill's idea of an Irish Brigade seems to have been the result of a desire to make the Irish contribution to the war effort more visible; he was aware of the many Irish men and women in the three fighting services and knew that most hailed from a neutral country. However, his suggestion was not received well by Northern Ireland's government. John Andrews, Prime Minister of Northern Ireland, wrote to say that his government found the very title 'Irish Brigade' unacceptable, since it

> would inevitably be associated with the Irish who fought against England in the days of Marlborough and the Irish Brigade which fought against Britain in the Boer War.

And, since the Army's three remaining Irish infantry regiments, that would form the brigade, were all territorially associated with Northern Ireland, Andrews further

---

* The O'Donovan said that he felt 'the mantle of Sarsfield' fall on his shoulders when he was told of his appointment to command the Irish Brigade (Col. K.G.F. Chavasse, notes to author).

claimed that the people of Northern Ireland would 'strongly object to the absorption of Ulster regiments into an Irish Brigade'. Andrews also objected to any act of British policy that might obscure the fact that Ireland was neutral, but his protests were pointless; Churchill, in full spate with enthusiasm for his idea, was not to be stopped.

In mid-1942, the Irish Brigade joined 6th Armoured Division as its lorried infantry brigade; it was also joining First Army, then being formed for Operation TORCH, the invasion of French northwest Africa. Brigadier The O'Donovan had to relinquish command as he was considered too old for active service and was succeeded by Brigadier Nelson Russell, who would take the Irish Brigade into action and lay the foundations of its outstanding reputation. Nelson Russell, born in the County Antrim town of Lisburn in 1897, was seventeen when the Great War broke out in 1914 when he was a pupil at Campbell College. Determined to become a soldier he entered Sandhurst from where he was commissioned into the Royal Irish Fusiliers, the Faughs, on, appropriately, Saint Patrick's Day 1915 and posted to the regiment's 3rd Battalion. By his eighteenth birthday he was serving with the 1st Battalion in France.

On 17 April 1916 Nelson Russell earned an immediate award of the Military Cross when he led a daylight raid on German trenches, believed to be the first-ever daytime raid. Commanding a party of three officers and thirty-three men, Russell created havoc in the enemy positions during a ten-minute battle. His soldiers laid demolition charges and killed at least fifteen enemy soldiers; many more were wounded but only one of Russell's group was injured slightly. In addition to Russell's Military Cross, two of his NCOs were also awarded the Military Medal. Shortly after this, Nelson Russell was Mentioned in Despatches and, in September, the citizens of Lisburn presented him with a silver Loving Cup in recognition of his earning the Military Cross.

Between the wars Nelson Russell served with the Royal Irish Fusiliers in Egypt, India, the Sudan and Palestine and was involved heavily in sport, especially cricket and hockey, representing both the Faughs and Ireland, such was his prowess. Appointed to command 6th Royal Irish Fusiliers in 1940, he remained with the battalion for two years until he succeeded The O'Donovan as Irish Brigade commander in July 1942.

In November the Irish Brigade, part of 6th Armoured Division, sailed for Algeria, from where it advanced into Tunisia. The Germans had reacted very quickly to the Allied landings and a strong German force, provided by XC Corps, pushed out from Tunis to seize and hold the mountain range that cuts the country in two. XC Corps' task was to expand the German bridgehead in Tunisia to the Algerian border, if possible. An Allied attempt to reach Tunis by a rapid advance failed narrowly and when the Irish Brigade reached the front in early-December the Germans already held strong defensive positions while the Luftwaffe had achieved local air superiority, thanks to being able to operate from hard-surfaced airfields whereas the Allied forward landing grounds had been turned into quagmires by heavy rain.

The Irish Brigade battalions fought a series of skirmishes and battles in the Goubellat area in late-December and early-January and so stretched were the Allied forces that the infantry battalions were committed to holding a very attenuated line. All three Irish battalions – 6th Royal Inniskilling Fusiliers, 1st Royal Irish Fusiliers and 2nd London Irish Rifles – were, as Nelson Russell described it, 'in the front window', which was against his every instinct as a soldier. Every commander wants a reserve: this was 'one principle of war for all commanders. It is my only one, I think. Always have a good reserve'. However, such a happy situation was not to prevail for quite some time. On 11 January 2nd London Irish were engaged in a battalion-level battle when they executed a successful operation to cover the withdrawal of the tanks of a Scottish yeomanry regiment that was in danger of being cut off and captured. Two days later the Inniskillings attacked a feature known as Two Tree Hill but, in weather conditions that precluded the use of armour and prevented vehicles from bringing forward extra ammunition, the Inniskillings were beaten off the hill, although the enemy's ammunition situation was also precarious and some German paratroopers resorted to throwing stones at their attackers.

Following the Inniskillings' withdrawal, planning began immediately for another assault, this time using the entire Irish Brigade. Nelson Russell was none too happy about this plan but was obliged to carry it out. Fortunately the attack was delayed by a day so that additional artillery could be moved up to support the brigade – the artillery commander of V Corps felt that the original planned support was insufficient. That delay may well have saved the Irish Brigade from destruction since, twenty-four hours before the attack was due, the Germans launched their own assault – on the Irish Brigade. However, the presence of all three battalions, plus three regiments of artillery, took the attackers by surprise since they had expected to meet but one battalion, the Inniskillings, and, at most, a single artillery regiment. In the ensuing battle the Germans suffered heavy losses and were forced to withdraw, although further attacks would follow. Brigadier Russell was then amazed to receive an order from V Corps to seize and hold Point 286, a feature overlooking the main road but so rocky and devoid of cover that it could not be held by either side. Russell argued that trying to hold Point 286 would be a tactical error but at First Army headquarters his view was not accepted; V Corps' commander was sent to tell him to carry out the order and Nelson was left with no choice but to conform.

The task of attacking Point 286 was assigned to the London Irish who, after great difficulty, reached the top and drove off the Germans. But Nelson Russell was then proved right as it was impossible to dig in since the ground was so rocky, and the Germans bombarded the Rifles with mortars and artillery. Then a counter-attack was launched. Tanks and infantry broke through the Rifles' positions and down onto the road below; the attackers were not stopped until they met a company of Irish Fusiliers, who had been placed on the brigade's southern flank to secure the road on the initiative of Pat Scott, the Faughs' commanding officer.

Casualties in the Rifles were severe with twenty-six dead, eighty-six wounded and 130 missing; many of the latter had been taken prisoner. The Germans who had forced the Rifles off Point 286 made no attempt to stay there themselves, thus proving the truth of Russell's original point. Instead, both sides tried to dominate the main road by patrolling the ridges. It was a very difficult time for the infantry, which they endured in slit trenches with no opportunity for relief and rest out of the line; the only change of scenery available was through exchanging positions with another front-line battalion. Because of the heavy losses sustained by 2nd London Irish Rifles, the Irish Brigade was augmented, temporarily, by 3rd Grenadier Guards.

In the brief period of relative stability that followed, Nelson Russell had time to reflect on the performance of his brigade. By now it was a well-drilled fighting machine and the Plains of Goubellat had been its war nursery.

> There we first heard the zip of the bullet, the quick stutter of the Schmeisser, the whine of the shell, followed by his bark, and that bloodsome crump of the mortar, the most formidable of the lot. And all fired with malicious intent.

During the following weeks the Irish Brigade patrolled and fought small actions along their sector of the front. Nelson Russell considered that his men were dominating the enemy; during this period the Inniskillings virtually annihilated Marsch Battalion A24, which had been sent to help the Hermann Göring Jäger Battalion while the Irish Fusiliers 'gave the latter some very unpleasant times'.

In mid-February the Germans, under Field Marshal Erwin Rommel, attacked the American II Corps at Kasserine Pass. The raw GIs were beaten badly in what, after Pearl Harbor, was the United States' greatest military disaster of the war. A rapid realignment of Allied forces was needed to contain the enemy, and troops were taken from the Bou Arada sector to secure the southern part of the line. Around Bou Arada a scratch division was assembled and designated Y Division. This *ad hoc* force included the Irish Brigade, a Parachute Brigade, a French regiment, which equated to a British brigade, and sufficient artillery for its needs as well as some armour. Nelson Russell was appointed to command Y Division, thus demonstrating the reputation that he had already earned. Typically, he commented that 'lack of competition placed me in command of this outfit, and Pat Scott took over the Brigade'.

However, it was not lack of competition that earned Nelson this command but his own proven ability as a battlefield commander, who had already seen his brigade through a series of battles in the Bou Arada sector. His handling of those battles had been first class. Nor had he been afraid to question the decisions and plans of higher authority when he felt that those above him were wrong. When he had challenged the need to take Point 286 he had been overruled and told to get on with the job; he had done so, but made it clear that he was acting against his own better judgement. The results of that action had proved him to have been right all along. And this had not been the sole instance where he had shown a firm grasp of the realities of the situation. It was the clear-headedness that he displayed in his command in such circumstances that qualified him for command of Y Division. His ability was to be tested yet again in the Bou Arada sector.

After the new division had been created, Nelson's staff began to take shape over the next five or six days: 'a G3 from here, a DAQMG from there – odd clerks out of some curious bag – and here and there a W/T set discharged from some unwilling source'. While this was happening, and the command structure was being sorted out, Nelson Russell embarked on what he described as a 'little secret plan'.

> I found a RESERVE. This erratic and unusual attitude to war in North Africa naturally met with a good deal of local opposition, but two days after the formation of Y Div. I had a divisional reserve of one battalion – THE FAUGHS – a squadron of Churchills (scrounged from Corps) and a squadron of Derby Yeomanry. It is true that the remaining battalions – previously very stretched – were now more than very stretched, and the battalion commanders disclaimed all responsibility for forcibly extended line fronts. But I had my RESERVE – I almost felt comfortable.

Only two days later, at dawn on 26 February, a German attack on the Bou Arada plain began. This was a determined assault with four German battlegroups striking against their British and French opponents. Y Division's right flank was held by the British Paras and the French regiment, for whom their German foes, four battalions strong, were no match. Similarly Marsch Battalion A33, the German unit that hit the Inniskillings, provided no worries for the Irishmen. However, on the left flank and to the rear it was a different story. That sector was attacked by German paratroopers, or Fallschirmjäger, while the final battlegroup, two Fallschirmjäger battalions and ten tanks, struck through the southern end of the Mahmoud Gap and made for El Aroussa by way of Steamroller Farm, thus threatening Y Division's rear and the divisional headquarters.

The London Irish were in extended positions and two of their companies were overrun by the Germans who captured Stuka Ridge; the battalion's other two companies held firm and were given artillery support from the Ayrshire Yeomanry. Although the situation was 'quite unpleasant' it was, according to Nelson Russell, also quite clear and 'it wasn't a difficult matter to decide on the (we hope) counters'. Pat Scott, commanding the Irish Brigade, was allocated six Churchill tanks and two Irish Fusilier companies to clear up his brigade front while the remainder of 1st Royal Irish Fusiliers with the Derbyshire Yeomanry, an armoured car regiment, and nine Churchills in support were deployed to delay and destroy the Germans advancing on El Aroussa and divisional headquarters.

On the Irish Brigade front Pat Scott's tanks and the Faughs launched counter-attack after counter-attack against the Germans and were joined by a company of Inniskillings; the Ayrshire Yeomanry* were able to fire, often over open sights, at their foes. By nightfall the situation had been stabilized and Stuka Ridge was clear of Germans.

---

* In the Second World War the Ayrshire Yeomanry were re-roled as two Royal Artillery field regiments, 151st and 152nd Regiments.

In the rear area there had also been much action. When Nelson Russell ordered the tanks to intercept the enemy armour he realized that it would take the Churchills some two hours to reach a position where they could block the Germans effectively. To slow the enemy advance he put the armoured cars of the Derbyshire Yeomanry squadron to work on a six-mile stretch of road through the hills. The Derbys laid mines, put down smoke and scurried in to fire their two-pounders whenever possible, thus doing all in their power to delay the German advance. Meanwhile the Churchills were grinding their slow way towards the last possible tank stop before the divisional headquarters.

> I doubt if I will ever forget the closing stages of this race – it quite beat Battleship's National* when I'd backed a 1st and 2nd – TEN panzers and NINE Churchills converging from right angles, quite unseen to each other, but the panzers didn't know about the Churchills, and the Churchills knew all about the panzers.
>
> From my seat at the tip of the right angle I could watch both sides. It was anybody's race. And the Churchills won. They reached 'THE SPOT' with three minutes to spare. Short but sufficient. Three minutes later saw the death of six panzers while you could count 'twenty'. Rather an inspiring sight, aptly described by the Churchill commander as 'a piece of cake'. But it was only made possible by the best squadron of Yeomanry I have ever seen in action.
>
> The remaining panzers withdrew and the enemy infantry went with them – to dig themselves in around Steamroller Farm. They were still a threat, but after our exciting morning they didn't seem quite such a ... threat.

Y Division had acquitted itself well but a significant force of Germans, including a number of tanks, was established inside the Allied positions at Steamroller Farm and represented a considerable threat to Bou Arada, or the main line of communication to Medjez el Bab. Since the Germans could call on reinforcements, it was necessary for Y Division to adopt an offensive posture but Nelson had used up his reserve and also needed to call in reinforcements. These arrived in the form of 1 Guards Brigade, an American Regimental Combat Team (RCT) – the equivalent of a British brigade – a tank regiment of Churchills and 'enough anti-tank guns to blow up all the panzers in North Africa'. Once the reinforcements had been assembled, Y Division attacked and, thirty-six hours later, the Germans in Steamroller Farm had been evicted with considerable force. It had been a combined armour and infantry attack with the Churchills doing more than Nelson Russell had ever considered possible for tanks. Pat Scott had also tidied up the Irish Brigade's area and Russell commented that 'all through this affair, Pat handled the brigade with a sure hand and was a great comfort'. Major John Horsfall MC, of the Faughs, had also carried out a patrol deep into the Goubellat Plain, cutting right across the enemy lines of communications.

* The Grand National, which was won by a horse called Battleship in 1938.

Effectively the patrol was a route march that ended with a bayonet charge on the Germans; it earned John Horsfall a Bar to his Military Cross.

In the early days of March the enemy threat around Bou Arada diminished considerably and Y Division declined in importance and size, losing, first, the Paras, then the Guards and then the Americans; Nelson Russell now had slightly less than the original divisional order of battle. He was quite certain that Y Division had never been intended as a fighting formation but, not only had it become involved in battle, it had also acquitted itself well. The performance of such a division, created from scratch with formations and units that had never operated together, and represented different nationalities and military cultures, was a signal tribute to the way in which it had been commanded. There can be little doubt that much of Y Division's success was due to Nelson.

Following the demise of Y Division, Nelson was faced with another battle – to protect the identity and integrity of the Irish Brigade. The London Irish had suffered heavy casualties in January on Point 286, to which had now been added the losses at El Aroussa. As a result the battalion was very much understrength and, at First Army headquarters, it was suggested that 2nd London Irish be disbanded. However, Brigadier Russell argued for the battalion's retention and eventually won; however, most of the battalion's officers were replaced, the blame for the tragedy of Point 286 being placed on the Rifles rather than on those who had planned the operation. Although the London Irish were to be retained the battalion was to be withdrawn for a time to absorb reinforcements and reorganize. The commanding officer was to be succeeded by Pat Scott, who was transferred across from the Royal Irish Fusiliers as Nelson felt that his fellow Faugh was the right man to rebuild the London Irish. Until the battalion could rejoin the Irish Brigade its place was taken by a battalion of the Hampshire Regiment, who would become honorary Irishmen.

After a fortnight with little fighting, 78th Division, to which the Irish Brigade had now been assigned, was allocated the first step in the final Allied push for Tunis. The Battleaxe Division was to clear the high ground north of the Oued Zarga–Medjez road; within the divisional plan the Irish Brigade's objective was Jebel el Mahdi, a pear-shaped prominence some four miles long, two wide at its broadest and about 1,400 feet high.

The only approach was through a narrow valley which was mined, booby-trapped and within mortar range. It also possessed no tracks, and ammunition and equipment had to be mule borne.

Nelson sought, and obtained, substantial artillery support for the attack and about 150 guns – almost a third of them mediums or heavies – fired in support of the Inniskillings who led the attack, followed by the Faughs. The Irish Brigade was successful but their achievement was tinged by loss, including the death of the Inniskillings' popular commanding officer, Lieutenant-Colonel 'Heaver' Allen. Success also crowned the efforts of 78th Division's other two brigades in what

Nelson Russell described as 'a well-planned co-ordinated divisional attack, the first of its kind I had seen in North Africa'.

The next phase of operations was to be the capture of the features of Jebel Tanngoucha, Longstop Hill and Jebel Ang, which would unlock the routes for the final advance on Tunis. Before, that, on 10 April, the Irish Brigade captured Jebel Guernat, supported by North Irish Horse tanks. But they had almost lost their commander: Nelson Russell's command car had been caught in a mortar blast and his signals officer, who had been sitting beside him, was killed; he had also been strafed four times in the same day by German fighters. From Guernat the Irish Brigade moved quickly to the relief of 11 Brigade in the Bettiour area.

> This hilly country north of Medjez merits description – but I doubt if I am able to describe it; I've never seen anything like it before. Five miles from Medjez the hills begin. In a width of a couple of miles are the mountain villages of Toukabeur, Chaouch, Kelbine and Heidous – this latter perched on top of a rock which has steep fifty-foot sides. Between these villages are tracks, passable to goats, but which could be, and were, bulldozed into tracks for MT. To the east and west of these villages are a jumble of bare rocky hills – with no tracks at all; and north of Heidous, the last northern village, one runs into real tiger country and all civilisation is left behind.

Attack after attack was launched against the brigade's objectives. The Rifles, who had returned to the fold under Pat Scott, assaulted Heidous, the Inniskillings Tanngoucha and the Faughs Kef el Tior and Point 622. Following several attacks, the Faughs with the support of three Churchills of the North Irish Horse, took Butler's Hill, followed by Point 622. The German surrender was taken by the remnants of the attacking company, fewer than ten men. That success unlocked Tanngoucha for the Inniskillings while the Rifles finally took Heidous. Although the Irish Brigade had suffered heavily it was still committed to pursuing the retreating Germans, which its soldiers did for three days before being withdrawn. It was their last operation in Tunisia; although they were detailed for the attack on Tunis itself in early-May, the Germans did not defend the city and the Irish Brigade had the distinction of being the first Allied infantry to enter it. Nelson Russell's services in Tunisia were rewarded with the DSO.

With the North African campaign over attention turned to Sicily, which was invaded in Operation HUSKY on 10 July 1943. The island fell after a brief but sharp campaign during which the Irish Brigade achieved worldwide fame when it captured the mountain town of Centuripe at the beginning of August. Originally Centuripe was to have been taken by 36 Brigade with the Irish Brigade then passing through to lead 78th Division in the crossings of the rivers Salso and Simeto. However, 36 Brigade's battalions were held up en route to Centuripe by German troops and the Irish battalions were assigned to capture the town, which was defended by men of the Hermann Göring Division and 3rd Fallschirmjäger Regiment. The town was a vital element in the German plan to withdraw to the northeast of Sicily and evacuate to mainland Italy. Centuripe could be reached only by a single road and a series of corkscrew tracks, while off the road were forty-five-degree slopes with six-foot terraces cut into them for cultivation. It was the strongest defensive mountain position that 78th Division had yet encountered.

Nelson Russell decided on a two-battalion reconnaissance in force to determine what vantage points were held by the enemy and what might be in friendly hands. The reconnaissance would also place the two battalions, Inniskillings and Faughs, within striking distance. Both were to be ready to move on into Centuripe 'if the going was good'. Both were, however, pinned down; Nelson planned a new attack with the London Irish seizing three points on the left flank after which the Inniskillings would advance on the town with the Faughs, on the right flank, moving up through the cemetery and the northern part of the town.

In fact, the Inniskillings jumped the gun and attacked earlier than planned, seemingly unaware of the brigade plan. The Inniskillings' attack was 'by the front door' with C Company scaling a hundred-foot-high cliff to enter the town. Artillery support was provided and A Company then followed through C Company and into the town itself. Russell adjusted his plan rapidly and the other two battalions joined in the battle. Although the Rifles were held up by fierce resistance, the Faughs went forward on the right flank to support the Inniskillings who were fighting from house to house in the town. By 3.00am Centuripe was in Irish hands. Its capture made headline news and drew comments in the house of commons and from Reuters News Agency which commented that 'the capture of Centuripe by Irish infantry must rank as one of the greatest achievements in storming almost impregnable heights'. The brigade continued its successful advance, led by the Faughs, over the Salso and Simeto rivers. Following a brief rest it was back in action for the advance on Randazzo in which it saw its last fighting of the campaign.

In September the Allies invaded Italy but 78th Division was not involved in the early fighting. In fact, the Irish Brigade did not go into action until early-October when they were shipped round the coast from Bari to Termoli, arriving at the latter just as a massive German counter-attack was being fought off. The three battalions disembarked with shells falling around the port and in the sea; they were ordered to be ready for action at first light while Nelson made plans for an attack out of Termoli against the high ground overlooking the harbour. On the morrow the Irish Brigade launched its attack and drove the Germans off the high ground. The battle for Termoli had been won.

As part of Montgomery's Eighth Army, 78th Division was operating on the eastern coast of Italy and advancing against the German winter line. Ahead lay numerous river valleys and mountains, all providing excellent defensive positions. Having secured Termoli the Irish Brigade's next action was the capture of Petacciato ridge, taken in a model operation by the London Irish, supported by artillery and a squadron of tanks from 44th Royal Tank Regiment. The first major river obstacle followed. This was the Trigno, over which, it was discovered, a bridge still stood intact. As a result the divisional commander ordered the Irish Brigade to 'capture the bridge intact and forthwith'. Nelson asserted that 'the ruddy thing will go up' but the divisional commander was confident that he was about to take possession of a perfectly good bridge, and so an attack was mounted. The Rifles secured a ridge to the right of the bridge while the Faughs were to force the crossing. However, just as the leading Irish Fusiliers reached the bridge 'it went up like Vesuvius at the top of her form'. The attacking troops had to wade across but succeeded in making the crossing and establishing a bridgehead. It proved a very uncomfortable bridgehead with enemy shelling inflicting casualties and creating difficulties in getting supplies across to the Faughs. To secure the bridgehead the town of San Salvo, on a ridge some 4,000 yards away, had to be taken. Once again the Rifles and the Faughs were given the task while 2nd Lancashire Fusiliers would attack San Salvo railway station.

The attack was planned for 27 October but very heavy rain that afternoon prompted Nelson Russell to ask for a postponement. However, this request was refused and the two battalions advanced behind an artillery bombardment. German machine-gun fire and muddy ground impeded the progress of the advancing infantry and the Faughs were eventually pinned down. B Company's commander, Dennis Dunn, was killed by a shell while Paddy Proctor, commanding A Company, was killed alongside his platoon commanders as they planned an attack on the final ridge. And the commanding officer, Beauchamp Butler, from County Carlow, fell to machine-gun fire as he organized his men. To the right the Rifles had also been pinned down and were suffering casualties. It was obvious that both battalions would have to be withdrawn; this was done before daylight and both returned to the bridgehead where the Rifles' second-in-command, Major Kevin O'Connor, was killed by a bursting shell.

San Salvo was taken eventually in a divisional attack that included the Inniskillings and Eighth Army's advance then continued to the Sangro river. At first the assault across the Sangro was to be made by 8th Indian Division who would break the enemy line at Mozzagrogna, after which the Irish Brigade would clear high ground between Mozzagrogna and the coast. But the Indian troops were beaten back and a fresh plan had to be devised. This came from the brains of Brigadiers Nelson Russell and John Currie* – of 4 Armoured Brigade – and was accepted by V Corps' commander following Nelson's guarantee that 'when we took a place we knew we had it'. On the morning of 29 November the attack was launched with the Irish Brigade augmented by 8th Argyll and Sutherland Highlanders. The attack was highly successful and 'a triumph for planning and organisation'. The Germans were routed, their line rolled up and the Rifles and Faughs pushed on towards Rocca and St Vito. With the latter taken, 78th Division moved on across the Feltrino river and towards

---

* John Currie had commanded 9 Armoured Brigade at El Alamein and was one of the Army's best armoured brigade commanders. Tragically, he was killed by a shellburst on his first day in action in Normandy at the end of June 1944.

the Moro. In this advance further casualties occurred and when London Irish patrols reached the Moro they found it well defended. A brigade attack was planned before it became known that 78th Division was to be withdrawn for rest and re-organiza-tion; it would be relieved by a Canadian division, to which would fall the task of crossing the Moro.

The Irish Brigade enjoyed a short spell of rest before being deployed to hold part of the Allied line in the Apennine mountains in January 1944. Here occurred a series of small actions which Nelson Russell believed that the higher command would see as a rest cure for 78th Division, which could then be looked on as 'fresh troops' for further offensive operations. Fortunately, Major-General Charles Keightley, 78th Division's commander, shared this view and was able to persuade his seniors to pull the division out of the line so that it might get some training before being committed to a new offensive. The Polish 3rd Carpathian Division then relieved 78th Division and the Irish Brigade moved back to Campobasso for training. Snow wrote *finis* to those plans and when the weather cleared the division was ordered to move to Capua to join Fifth US Army. Based in the Caserta area in Fifth Army reserve, the Irish Brigade at last had the opportunity for training. But it was at Caserta that the Brigade had to say farewell to its commander; Nelson Russell suddenly and, in his own words, 'inexplicably became worn and was placed in hospital'.

The doctors' verdict was that Brigadier Russell would not be fit enough to resume command of the Irish Brigade and would have to be evacuated to the United Kingdom. In a Special Order of the Day dated 18 February 1944, Nelson said his goodbyes to his Brigade:

> The time has come when I say farewell to the Brigade. We have fought many battles together during three campaigns and it will always be my proud memory to have had the honour and privilege of commanding this fine brigade – to my mind the best Brigade in the Army.
>
> My successor is well known to you all. In his sure hands you will certainly maintain your great reputation.
>
> I wish all ranks 'good luck' and 'good fortune' in the battles still to come.
>
> I also thank you for everything you have done in fifteen months hard fighting. 'Everything' means a great deal.

Nelson Russell held no further active service commands in the Second World War, serving instead as Belfast Sub-District and Garrison commander. His reputation as a brigade commander in action, however, was of the highest standing. He had led his brigade from its first landings in Africa though the mountains of Tunisia, across the Mediterranean to Sicily and the brief, bitter campaign on the island, and then on to the Italian mainland with a series of tough actions in a matter of weeks before moving into the Apennines. Small wonder that he had collapsed: he was forty-six years old, had always shared the risks faced by his soldiers, had come close to death on several occasions and had borne that lonely burden of responsibility that is command.

Nelson's own experience and skill, as well as his leadership ability – which included, or perhaps was based on, his great understanding of the soldiers under his command – were tremendous assets to the Irish Brigade in its first campaign in Tunisia. Colonel Desmond Woods, who lived near him in County Down, recalled for me how Nelson had once described his regard for the battalions of the Irish Brigade: his command technique, he explained, was to know each battalion's strengths and, accordingly, use each where those strengths would be of greatest use. And, of course, he did his best to protect his men from what he regarded as the less sensible ideas of those in higher authority, an attitude that would not have endeared him to some of those individuals but that certainly earned the total support of those who served under him. He was very often right in his criticism of plans that were handed down to him but his own planning could rarely be faulted and he did his best to ensure that the risks faced by his soldiers were minimized to the greatest possible extent. The superb reputation earned by the Irish Brigade in Tunisia, Sicily and Italy was due very much to the outstanding command qualities of Nelson Russell.

~ 10 ~

Scott

When Nelson Russell fell ill and relinquished command of the Irish Brigade in February 1944 he regarded his friend and fellow Irish Fusilier Pat Scott as his natural successor. Scott had already served in the Irish Brigade before being promoted to command an English brigade and had, temporarily, commanded the Irish Brigade as part of Y Division under Nelson Russell. The latter's recommendation on the succession was accepted and Pat Scott took over command, holding the post for the final fifteen months of the war and then until the Irish Brigade was disbanded in Austria in 1947. He was regarded widely as one of the Army's finest brigade commanders.

Pat Scott was born into the Army in 1905. His father, Thomas, was an Indian Army officer and Pat was born in the Punjab, although the Scott family's roots were in County Fermanagh, where Pat died in 1976. It was almost natural that the young Scott would join the Army and Pat was commissioned into the Royal Irish Fusiliers from Sandhurst in 1924. There was a family connection with the Irish Fusiliers: his father, now Lieutenant-General Sir Thomas Scott, had been appointed Colonel of the Regiment in 1923. Pat Scott's early service took him to Egypt and India with his regiment, but he also served in staff and training posts. During his service in India the Faughs were commanded by Lieutenant-Colonel Donagh McCarthy-O'Leary DSO MC, who made a profound impression on the young Pat. Donagh McCarthy-O'Leary had a deep sense of duty and responsibility towards his soldiers which, combined with an intense Christian faith, made him a substitute father figure for many young officers. Pat Scott considered that he learned more about duty and responsibility from his commanding officer than he ever had from his father, a rather distant and severe figure. It is interesting to note that Donagh McCarthy-O'Leary was a Roman Catholic whereas Pat Scott was Church of Ireland.

When war was declared in September 1939, Pat was a student at Camberley but all students were returned to their regimental depots upon the outbreak of war. Captain Scott went to Ballykinlar in County Down, shortly to become the Infantry Training Centre for the three Irish infantry regiments. He was then appointed brigade-major to an infantry brigade due to deploy to Norway as a reserve formation for the Norwegian expeditionary force. However, Norway was evacuated before the brigade could sail from Britain; it was diverted to assist in occupying Iceland, which had declared its total independence from Denmark after the German invasion.

By August 1940 Major Pat Scott was back in the United Kingdom to help form an officers' school in Wales and remained there until being appointed to command a divisional battle school at Poyntzpass in Northern Ireland. Pat was an eminently good choice for such a post, as he possessed a sharp eye for detail and a feel for battle. The latter quality was all the more surprising since, at this time, he had not seen any action at all; but his feel for battle would be demonstrated time and again in the years ahead. And Major Scott was also able to inspire confidence in the soldiers who served under him; I can recall the respect that my own father had for Pat Scott, under whom he served in the Royal Irish Fusiliers in India.

At the end of 1941 Pat Scott was promoted to lieutenant-colonel and returned to the Royal Irish Fusiliers to command its 1st Battalion. The Irish Fusiliers, better known as the Faughs from their Gaelic motto Faugh a Ballagh!, or Clear the Way!, were stationed in England and about to become a battalion of the new 38 (Irish) Infantry Brigade. The Irish Brigade spent much of 1942 training in England and Scotland. That training was to be put to good use as part of First Army in the Tunisian campaign. The Allies were planning to invade French northwest Africa at the end of 1942 in Operation TORCH. Allied troops began landing in the French colonies in November while Montgomery's Eighth Army, having defeated the Italo-German army at El Alamein, was pushing Rommel's forces westward towards Tunisia. If all went to plan, First Army's arrival at the western end of the Mediterranean would catch the enemy forces in a nutcracker movement and finish off the Axis in Africa. However, the Germans had other ideas and, in a superbly organized operation, moved troops and equipment from Sicily and Italy into Tunisia. First Army, which had hoped to take Tunis before the end of December, found itself on the defensive against General Jürgen von Arnim's newly created Fifth Panzer Army in Tunisia. Such was the situation when the Irish Brigade arrived. Both Allies and Axis tried to secure the hills overlooking the routes to Tunis and it was in these actions that Pat Scott first demonstrated his feel for battle and showed that he, too, possessed what the Germans called *Fingerspitzengefuehl*.

On the morning of 18 January 1943 the Irish Brigade was on Grandstand Hill, preparing for an attack on the neighbouring Two Tree Hill from which the Inniskillings had been repulsed three days earlier. However, instead of attacking, the Irish battalions were forced onto the defensive when five German battalions, supported by about a dozen tanks, attacked Grandstand. The ensuing battle raged for several days and Pat Scott was fortunate to escape only slightly injured when German aircraft dive-bombed his headquarters. German troops captured a ridge overlooking the British main supply route; the highest point of that ridge was Point 286. When the Irish Brigade was ordered to take Point 286, Brigadier Nelson Russell objected on the grounds that 286 could not be held by either side but his objections were overruled and 2nd London Irish Rifles were ordered to attack.

The London Irish took Point 286 but the hilltop was solid rock and it proved impossible to dig in for shelter against shells and mortar bombs. It was then that Pat Scott's intuition came into play. Believing a heavy German counter-attack to be inevitable, and that the Rifles would be unable to stop it, he sent a company of Irish Fusiliers to act as a longstop, securing the main road and guarding the brigade's southern flank. John Horsfall, then commanding D Company of the Faughs, described the events that followed in his book *The Wild Geese are Flighting*:

> There was no delay at all before the storm burst and the German counter-attack came in like a visitation from the angels of hell complete with chariots of fire. The force and vigour of the onslaught was only matched by its audacity. True disciples of Rommel, the tank commanders rode in, sitting on the turret tops, armed with Verey pistols and star shells to guide them. They simply charged along the ridge, from one end to the other with a solid phalanx of tanks, leaving their jaegers to pick up the bits later. Driving straight over the top of the feature in the starlight they went on and down and over the road itself in an ever-widening torrent and our defence dissolved into fragments before them.

Although the Germans had broken through the riflemen on the ridge they had failed to turn the Irish Brigade's flank and thus did not gain the major objective of their attack. Pat Scott's positioning of a company of Irish Fusiliers had paid off.

In the closing days of February the brigade fought off another major attack at Bou Arada and, again, Scott showed his ability as a commander. However, on this occasion he was commanding the Irish Brigade rather than 1st Royal Irish Fusiliers, since Nelson Russell had been given command of the ad hoc Y Division. In spite of determined German attacks in his sector, and severe casualties among the London Irish, he organized defence and counter-attack to such effect that the Germans lost virtually all their early gains within a matter of hours. Subsequently, he set about clearing the Irish Brigade's area of Germans; in Nelson Russell's words he 'handled the brigade with a sure hand'.

At Bou Arada the Rifles again suffered badly and the disbandment of the battalion was proposed at army headquarters. Brigadier Russell opposed this suggestion, since he believed that losing the London Irish would endanger the identity of the Irish Brigade. As there were no other Irish battalions in Tunisia, it was unlikely that another Irish battalion would replace the Rifles. This assessment was undoubtedly correct. Nelson won the argument: the Rifles would survive but, in the short term, they would have to be withdrawn from the front line to be rebuilt as a fighting battalion and, for that task, he transferred Pat Scott from the Faughs to the Rifles.

Using the strength of the surviving men, especially the older regular soldiers, Pat Scott soon had the Rifles fit to take their place in the front line again. Towards the end of the Tunisian campaign the battalion was back in action as part of the Irish Brigade in 78th Division, which had been given the task of breaking through the

Oued Zarga mountains. Known to the Germans as the Siegfried line of Tunisia, these included mountaintop fortresses held in strength, and hillsides that the defenders were able to sweep with machine-gun fire. The Irish Brigade was to capture Jebel Tanngoucha.

The Rifles' role in this operation was to take the village of Heidous, known to the soldiers as Hideous. They were successful while the Faughs and Inniskillings forced the enemy off Tanngoucha, suffering heavy casualties in doing so. Pat Scott had imbued the Rifles with a tremendous sense of confidence and had built up their morale considerably. Jim Hamilton MM, then a warrant officer in the battalion, said that he was 'the best commanding officer [I] ever served under; he told you everything, just like Monty'.

The Tunisian campaign ended in May 1943 and the Allies began preparing for their next campaign, the invasion of Sicily in July. By then Pat Scott had moved on from the London Irish. His ability had been recognized and he had been promoted to command 12 Infantry Brigade,* in 4th Division, from which he moved to command 128 (Hampshire) Brigade,† in 46th Division. He retained the latter command until he broke an ankle in early 1944. As Pat was recovering from his injury, Nelson Russell collapsed and was admitted to hospital. When the doctors decreed that the Irish Brigade commander would have to return home, that created a vacancy for which Russell recommended Pat Scott. Although not fully recovered, Pat arrived to take command of the Irish Brigade in March.

By now the Irish Brigade was in Italy and the Allies were facing the Germans' Gustav line, which cut across Italy from coast to coast south of Rome. The best-known feature of the Gustav line was the hill on which stood the monastery of Saint Benedict, Monte Cassino. Almost as soon as Pat took over, the Irish Brigade deployed around Cassino with brigade headquarters in the village of Cairo, probably the most shelled spot in all Italy. Since his ankle had not yet fully healed, Pat Scott was not particularly mobile and needed a jeep to travel any distance at all. However, jeep travel was out of the question because of the terrain and the fact that the Germans overlooked the tracks and could bring down artillery or mortar fire at will. The spell in the mountains proved a difficult one but the morale of the brigade was very high with the Inniskillings dominating the no man's land between their positions and those of the Germans. The Faughs, based around Cassino, also patrolled actively. Regular German artillery bombardments were a particular nuisance; during one bombardment, the brigade's Catholic padre, Father Dan Kelleher, a Kerryman, earned the Military Cross for rescuing wounded men under fire. At one stage the divisional commander asked Pat Scott to devise a plan for capturing the monastery, to which Pat replied that he 'thought the best plan was for someone else to capture it'.

---

* The brigade included 2nd Royal Fusiliers, 6th Black Watch and 1st Royal West Kents.
† The Hampshire Brigade included 2nd, 1/4th and 5th Hampshires.

Needless to say, Pat Scott was not sorry when, after three weeks of living on mountaintops, the Irish Brigade handed their positions over to the Poles during three nights in late April. It was far from being a straightforward handover, as he himself described:

> The essence of this relief was a race against time. The hours of darkness were barely sufficient to get the Poles across the Rapido valley and into their mountain positions and our people out and back before daylight. The business of getting the Poles to the right place with no common language and a fair amount of shelling to impede [the operation] was no ordinary undertaking. To avoid being caught in the open at dawn, we had smoke canisters laid out across the valley thickened up by the 25-pounders. Cassino itself was kept in an almost continual pall by this means.

There is a certain irony in the fact that the relief of 1st Royal Irish Fusiliers by a Polish battalion was overseen by the adjutant of the Faughs, Captain Brian Clark, and his Polish counterpart in a common language: German.

By this stage in the war the Irish Brigade had suffered many casualties and these men had to be replaced. In a normal peacetime situation, replacement soldiers would have come from the training depots of the Irish regiments but the strain of war meant that infantry units, other than Guards, had to accept whatever reinforcements were sent to them. (This was especially true in Italy; the manpower demands of Operation OVERLORD meant that no reinforcements were sent from Britain after February 1944. Eighth Army had to find casualty replacements from within the Mediterranean area; these were provided by retraining gunners from disbanded anti-aircraft regiments, and surplus personnel from both the Royal Navy and Royal Air Force.) The effect of this on the Irish Brigade was that the infantry battalions now contained many men with no connection at all with Ireland. However, Pat Scott was determined that these men should at least feel Irish and in this he was remarkably successful. Officers and men were encouraged to learn and sing Irish songs while the brigade's Irish pipers were called on to play at every possible occasion. Officers were even expected to learn Irish dancing and nights in the officers' messes included traditional dancing and singing from the Irish Brigade songbook, which Pat had also had produced.

The songbook contained a wealth of Irish songs with a very large element being 'rebel' airs, including the Irish national anthem, 'The Soldier's Song'. Not only did the songbook catch the imagination of the Irish Brigade's soldiers but it also had an effect on anyone who came into contact with the Brigade. Historian James Lucas, who served in a Home Counties Brigade, was in hospital with a number of Irish Brigade soldiers and came under the effect of the songbook. Until his later years he could sing songs such as 'Kevin Barry', 'Kelly, The Boy from Killane', 'The West's Awake', and 'The Sash', all of which featured in the book. Many of the titles included could have caused a riot in Belfast or Dublin, but in the midst of war and far from home they had a unifying rather than a dividing effect.

Pat Scott was an exceptionally capable and popular commander and the soldiers of the Irish Brigade respected him. They also had complete confidence in him and knew that when they were sent in to an attack their commander would have obtained for them the best possible support. Time and again he justified that confidence. The Irish Brigade had a field artillery regiment attached as part of the brigade group. This was 17th Field Regiment, Royal Artillery, who were wont to refer to themselves as the Royal Hibernian Artillery and whose twenty-four 25-pounder guns were on hand to support any brigade operation. If that firepower were not enough then Pat Scott ensured that more guns were obtained from somewhere. John Horsfall summarized the brigade's feelings for their new commander in his 1976 obituary for Pat Scott in *The Blackthorn*, the journal of the Royal Irish Rangers.

> Pat was interested in his men and it was not possible for anyone to serve long in the Irish Brigade without being made aware of this fact. They knew that he put their welfare above other considerations and that he was their champion and protector against all comers.

General Alexander's plan to break the Gustav line and the deadlock in Italy was codenamed Operation DIADEM; Eighth Army's part in that was codenamed Operation HONKER.* With most of Eighth Army moved from the east coast to the west, except for a corps maintained on the east coast, the Allies were ready to open their offensive on 11 May. That evening over 1,000 guns opened fire on German positions. Alexander had achieved complete success as several senior German officers were on leave, not expecting an assault so soon.

The Irish Brigade was not involved in the initial infantry operations as 78th Division was to pass through a bridgehead created by 4th Division and 8th Indian Division to attack a number of objectives; their ultimate task was to cut Highway 6, the main road to Rome, thereby isolating the Monte Cassino strongpoint. Once that had been done the German paratroopers on Monte Cassino would be forced to withdraw or surrender. A Polish frontal attack on the monastery had failed with the Poles suffering heavily. When the Irish Brigade went into action the first part of their operation was carried out by 6th Inniskillings. Supported by Sherman tanks the Skins crossed the Piopetto river and thrust into the heart of the enemy defensive positions. The next phase involved the London Irish attacking a village called Sinagoga but as the Rifles' commanding officer and the commander of their supporting tanks were finalizing their plans they came under fire from German artillery and mortars. The COs were killed or fatally wounded and Pat Scott immediately made his way to the Rifles' tactical headquarters where he met Lieutenant-Colonel Bala Bredin, commanding officer of the Inniskillings, and John Horsfall, to whom he gave command of the Rifles. This meeting was described by John Horsfall in his book *Fling Our Banner to the Wind*.

---

* The Poles believed that HONKER was a reference to themselves as wild geese exiled from their homeland; they appear not to have been aware that the same soubriquet had been applied to Irish soldiers. In fact, the operation's title was coincidental.

Pat was as lucid and as helpful as usual, in spite of the incessant screams of shells ripping over our heads in both directions. He knew that both his forward battalions were in trouble, but he in no way pressed me beyond pointing out our exposed position and the danger of delay. This, of course, [meant] that the enemy had to be hit again while reeling, otherwise it was only a matter of hours before his counterthrust slammed into us.

Pat Scott assigned a tank to John Horsfall as a mobile command post and he was able to keep in close touch throughout the battle. As John commented, 'Thank God for the headphones and Pat's quiet voice coming through'. The Rifles took Sinagoga; the Faughs moved through them and went on to take their objective. Four hours later, the Irish Fusiliers were on Massa Cerro; before the end of the day German troops on Highway 6, the Via Casalina, were being mortared by the Faughs. The latter's part had gone so well that Pat had ordered the other two battalions to move up to their left. That afternoon the Inniskillings were given the task of seizing the village of Piumerola. Once again the operation was swift and successful. An hour of fierce fighting saw the Skins capture the village and take a hundred prisoners from 1st Fallschirmjäger Division. The Rifles had also moved forward again; they, too, captured a number of German paratroopers.

The Irish Brigade had done remarkably well, moving quickly and beating the best of Germany's soldiers. On the last day of intense fighting, 17 May, all three battalions and their support units were on the move throughout the day and were involved in tough, bloody action for most of it.

As a CO of one of them, I was never conscious of the slightest pressure from our commander, who at all times drawled his instructions to us in the bored and disinterested manner which he sometimes affected. But however Pat gave out his orders, laughter usually found its way into the procedure somewhere.

The Irish Brigade had played an important part in breaking the Gustav line. Although most accounts of the war in Italy tell of the Poles capturing Monte Cassino, that feature had been abandoned by the Germans when the Poles launched their final assault. With Highway 6 threatened the paratroopers had withdrawn and on the morning of 18 May soldiers of the Podolski Lancers were able to hoist a hastily-made regimental pennant – not the Polish flag as is often claimed – over the ruins of Saint Benedict's monastery. The suffering of the Poles in earlier assaults caught the imagination of the world and so they have been credited with more than their due, to the detriment of the Irish and French soldiers who did so much to win the battle.*

Following the smashing of the Gustav line the Allies then broke through the next Axis barrier, the Hitler line, before pushing on to link up with the troops breaking

---

* In launching his North African soldiers through the Aurunci mountains, General Juin of the French Expeditionary Corps made what was probably the most valuable contribution to Allied success at the Gustav line.

out of the Anzio bridgehead. Once again the Irish Brigade was engaged in tough fighting, throughout all of which their commander retained a calm control over his battalions. As the London Irish advanced on the little town of Ripi they were left without tank support for a time while ahead of them the enemy defences were beginning to harden. John Horsfall was reluctant to commit his soldiers to battle against armoured opposition without the support of their own armour. However, at higher level, the situation was not appreciated fully and it was believed that the Rifles had simply to execute an advance guard movement rather than attack a position that was held in depth. John Horsfall appealed to Pat Scott to 'pacify our chiefs' until he had the resources needed to carry out his attack. This was the type of situation in which Pat excelled and in which his concern for his soldiers shone through. Those above him suggested that the Irish Brigade was slow to perform its task but Pat trusted his commanding officers and accepted their assessment of the situation on the ground. He ensured that the Irish Brigade's artillery was ready to open fire when needed and even added targets to their fireplan as well as ensuring that the tanks were in position for the advance. He came up to John Horsfall's headquarters where he remained until the attack started, giving Horsfall the opportunity to observe his commander's technique with generals, since much of the Brigadier's time was spent on the radio to 78th Divisional headquarters. Capable of summarizing a complex tactical situation in a few crisp sentences, Pat could even make his friend Charles Keightley wilt in the face of his appreciation of a situation. The usual outcome was that Keightley would say 'Go on, Pat – have it your own way – you are usually right'. John Horsfall observed 'That was just the trouble, Pat was *always* right and no man ever had such a gift for reading the mind of the enemy'.

In spite of delaying actions such as that at Ripi, the Germans were falling back rapidly to establish their next major defensive line at Lake Trasimene where the Irish Brigade would fight another pitched battle. Before that, however, Pat Scott took the Irish Brigade to Rome to meet the Pope. The Brigade marched into the Vatican on 12 June; Irish pipes and drums played in Saint Peter's Square and His Holiness greeted the Irish soldiers:

> Dearly beloved sons, we bid you welcome. You belong to the nation which has ever belonged to God's church since Saint Patrick. We are well aware of the good which the Irish have done in spreading the faith from the shores of their green isle to the shores of many nations. We greet you and bless you with all our heart's affection and your dear ones at home. God be with you always.

When Pat Scott asked the Pope if he would like to hear the Irish pipes he was told yes. The tunes that were played included 'The Wearing of the Green', 'The Minstrel Boy', and 'The Boys of Wexford'. These were described in the following day's Vatican newspaper as 'sacred music' which, at least as far as the pipers were concerned, was probably an apt description. Pat Scott was impressed by the Irish priests in the Vatican, many of whom had helped Allied prisoners of war to escape. He expressed the hope that one day their story would be told and also commented:

It is a matter of great concern to all of us who come from Ireland that when the war is over it will only be remembered against her that Éire was neutral. What we hope is that all the magnificent deeds wrought by the sons of Éire in this war may be remembered to her credit. It is sometimes overlooked that the services of every Irishman from every part of Ireland are given of their own free will for the good of the cause, be they fighting men or those priests who helped the English prisoners in Rome.

From its meeting with the Pope the Irish Brigade went to a further meeting with the Germans at Lake Trasimene. By the evening of 20 June the other two brigades of 78th Division were in close contact with the enemy at Trasimene and both had suffered heavily. Pat Scott went to meet the divisional commander, Charles Keightley, to plan the breaking of the German positions. Keightley suggested embarking 2nd London Irish Rifles in amphibious DUKWs and sailing ten miles down the lake to land behind the enemy. Pat Scott was not impressed; first, however, he went to see John Horsfall and asked what he thought of the general's idea. Lieutenant-Colonel Horsfall was horrified: the DUKW was slow, had a very noisy engine and would give the Germans several hours' notice of the Rifles' coming. He suggested that his battalion would be met by a reception committee complete with car headlights and heavy artillery; he also suggested that the idea might bring an end to Keightley's career, and Pat's for allowing it. The latter replied with a grin: 'I thought I'd try it out on you. I'll pass your comments and mine on to himself.'

So ended the idea of amphibious operations. This incident also illustrates another aspect of Pat Scott's character. He was forthright in his beliefs and as likely to tell a general what he thought of him as he was a major. Major-General Keightley, however, was a very good friend of Pat Scott and often relied heavily on Pat's advice. He accepted it on this occasion and on many others to the extent that 78th Division, under Keightley's command, was run effectively by the partnership of Keightley and Scott. The Irish Brigade went into action at San Fatucchio on the morning of 21 June, with the Rifles the first to go forward – without the benefit of artillery support. This was because men of 2nd Lancashire Fusiliers were pinned down by enemy fire so close to the village that an artillery bombardment on the Germans would also have fallen on the Lancs. The Rifles took San Fatucchio and pressed on into the German lines to establish a foothold on the Pucciarelli ridge. There they met with very heavy opposition that eventually brought their advance to a standstill.

Pat Scott had been prepared for this and the Inniskillings advanced to exploit the Rifles' gains. By now 17th Field Regiment's guns were able to lend their full support while Canadian tanks also backed up the Irish infantry. There were several fierce counter-attacks but Scott had a very effective force and by the evening of 23 June the Faughs were able to launch the next phase of the operation on the villages of Pescia and Ranciano. Following heavy fighting the Irish Fusiliers took their objectives and, by the evening of the 24th, the operation moved into a further phase with 36 Brigade passing through the Irish Brigade to renew the attack. Commenting on the Trasimene battle, Pat Scott said that it had been 'marked by as fine a demonstration of leader-ship and guts as one may expect to see anywhere'. He was referring to the courage of his soldiers and the leadership provided by their officers, but the men of the Irish Brigade had no doubt that Pat's own inspiring leadership was stamped on the entire operation.

Following a spell in Egypt, the Irish Brigade returned to Italy and positions in the northern Apennines, facing the Gothic line. Their corps was under American command in Fifth Army and in October 1944 the Faughs were placed under command of 36 Brigade to attack Monte Spaduro.* This operation was undertaken in the mistaken belief that Spaduro was held only lightly and that other features over-looking the area had been cleared of enemy troops.

> None of us in the Irish Brigade was ever at ease for long when detached like that. Anyway, the splitting up of the brigade was another thing to worry about, and the fact that it happened almost nonstop at this time leaves a good many questions at Fifth Army Headquarters unanswered, as well as in the Division.

By now Charles Keightley had been promoted to command V Corps and the new leadership of 78th Division had yet to settle down. The result of all this for the Faughs was that two companies, less than 200 soldiers, were deployed to capture Monte Spaduro. A full German regiment, almost 2,000 men, was located in the area. Amazingly, the Faughs took their objectives but were very quickly counter-attacked and suffered heavy losses. The survivors of the two companies were forced to with-draw; only about forty returned to their battalion's positions. Later, their comrades found evidence of the bravery shown by the attacking Faughs: Major Maurice Crehan's body was found with that of several of his men and the bodies of many more dead Germans around them; the Faughs had fought to the death.

Pat Scott had never believed that a single battalion could take Monte Spaduro. Had Keightley still been the divisional commander it is unlikely that such an attack would have been made. As it was, however, Pat decided to move the London Irish up close behind the Faughs to provide a firm base should anything go wrong. At that stage it was not his battle, and his actions once again reflect his uncanny feel for the battlefield and for reading the enemy's mind. When the Rifles appeared in his head-quarters area, John Horsfall felt much happier. 'I knew then that Pat was in charge now, and whatever might happen the battle was an Irish Brigade one.' And so it was, although it took the combined strength of the Irish and 11 Brigades before Monte Spaduro finally fell several days later. Had Pat Scott's advice been listened to before the first attack it could have been a very different story.

---

* John Horsfall was now commanding 1st Royal Irish Fusiliers while Lieutenant-Colonel Bala Bredin commanded 2nd London Irish.

In April 1945 Eighth and Fifth Armies finally broke through into the plain of Lombardy in northern Italy. The Irish Brigade, augmented almost to the strength of an armoured division, played a central role in this operation with 2nd London Irish serving as armoured infantry in Kangaroos – tanks or self-propelled guns converted into armoured personnel carriers. Once again, Pat Scott's steady hand exercised control and his ability to anticipate what the Germans might do led to a hastily-improvized force of Inniskillings, Royal West Kents and Commandos thwarting a counter-attack that threatened both the advance of 6th Armoured Division and the Allied rear area. Not surprisingly, shortly after the war, Pat Scott was the commander asked to give a full-scale presentation on the final operations in Italy.

When the war was over the Irish Brigade moved into the Austrian province of Carinthia and the task of rounding up thousands of German soldiers. However, this proved a minor concern compared with what followed. The Royal Irish Fusiliers were asked to accept the surrender of Cossack soldiers who had fought for Germany and found thousands of men accompanied by their families. A small group of Faughs managed to get the Cossacks into the British sector and away from the approaching Red Army. Pat Scott then found himself dealing with what appeared to be virtually the entire Croatian nation who were trying to move into western Europe. During the war the Croatians had sided with Germany and the Nazis had established a Croatian state, carved out of Yugoslavia. The Yugoslavs now sought the return of the Croatians. Pat Scott eventually persuaded the Croatians to accept the terms of the general surrender, which meant that they should surrender to Tito's Yugoslav forces. The Croatians – an army and its civilian followers – were returned to Yugoslavia where many were massacred by Tito's men.

Alongside such problems the settling of frontiers between the Western Allies and the Soviets must have seemed minor, but Pat Scott also handled this problem. During negotiations with the Soviets he had to allow Red Army generals to believe that he was a major-general and his divisional commander, who was a major-general, was ordered to stay out of sight lest he compromise Pat's standing with the Soviets. That order came from Charles Keightley, V Corps' commander, who seems to have had more confidence in his old friend's ability to deal with the Soviets than he had in that of 78th Division's commander.

Pat Scott rose to the rank of major-general before retiring from the Army. His forthright honesty probably denied him further advancement. Although told that he was to be appointed GOC, Northern Ireland, a lieutenant-general's appointment, this did not happen as another officer was appointed in his stead. He was also approached to become Inspector-General of the Royal Ulster Constabulary in succession to Sir Richard Pim but this went no further than discussion. However, he was appointed Colonel of the Royal Irish Fusiliers in succession to Sir Gerald Templer. This was an appointment that his father had also held and it was believed to be a unique occurrence as no other regiment in the Army had had both a father and son as colonel. Pat was the last Colonel of the Faughs; his regiment became part of the new Royal Irish Rangers in 1968 and his enthusiasm for the amalgamation and the new regiment did much to ensure its success.

As a brigadier in the Second World War Pat was also, in American parlance, a one-star general. He could have achieved higher rank since he undoubtedly had the ability to do so. His eye for battle, that *Fingerspitzengefuehl*, was an attribute he shared with many great commanders of history – with Rommel, for example, or with another Irish general, Wellington.

> He never relied on the personal magnetism factor in leadership. Like the Iron Duke he owed his success to painstaking preparation both in training and in planning operations so that nothing that could be done was left undone in the prelude to battle. These characteristics were amply matched by the skill with which he fought [his battles].

Pat Scott preferred to remain with the Irish Brigade rather than move on to greater things. And his ability would have guaranteed a rapid rise. Perhaps the greatest tribute to his leadership was paid by John Horsfall when he wrote in Pat's obituary:

> The only anxiety the Brigade ever had when serving under Pat was the ever present fear of his promotion to higher things and thereby losing him. Fortunately for all of us this never happened until Hitler's war was safely over.

~ 11 ~

McCreery, Horrocks and Adair

Those generals studied in the previous chapters were not the only Irishmen to achieve such rank during the Second World War, although they were the most successful and include those best known to the public. But there were other men, some who were also successful and some whose command was not distinguished, who commanded brigades, divisions and corps while at least three commanders with Irish family backgrounds achieved distinction. Those three were General Sir Richard McCreery, Eighth Army's last commander, Lieutenant-General Sir Brian Horrocks, an outstanding and inspiring corps commander, and Major-General Sir Allan Adair, who commanded Guards Armoured Division in north-west Europe in 1944–5.

Richard McCreery, the only cavalryman to command Eighth Army, was born in Bilton Park, Rugby in 1898, the son of Walter McCreery. The McCreery family's Irish roots were in County Tyrone, where they had farmed at Killyclogher near Omagh. Dick McCreery's grandfather, Andrew, left Ireland with his brother, James Buchanan, for the United States 'soon after the American civil war' and worked for a time in Philadelphia before going to California where he 'became a man of some substance'. Andrew had three sons, of whom Walter was the middle one. In turn, Walter had four sons, of whom Richard was the oldest. The next son, Bob, was murdered by republican terrorists in 1920.

Dick left school to join the Army as soon as he possibly could – he was sixteen when war broke out in 1914 – and from Sandhurst was commissioned in XII Royal Lancers, with whom he served in France from 1915 to 1917 and in the final four months of the war, from August to November 1918. For much of its duration on the western front the Great War was not suited to the deployment of cavalry in their traditional role and thus cavalry regiments, including 12th Lancers, were held in reserve for the breakthrough that was always being sought, or carried out duties in the rear or relieved infantry units in the trenches.

> in spite of many actions involving flank protection, getting information and covering the movement of infantry and guns, it was not until the autumn of 1918 that the 12th Lancers were able once more to practise their traditional tasks of wide, deep reconnaissance and thrusting forward in the van of the army.

A fellow officer regarded McCreery as having no equal as a troop leader while another described him as 'a very courageous and efficient troop leader'. On 9 November 1918 it was an action by Lieutenant McCreery's troop, which cleared up a machine-gun post at Les Fontaines, that allowed a half squadron of the regiment under Captain Spicer to advance beyond Solre le Chateau. For this action the commander of 50th (Northumbrian) Division recommended McCreery, whom he described as 'a very young officer ... who looked, as he was, a mere boy and as if he had only just left Sandhurst', for the Military Cross. Richard McCreery therefore returned from France with the first of many decorations but having lost the toes of his right foot and suffered a serious wound to his right leg.

The interwar years were filled with regimental duties in a number of stations, including Germany, Ireland and a spell in Egypt when McCreery was commanding 12th Lancers. Arriving in Egypt in January 1936 the regiment began a period of desert training based around Mersa Matruh that would stand them in good stead in the war that was soon to come. McCreery also became familiar with the desert and the problems of mechanized warfare in that setting – 12th Lancers had given up their horses in favour of armoured vehicles in 1929. For McCreery the years between the wars included a time as adjutant of 12th Lancers, attending Staff College and acting as Brigade Major to 2 Cavalry Brigade at Tidworth. In 1934 he returned to 12th Lancers as Commanding Officer and did much to prepare the regiment for the forthcoming war. At the time he commanded one of the only two cavalry regiments to be mechanized.

The quality of McCreery's preparation was demonstrated amply by the regiment's performance in the retreat to Dunkirk, during which it earned three DSOs, three DCMs, three MCs and three MMs for a few days in action. By then the regiment was commanded by Herbert Lumsden, later to command X Corps at El Alamein.* When the BEF went to France in autumn 1939, McCreery was the principal staff officer – GSO1 – of 1st Division, commanded by Major-General Harold Alexander. Since McCreery had been appointed in mid-1938, he and Alex had had time to build up an excellent rapport from which sprang excellent teamwork.

> In the winter before the war started, McCreery remembers that 1st Division was concentrating on defensive problems. He remembers too that the principles on which they worked – all-round mutually supported defence in depth with a mobile reserve to deal with enemy penetrations – held good for the rest of the war.

However, in January 1940, McCreery took command of 2 Armoured Brigade[†] and it was as commander of that formation that he saw action against the attacking

---

* Lumsden was to become the scapegoat for Montgomery's lack of appreciation of what tanks could do. He was killed in the Pacific in a kamikaze attack on the American battleship USS *New Mexico* in 1944.

† The brigade included The Bays, 10th Hussars and 9th Lancers. The latter was later to amalgamate with McCreery's own regiment to form 9th/12th Royal Lancers.

German forces. For a time his brigade fought alongside a French formation commanded by Charles de Gaulle whose bearing very much impressed McCreery. Two Armoured Brigade put up a stout rearguard action in difficult circumstances between the Somme and Seine rivers and was eventually evacuated from Brest. For his 'gallant and skilful conduct' of the retreat, Dick McCreery was awarded the DSO. His Brigade Major, John Anderson, recalled McCreery's energy.

> General Dick kept going literally night and day, contriving to be where it mattered all the time. He was essentially a leader by personal example, utterly fearless and always in the lead, never asking anyone to do what he wouldn't do himself ... When not in some primitive armoured vehicle on reconnaissance or in personal command, he was driving his own staff car, night and day, at high speed since no driver could go fast enough for his liking. I ventured once to say to him that I didn't understand how he managed to go on driving like that. He replied simply: 'You'd get tired. I don't'.

As the reforming of the Army got underway Dick McCreery was promoted to major-general commanding 8th Armoured Division. He took up this appointment on 14 December 1940, the division having been formed only a month earlier, on 4 November. Although equipment was in short supply following Dunkirk, McCreery was determined that the training of his new command should be based on sound principles and he set about this task with typical enthusiasm and a clear sense of purpose. He was described as the first British commander 'to appreciate and demonstrate the power of an armoured division employed on the ground in defence'. By October 1941, when large-scale manoeuvres were held, the prowess of 8th Armoured Division was such that McCreery was praised by both senior commanders and the press for the skilful and decisive way in which he handled his tanks. Brooke commented that the division was 'going on well under Dick McCreery'. (Although 8th Armoured Division was later sent to North Africa, it was never deployed as a complete division and was disbanded after El Alamein.)

From 8th Armoured Division, Richard McCreery was posted to Egypt where, in March 1942, he became General Sir Claude Auchinleck's principal adviser on armoured warfare. Major-General McCreery's main role was to ensure that Eighth Army was equipped with tanks that were fit for action, a role that he was to describe as 'thankless ... because of the mechanical unreliability of the Crusader tank'. It was not long before McCreery was faced with a task that would have daunted Hercules, following Rommel's attack on Eighth Army along the Gazala line. The bloody fighting over three weeks led to Eighth Army's withdrawal from Gazala and the fall of Tobruk. But its effect on the tank strength of Eighth Army was devastating. On 11 June Eighth Army could deploy some 300 tanks,[*] outnumbering Rommel's Panzer Armee Afrika by two-to-one whereas, three days later, the Army's tank strength was

---

[*] This exceeds the total tank strength of the modern British Army.

down to only seventy, of which twenty were I-tanks and the remainder cruisers. It was McCreery's job to ensure that Eighth Army had sufficient tanks with which to fight the battles that lay ahead. His efforts, coupled with those of Auchinleck, ensured that there were enough tanks to meet Rommel's advance after the fall of Tobruk and to fight the Panzer Armee to a standstill along the El Alamein line.

Although the fall of Tobruk was a catastrophe in Churchill's eyes it brought an unexpected bonus for Eighth Army in the form of 300 new American tanks. These were Shermans that were diverted from the US Army and shipped to Egypt. They were supplied at the behest of Roosevelt to whom had fallen the task of telling Churchill of the loss of Tobruk; the prime minister was a guest at the White House at the time. For Eighth Army the Shermans were a godsend; the US tanks were much more reliable and were fitted with a 75mm gun. (Eighth Army already had some American Grant tanks which were also fitted with the 75mm, but the Grant had the disadvantage of having its main armament fitted in a side sponson, thus limiting its traverse and preventing the tank from taking up a hull-down position; nonetheless, Grants provided the Germans with a considerable shock during the Gazala battles.)

Although McCreery ensured that the base workshops repaired tanks quickly enough to return them to battle when Eighth Army was most in need, he and Auchinleck did not see eye to eye on the employment of armour. McCreery's ideas contradicted those of the Auk and this came to a head when

> the Commander-in-Chief who had General Dorman-Smith with him had a long talk to me and John Harding. I knew the views of all the armoured brigade commanders, and I stuck to my guns and refused to endorse the many changes in armoured organization which the C-in-C wished to make.

The result of this impasse was that McCreery was dismissed, only to be re-appointed as the C-in-C's chief of staff when Alexander took over from Auchinleck. Once again he proved his worth as a staff officer and no more so than when Montgomery was forced to rethink his strategy during the battle of El Alamein. With his first assault fought to a standstill, Monty planned to launch a fresh assault along the axis of the coast road but Rommel had foreseen this and moved the bulk of the German forces into the northern sector ready to meet that renewed offensive. On 29 October, at 11.00am, Montgomery decided that the attack would instead be made against the junction of German and Italian troops. The timing here is significant since it indicates that the decision was made during a conference at which Alexander and McCreery were present. In his *Memoirs* Alex notes that it was McCreery's suggestion 'as an experienced armoured commander ... that it should go in just north of the existing northern corridor'. Montgomery's biographer, Nigel Hamilton, argues that it was Freddie de Guingand, Montgomery's chief of staff, who persuaded his master to change his mind; but change it he did. Montgomery wrote that

> What ... I proposed to do was to deliver a hard blow with the right, and follow it the next night with a knock-out blow with the left.

Although Lord Carver suggests that neither Alexander nor McCreery could make Montgomery change his mind, it was de Guingand's feeding Monty the information of Rommel's latest dispositions that brought about the change in plan. The most likely explanation is that de Guingand managed to make Monty believe that McCreery's proposal was his (Monty's) idea all along. Whatever the course of events the fact remains that McCreery played a significant part in ensuring the British victory at El Alamein.

Over the next several months McCreery remained at Alex's side as his chief of staff but when Brian Horrocks was wounded at Bizerta in June 1943 his place as commander of X Corps was taken by McCreery. X Corps was to be an assault formation for Operation AVALANCHE, the invasion of Italy at Salerno but it would no longer be part of Eighth Army. Instead McCreery was to command a British corps in an American army, Fifth US Army under Lieutenant-General Mark Clark; the other assaulting corps was VI US Corps. Operation AVALANCHE was intended to allow Allied forces to seize Naples and thus create a firm base from which operations on the Italian mainland could be maintained but it came close to disaster and even Alexander admitted to suffering anxious days.

> but it was the personal example and dynamic influence of Dick McCreery and his Corps which ensured that a firm footing was obtained. Indeed, there are those who maintain that had not Dick McCreery advised his American colleague as to what should be done, the US Corps would have been driven into the sea.

It will be recalled that Alexander paid a personal visit to the beachhead and advised Clark to replace VI Corps' commander, as well as releasing 82nd US Airborne Division to help stabilize the beachhead. One of the reasons for the lack of stability was the gap between the two corps in the beachhead, which the Germans had identified as the principal Allied weakness and attempted to exploit. McCreery ensured that this gap was closed and thus deprived the enemy of a tactical opportunity.

As the commander of X Corps, McCreery set an example of leadership and courage that had few equals. Gerald Templer, commanding 56th (London) Division recalled meeting McCreery, his corps commander, coming down a front-line mountain in Italy when he (Templer) was going up and being greeted by McCreery with 'Ah – it's all right for you to go on now'. Visiting the Italian front, Brooke considered that he had found more life in X Corps' area than in the rest of the front and was impressed with the way McCreery 'was running his Corps'. In the Cassino battles of 1944, X Corps had only a supporting role and thus McCreery had few opportunities to show his mettle. At Eighth Army headquarters it was said that McCreery was holding the X Corps front 'with a troop of armoured cars and a volley of oaths'. But his record and reputation were such that he was chosen to succeed Oliver Leese when the latter left Eighth Army in September 1944. He was to be that army's last commander and the only cavalryman to command what was probably Britain's most famous field army of all time. His predecessors had all been infantrymen, save for Alan Cunningham, Eighth Army's first commander, who was a Gunner.

When McCreery took command of Eighth Army the 1944 summer offensive – Operation OLIVE – intended to break through the Gothic line had ground to a stand-still and the Allied armies were faced with another Italian winter. Although operations continued on a limited scale, static warfare became the order of the day as winter set in. Eighth Army lost its Canadian Corps to North-west Europe and, as 1945 dawned, it seemed that the army was a tired body of which little more could be expected. Mark Clark, who had succeeded Alexander as commander of the army group in Italy, had no confidence in either Eighth Army or McCreery. Irrespective of Clark's opinion, McCreery, now Sir Richard, was preparing Eighth Army for its part in the final offensive in Italy. His handling of Eighth Army did much to build confi-dence and morale in its soldiers. Using dismounted cavalry regiments to hold sections of the winter line, he was able to allow infantry units to rest, recuperate and train.

> His preparation for the forthcoming offensive was another [element]; without the showmanship of a Montgomery he imbued Eighth Army with a level of confidence probably as great as at any time in its existence. McCreery was determined that Eighth Army would succeed while giving his soldiers the best possible chances of survival.

One veteran of the Italian campaign, John Strawson, summed McCreery up as the

> greatest cavalry soldier of his generation and at the same time that rare coali-tion of a brilliant staff officer and higher commander.

The preparations for Operation BUCKLAND, Eighth Army's part in the final opera-tions in Italy, prove the truth of Strawson's statement while the execution of BUCKLAND put that truth beyond any doubt. Overall, the 15 Army Group plan, Operation GRAPESHOT, owed much to McCreery and his American counterpart, Lucian Truscott, another cavalry officer and one of the best American generals of the war. Both men had given considerable thought to the new offensive and 'were deter-mined that Fifth and Eighth Armies should have the destruction of the German armies in the field as their objective' whereas Clark seemed set on a territorial objec-tive, in this case the capture of Bologna by US divisions from Fifth Army. In Clark's view Eighth Army would only be capable of subsidiary operations in support of Fifth Army but the combined persuasive power of his two army commanders forced a change of mind. But it is worth stressing that

> The final plan was not a compromise, a course invariably fatal, but contained the inputs of two highly professional army commanders.

The plan was for a double encirclement, what the Germans called *Keil und Kessel*, or 'wedge and trap', with Fifth Army's IV Corps striking into the Emilian plain, west of Route 64, before sidestepping II Corps on to an axis west of Bologna. One wing of Fifth Army would advance towards Verona while the other would strike north before swinging east behind Bologna and south of the river Po. McCreery proposed that Eighth Army would push northwards to cross the Po but Clark ordered an eastward strike along Route 9; he considered a breakthrough on Eighth Army's sector unlikely but felt that McCreery's troops could draw German reserves to that sector.

Operation BUCKLAND was to open on 9 April with the entire Allied air effort providing support. This would be the case until Fifth Army launched Operation CRAFTSMAN on the 12th. McCreery's plan was crafted carefully but with imagination and flair, of a type Montgomery never demonstrated. Although the Germans had deliberately flooded the low lands around Lake Comacchio, McCreery did not consider this an obstacle; instead he determined to use it to assist Eighth Army's assault by deploying a brigade carried in amphibious assault vehicles, or Fantails, while other elements of the army would race through the Argenta Gap* in tanks and armoured personnel carriers. The latter, converted from tanks and self-propelled guns, were known as Kangaroos and the force carried in them became known as the Kangaroo army. In addition, an armoured engineer brigade had been created with local REME workshops carrying out much of the work to produce some 200 specialized armoured vehicles. Eighth Army's artillery disposed 1,020 guns with about 2,000,000 rounds of ammunition.

McCreery gathered all Eighth Army's officers down to the rank of lieutenant-colonel into the cinema at Cesena four days before BUCKLAND was to be launched and explained to them his plans.

> In his quiet, almost apologetic voice, he said that the theatre had been stripped of troops for France; that the army was like an old steeplechaser, full of running, but rather careful; that it was his intention to destroy the Germans south of the Po, rather than to allow them to withdraw to further defence lines in the north. The plan was then outlined.

The old steeplechaser produced the best performance of its life. McCreery left nothing to chance in his preparations; all the painstaking care of a Montgomery was evident but the execution of BUCKLAND was carried out with the élan of a Rommel or a Patton. In a battle that lasted into May the enemy armies were smashed in spite of all the tactical advantages the Germans had: rivers, inundations and extensive minefields. In McCreery's own words the 'battle [was] a model of Army and Air co-operation' with the Desert Air Force providing 'wonderful support' while the 'skill, determination and endurance shown by *all* Ranks, and excellent co-operation of all

---

* McCreery had flown over the area in an Auster AOP (Air Observation Post) light aircraft and had identified the existence of the Argenta Gap.

Arms' were decisive factors in Eighth Army's victory. The smashing of the German forces south of the Po made any further resistance impossible and on 2 May the Germans surrendered in Italy.

Sir Richard McCreery had managed one of the finest performances of a British army in the course of the war. He had done so through attention to detail, careful planning and a strategic flair that had few superiors. His own confidence was based on a deep Christian faith that often seemed at odds with the fact that he could swear like a trooper. Victor Pike, Eighth Army's Chaplain General, a future bishop of Sherborne and an Irishman, was close to McCreery and recalled that, before each battle,

> General Dick would ask him to come to his caravan where they would pray together that he would receive the right guidance during the battle in order that he should – not specifically win it – but make the right decisions and do the right things.

Not a self-publicist in the manner of Montgomery, McCreery managed nonetheless to gain the confidence of his soldiers who trusted him in peace and war. In the aftermath of victory he commanded Eighth Army in Austria and continued to command it when it became British Troops Austria. His care for refugees, his firmness in dealing with the Russians, his concern for the welfare of his soldiers all added yet more supporting proof to the argument that he was an outstanding commander. He was one of the great commanders of the war, even if history has not acknowledged fully that greatness.

Dick McCreery moved from Austria to command the British Army of the Rhine (BAOR) in Germany and served as the Army's representative on the Military Staff Committee of the United Nations before retiring from the Army in 1949. However, he was to continue his association with his beloved 12th Lancers, serving as Colonel of the Regiment until 1962, by which time 12th Lancers had amalgamated with 9th Lancers to form 9th/12th Royal Lancers.* When he was being dined out by the officers of the Regiment on relinquishing the Colonelcy, the official dinner was held in Lisanelly Barracks in Omagh, County Tyrone. It was an appropriate venue for a general with Tyrone blood flowing through his veins.

Sir Richard McCreery GCB KBE DSO MC died peacefully at home in 1967.

* * *

Brian Horrocks was born at Ranniket in India where his Lancastrian father was serving as a doctor in the Royal Army Medical Corps. It was in India that Horrocks

---

* He was also Colonel of 14th/20th Hussars and Honorary Colonel of 3rd/4th County of London Yeomanry (Sharpshooters) as well as being involved with the British Legion.

senior met his wife 'who had all the gaiety and charm of the Irish'; her family, the
Moores, came from County Antrim. Horrocks was to demonstrate that same gaiety
and charm throughout his military career and then in retirement as the presenter of
a memorable television series. In October 1912 Brian Horrocks entered the Royal
Military College at Sandhurst. His entry position – second from bottom – was no
augury of the outstanding career that was to follow. When Britain declared war on
Germany in August 1914 Horrocks was waiting for his passing-out examination
results. He need not have been concerned; he was commissioned into the Middlesex
Regiment and, before the month was out, was in charge of a draft of reinforcements
for 1st Middlesex, already in France with the BEF. Horrocks joined the battalion
during the retreat from Mons and became a platoon commander. He considered
himself fortunate in having a company commander, Captain Gibbons, and a platoon
sergeant, Sergeant Whinney, who 'were both first class at their jobs'. Gibbons reinforced the lesson that an officer's first duty is to his soldiers.

> Woe betide me if I attempted to have my own meal without first reporting to
> him, 'All ranks in number sixteen platoon fed, sir.' Once we arrived in
> pouring rain to find that a muddy field which had previously been rather
> over-populated by cows had been allocated as our bivouac area for the night.
> It was a depressing thought, but my spirits rose when the adjutant appeared
> and said that the officers could sleep in a house nearby where battalion H.Q.
> was billeted.
>   Gibbons was furious. 'If the men sleep out, we sleep out.' My heart sank
> but I knew instinctively that he was right.

However, Gibbons and Horrocks were soon to part company. On 21 October 1914,
as the first battle of Ypres began, Horrocks' No. 16 Platoon was surrounded by the
enemy and captured. Horrocks himself had been wounded in the stomach. Thus
ended his war for he would spend the next four years as a prisoner of the Germans.
While this undoubtedly contributed to his surviving to fight in the Second World War,
he also found it 'probably the best apprenticeship for the difficult business of
command in war'. Away from the support of fellow battalion officers, and platoon
NCOs he was alone and had to learn self-reliance.

> Life in a prison-camp was a severe test of character. The deadly monotony of
> it all, the same routine day after day, nothing to look forward to and always
> the sight of that eternal barbed-wire, with the German sentries marching
> round outside to remind us of our degradation. There was no getting away
> from it. At the back of everyone's mind was a lurking sense of shame at being
> a prisoner-of-war at all.

Another lesson he learned was the degree to which British soldiers in captivity maintained their morale and their sense of humour. In later years he would tell young

37 In the final phase of operations in Italy, General Sir Richard McCreery commanded Eighth Army in what was probably its most successful action ever. McCreery is seen with a Royal Air Force officer observing events on the ground and in the air. (McCreery family) 38 Brigadier Adrian Gore, commanding 61 (Rifle) Brigade, is seen with Major-General Nat Murray, GOC 6th Armoured Division, and a divisional staff officer as they discuss the Division's operations during that final phase of the war in Italy. (IWM, NA24400)

39 Gore is seen here with Sir Richard McCreery, GOC-in-C, Eighth Army, at Klagenfurt in Austria on 15 May 1945, shortly after the occupation of Austria by Allied troops. (IWM, NA 25148) 40 Major-General Freddie Loftus Tottenham became GOC, Iraq after the war and then went on to command 7th Division in Pakistan following the partition of the Indian sub-continent. His final appointment in uniform was as commander of the Home Guard in Northern Ireland from 1952 to 1956 when the author's father was one of his soldiers. The parachute wings that he earned early in the war may be seen in this photograph. (Gurkha Museum)

41 Field Marshal Sir Claude Auchinleck was Colonel of The Royal Inniskilling Fusiliers, 1941–7. This photo-graph was taken in 1945 before his promotion to Field Marshal. (Inniskillings' Museum)   42 As Governor General of Canada, Field Marshal the Earl Alexander of Tunis and Errigal visited the United States in 1947 where he laid a wreath on the grave of George Washington at the first president's home at Mount Vernon, near Washington DC. (US National Archives: 199511)

43 As Chief of the Imperial General Staff, Field Marshal the Viscount Montgomery of Alamein also visited the United States and helped bring about the creation of NATO. In this photograph he is pictured in the grounds of the White House with President Harry Truman in September 1946. (US National Archives: 199427)   44 Gerald Templer went on to become High Commissioner in Malaya and to win the war against communist terrorists in that country. Subsequently, as Field Marshal Sir Gerald, he became Chief of the Imperial General Staff. He was also Colonel of The Royal Irish Fusiliers from 1946 to 1960. In this photograph he is wearing the insignia of a general. (Royal Irish Fusiliers' Museum)

45 Sir Richard McCreery commanded the British Army of the Rhine (BAOR) and represented Britain on the Military Staff Committee of the United Nations before retiring from the Army in 1949. This portrait, which shows him in general's uniform, makes a fine contrast with plate 2. (McCreery family)

46 David Dawnay became Colonel of the North Irish Horse and also of 10th Royal Hussars (Prince of Wales's Own), into which he had been commissioned. He is pictured (left) on horseback with the commanding officer of 10th Royal Hussars during a visit to the Middle East. (King's Royal Hussars Museum)   47 Montgomery retired from the Army in 1958, after fifty years' service. He is seen in this photograph being honoured at a farewell ceremony at Supreme Headquarters Allied Powers Europe, near Paris, in September 1958. (SHAPE photograph)

48 In 1960 Major-General Pat Scott succeeded Sir Gerald Templer as Colonel of The Royal Irish Fusiliers. He was the last Colonel of the Regiment, which became part of The Royal Irish Rangers on 1 July 1968. (Royal Irish Fusiliers' Museum)   49 Field Marshal Alexander became Colonel of the Irish Guards and is seen visiting the Regiment at Elizabeth Barracks, Pirbright in October 1967 after its return from Aden (he had presented shamrock to them in Aden on St Patrick's Day) and meeting Shaun, the Micks' Irish wolfhound mascot. A new barracks at Pirbright was later named Alexander Barracks in memory of the Field Marshal. (Irish Guards)

50 David Dawnay. Following his Army service he became Clerk of the Course at Ascot and was also Colonel of the North Irish Horse and of 10th Royal Hussars. (King's Royal Hussars Museum)   51 A portrait shot of Lieutenant-General Brian Horrocks as commander of XXX Corps in North-West Europe. He was a popular and inspiring commander and one of the best corps commanders of the war. (IWM B 9301)

officers: 'There will be moments when your soldiers will drive you almost mad, but never forget this – that we are privileged to command the nicest men in the world.'

Horrocks attempted to escape from the PoW camp for which he was punished by being sent to Fort Zurndorf, at Custrin, a special-regime prison for habitual escapees. As with Colditz castle in the next war, this had the effect of putting many likeminded people together and created many further problems for the German guards. As the result of an agreement between the British and German governments, an equal number of those from either side who had been longest in captivity were to be given parole and sent to The Netherlands – a neutral country. This meant that they could take no further part in the war. Horrocks was selected for this scheme but refused to take part. However the commandant at Fort Zurndorf told him that he would be moved by force, to which Horrocks responded that he would escape. From the camp to which he was then sent, in readiness for his move into The Netherlands, he did escape but was recaptured after several hours and later sent back to Fort Zurndorf. In spite of many more escape attempts he was still a PoW when the war ended.

Horrocks found it difficult to settle into a normal life after the war, such had been the toll of four years' captivity. However, since he had lived for many months with one other British officer and fifty Russians he had learned Russian and so was able to volunteer for service in Russia 'to help the White armies in their struggles against the Bolsheviks'. Serving in Siberia was frustrating and the British officers found that the White Russian officers did not trust them. This became more obvious as the British proved excellent trainers; Horrocks was second-in-command of an NCOs' school at Ekaterinburg and as the quality of the trainees improved so did the hostility of the Russian officers. Cooperation was almost non-existent and even the civilian authorities in Ekaterinburg proved truculent, refusing to 'remove refuse from the barracks until they were made to do so by force of arms'. Eventually it was decided to remove the British military mission although Horrocks and one other officer, George Hayes, remained as liaison officers with First Siberian Army.

The civil war was developing very much in favour of the Bolsheviks, or Reds, and Horrocks noted that every time 'a White battalion arrived at the front – having been trained and equipped by us – it almost invariably deserted en bloc to the Red workers' paradise' across the lines. Inevitably, both Horrocks and Hayes were taken prisoner by the Reds and thus began Horrocks' second period as a PoW. It lasted almost ten months. Shortly before Horrocks and Hayes were to be repatriated, Horrocks fell victim to typhus and was fortunate to survive; only the efforts of Hayes and another British officer had ensured that he would live. They arranged for him to be taken to a hospital with beds, some doctors, nurses and medical orderlies; one nurse and six orderlies cared for 125 patients. At last Horrocks returned to Britain, via Moscow, Finland and Denmark.

Soon it was back to the business of regimental soldiering, a business that could be very frustrating in the economically stricken inter-war period. Military life, wrote

Horrocks, 'was not calculated to develop the qualities of robust initiative so necessary in a commander on the battlefield'. (And yet the Army produced so many
outstanding commanders.) Worse still was the situation of the Army at home,
'reduced largely to a flag basis'. On exercises junior NCOs carried boards declaring
'This represents a section' while weaponry was represented by coloured flags. As
Horrocks recorded:

> We have all been amused by the story of the young officer who, at the start
> of the last war, on receiving his orders to move out into the desert to fight the
> Italian Army, had asked his commander whether the Italians understood that
> a green flag represented an anti-tank gun. That was the depth to which we
> sank between the wars.

Horrocks represented Great Britain in the modern pentathlon in the 1924 Olympiad
in Paris, married, served as Adjutant to a Territorial Army battalion – 9th Middlesex
– and went to Staff College in 1931. His course was believed to contain more
students who later rose to divisional or corps commands than any other between the
wars; in its second year it included a Naval officer, Warburton-Lee, who would earn
the Victoria Cross in Norway in 1940. The Camberley commandant during
Horrocks' course was Sir John Dill.

From Camberley Horrocks went to the War Office in Whitehall, to the Military
Secretary's branch, a post which, to his surprise, he found interesting. Promotion to
major took him to 5 Brigade of 2nd Division at Aldershot as brigade major. As at the
War Office, he took over from Miles Dempsey, who would command Second Army
from D-Day to VE-Day. The division was commanded by Archie Wavell and then by
'Jumbo' Wilson, both of whom would become field marshals. Exercises organized by
Wavell 'were always a challenge and a joy, never a bore'. Horrocks so impressed his
superiors during this period that he was recommended for an instructor's appointment at Camberley. He was serving in this demanding post when war broke out and
students returned to their own units while the instructors were ordered to organize
'short war courses for regular and T.A. officers'.

With the German invasion of the Low Countries on 10 May 1940 much changed,
including Horrocks' life. That morning he was preparing for a move to France to take
command of 2nd Middlesex Regiment but the news from the continent meant that,
instead of leaving Camberley in two weeks' time, as planned, he left in two hours.
On 13 May he took over command of 2nd Middlesex at Louvain in Belgium where
the battalion was serving in Montgomery's 3rd Division. Horrocks' arrival cannot
have been greeted too warmly by many of his soldiers since he found them unshaven
for which he 'roundly abused them'. But he had good reason to do so.

> The one thing which is always in short supply in battle is sleep, and the
> refreshing effect of a shave is worth at least two hours' sleep. Moreover, if a

man keeps himself clean he will almost certainly keep his weapons clean, and this is vital. In my experience of two wars I have always found that the clean soldier fights better than the dirty one, however tough the latter may look with his unshaven chin.

Since 2nd Middlesex was a machine-gun battalion it came under divisional command and it was not long before Horrocks met Montgomery, who was 'probably the most discussed general in the British Army before the war' and far from being the most popular. But Monty had trained 3rd Division well and its soldiers were to pass the examination of battle with honours. Horrocks had one experience of Monty's efficiency on the night of 27–8 May. He was at Montgomery's headquarters when Brooke, the corps commander, arrived to order 3rd Division to make what became its famous night march from one flank of II Corps to the other. Horrocks' battalion was the first to move so that it might hold the gap on the extreme left until the remainder of the division arrived. Monty's training paid off, the gap was filled and the BEF saved from potential destruction.

Commanding a machine-gun battalion in action was a difficult task since the nature of the role meant that the battalion was dispersed throughout 3rd Division. However, Horrocks performed his task so well that, after seventeen days, he was promoted to command 11 Brigade in 4th Division in the Dunkirk perimeter. He had little opportunity to show his mettle as a brigade commander as the evacuation had already begun but on the voyage back to Britain, in a small Dutch cargo boat, Horrocks manned the vessel's forward anti-aircraft machine gun.

Within days of his return to Britain Brian Horrocks was appointed to command 9 Brigade in 3rd Division. His brigade was responsible for defending the coastline between Rottingdean and Shoreham. Although Horrocks thought it unlikely that the Germans would ever invade, given their lack of experience of amphibious operations, nonetheless he applied himself to his task with the enthusiasm that was his hallmark and ensured that his soldiers kept themselves alert by organizing short mobile exercises. Later in the year 3rd Division was re-assigned to a counter-attack role, carrying out many exercises in Dorset, often with units of the Home Guard. Then, in January 1941, came a fresh appointment, as Brigadier General Staff (BGS) of Eastern Command where over a five-month period, he organized large-scale exercises before moving on, as a major-general, to command 44th (Home Counties) Division, a formation that would be under his command at El Alamein in 1942.

Horrocks' new division was based on the coast from the Isle of Thanet to the channel ports of Dover and Folkestone and was under Montgomery's overall command. In March 1942 came a move to command 9th Armoured Division. As an infantry officer this would be a tough task and although Horrocks found the soldiers to be well trained as individuals the real task was to weld 9th Armoured into a fighting formation. All the division's officers were called to a cinema where Horrocks addressed them and criticized the state of their vehicles, only about half of which were able to move. When a REME* officer stood up to explain why this should be he was told, politely but firmly, that he would be making better use of his time if he were to ensure the vehicles would work, rather than explaining why they would not.

It was not long before 9th Armoured's officers were commenting on their good fortune in having such a spirited divisional commander. Horrocks was also learning about armoured warfare in which communication by wireless telephony (W/T) from tanks was critical. It was not long before he would be putting those lessons into practice for, on 15 August 1942, he was ordered to report to London where he was told that he was to be posted to Eighth Army, now commanded by Montgomery.

Arriving in Egypt, Horrocks was given command of XIII Corps in time to meet the Panzer Armee onslaught at Alam el Halfa ridge. This was Rommel's last attempt to break through Eighth Army and it had been anticipated, thanks to ULTRA decrypts of German signals. Horrocks proved a steady hand throughout the battle from which Rommel's forces eventually withdrew, battered and bloodied. Although XIII Corps had suffered casualties, Horrocks had ensured that it had not been unduly mauled; this had been stressed to him by Montgomery who now wished to form a mobile armoured reserve. X Corps was reformed as an armoured formation but Horrocks did not accept command, suggesting to Montgomery that Herbert Lumsden, a cavalryman from 12th Lancers, should fill the post. Lumsden appreciated armoured warfare much better than Montgomery but the latter was unaware of his own deficiency and blamed Lumsden for X Corps' failure to perform as Monty had expected at El Alamein in the final battle.

While X Corps was slugging against Panzer Armee Afrika in the northern sector of the El Alamein line, XIII Corps was deployed in the south where Horrocks was expected to give the impression of being Eighth Army's main thrust. Initially, things went well for XIII Corps but its formations then became bogged down in minefields and the corps reverted to an almost static role. Eventually, Horrocks was left with but a shadow of his command as more and more units were transferred to the northern sector. As the pursuit got under way, Lumsden was relieved of command of X Corps and Horrocks took his place for the advance into Tunisia from Libya.

Supported by the New Zealand Division, X Corps made a flanking move to break the Axis hold on the Mareth line. The manoeuvre was carried out with typical Horrocks drive and although described as 'one of the most desperate assaults of the war' proved successful with the British armour fighting its way through against a tenacious defence that, nonetheless, was surprised to see its foe appear from an unexpected direction. Next came the battle for the Gabes Gap, better known as the battle of Wadi Akarit, in which X Corps' tanks ran into an unexpected anti-tank ditch covered by 88mm anti-tank guns, which created mayhem among the tanks. Although the armour broke through this was largely because the Germans pulled back. After what he described as some of the 'most unpleasant' days of his life, in an attempt by Monty to break through the Axis Enfidaville–Takrouna position, Horrocks was

* Royal Electrical and Mechanical Engineers, a new corps formed in 1942.

transferred with several Eighth Army formations to command IX Corps in First Army.

For the final assault on Tunis, Horrocks' IX Corps included 4th British and 4th Indian Infantry Divisions with 160 Churchill tanks and 6th and 7th Armoured Divisions, supported by the tactical air force. Co-operating with V Corps, Horrocks planned the attack on Tunis. He later wrote that the 'capture of Tunis was the result of the closest co-operation between our two corps'. The battle 'went like clockwork' and at 3.00am on 6 May the two infantry divisions made the first breach to be followed through by the armoured divisions.

> It was a most inspiring sight to see these two well-trained and experienced armoured divisions being used in a role for which armoured divisions were specifically designed – to exploit a breakthrough deep into the enemy's heart.

Modestly, however, Horrocks accounted this no 'great feat of generalship' but a battle in which victory was a foregone conclusion. On 7 May the first Allied troops entered Tunis and a week later the final Axis surrender was made. Allied eyes now turned to the next phase of operations, the invasion of Sicily.

Horrocks was not to take part in the Sicily campaign. Once again commander of X Corps he was to prepare his soldiers for the invasion of Italy at Salerno – Operation AVALANCHE – in which they would fight as part of Fifth US Army. However, Horrocks was fated not to take part in that operation either. Visiting 46th Division at Bizerta to watch a rehearsal of their assault, he fell victim to a German fighter that machine-gunned the divisional commander's party. No one other than Horrocks was hit: one round entered the top of his chest, passed through lungs and intestines and emerged at the base of his spine; another struck him in the leg. His own description was: 'A sledgehammer hit me in the stomach.' Fourteen months would pass before he could persuade the doctors that he was fit enough for active service.

Horrocks returned to service in August 1944 when Montgomery sent for him to take command of XXX Corps in Normandy. He arrived in Normandy as the German defence was beginning to crumble and, by late-August, the Allies were racing for the Seine and then towards the Low Countries. At the end of the month Montgomery put XXX Corps in the van of 21 Army Group's advance and, on 3 September, Brussels fell to XXX Corps; Horrocks had advanced 250 miles in six days. He then pushed 11th Armoured Division towards Antwerp to occupy the docks there. In hindsight, this was a mistake: had he ordered Roberts' division to pass Antwerp, cross the Albert canal and advance some fifteen miles, he would have cut off the Beveland isthmus, thereby blocking a German escape route and preventing the bloody fighting that, subsequently, was required to clear the Scheldt estuary. However, Horrocks' attention was fixed on the Rhine, as was that of the Allied high command, and this dictated strategy.

There followed the tragedy of Arnhem. While the Allied Airborne Army was dropped to secure the bridges at Nijmegen, Grave and Arnhem, XXX Corps was to lead the advance of Second Army to secure each of those bridgeheads. Struggling forward on a single road, XXX Corps, led by Guards Armoured Division, failed to reach Arnhem in time to prevent the withdrawal or capture of 1st British Airborne Division. 'Horrocks blamed himself for not having insisted on having a high-ranking Dutch officer at his headquarters, who might have advised a left hook well west of Nijmegen'.

XXX Corps remained in the line until December when it was withdrawn to prepare for further operations. These operations constituted the battle of the Reichswald and XXX Corps was lent to First Canadian Army for Operation VERI-TABLE, designed to destroy German forces between the Meuse and the Rhine. The battle raged from 8 February to 10 March and resulted in almost 16,000 casualties in First Canadian Army, of whom two-thirds were British troops. But the Germans had lost some 44,000 men and been forced back to the Rhine. As the battle raged Horrocks suffered a recurrence of an illness that had afflicted him after Normandy but continued to lead from the front and none but his senior staff knew that anything was wrong, although his temper was frayed.

The Reichswald battle was followed by the crossing of the Rhine but XXX Corps was not in the spearhead. Following its own crossing the corps advanced into the heart of Germany, finding every crossroads fought for and every bridge demolished. There was one exception: a bridge over the Ems was taken intact through the courage of a company commander of the Coldstream Guards. Then followed the capture of Bremen, a bloody street-by-street struggle that lasted five days. Here Horrocks saw for the first time how the Germans had suffered as a result of war; the city was a shambles with, seemingly, not a single house standing in the port city. But his pity was tempered by the discovery of the Sandbostel death camp near Bremen. Visiting the camp Horrocks was physically sick when he saw the pitiful survivors and smelt the stench of death. So angry was he that he ordered the local burgomasters to send people into the camp to clean it up and to care for the survivors. Then, having taken the surrender of German forces in the area, he

> finished with these words. 'These orders must be obeyed scrupulously. I warn you we shall have no mercy if they are not. Having seen one of your horror camps my whole attitude towards Germany has changed.' The chief of staff jumped up and said, 'The army had nothing to do with those camps.' 'Sit down,' I replied, 'there were German soldiers on sentry duty outside and you cannot escape responsibility. The world will never forgive Germany for those camps.'

Horrocks' war was over. In 1946 he was appointed to command Western Command and then, in March 1948, became commander of BAOR. Less than a year later he became ill and was invalided out of the Army. In later life, he became Gentleman Usher of the Black Rod in the house of lords and also a celebrated television presenter with a series on various battles. The enthusiasm that had transmitted itself to his soldiers shone through in those TV programmes, all broadcast live. He was 'a natural actor, his stage presence was drama personified'.

Sir Brian Horrocks died in 1985, aged eighty-nine.

* * *

Allan Adair was born in London in 1897, Queen Victoria's Diamond Jubilee, into a family with strong connections in Ulster. Although the Adairs are most closely associated with Ballymena in County Antrim – where, in 1626, Charles I granted William Adair a charter to hold fairs and a Saturday market – the family also owned a home on the outskirts of Londonderry, which later passed into the hands of the Christian Brothers of Ireland. The family was descended from the Fitzgeralds, making them distant relations of the earls of Kildare and of Desmond. After school at Harrow, Allan Adair was commissioned directly into the Grenadier Guards as a Special Reserve officer in 1916. His family's only connection with the Grenadiers had been an ancestor who had served with the regiment – then 1st Foot Guards – under Wellington and had been killed at Waterloo. In January 1917 Allan Adair was posted to 3rd Grenadier Guards in France.

He was soon in action in the front line and became used to the routine of trench warfare where, on occasion, opposing trenches were less than a hundred yards apart. At this time the Germans were withdrawing to the Hindenburg line and a British advance began on 16 February, following which 3rd Grenadiers spent ten weeks on fatigue duties such as road mending. Guards Division moved to the Ypres sector where it began preparing for a major offensive at the end of July. Although the attack was successful, driving the enemy back over two miles and taking all its objectives, many from 3rd Grenadiers were killed. But Allan Adair did not take part. He was in hospital in London, recovering from a broken shoulder, sustained in a crash on a bicycle in early-July. He rejoined his battalion in January 1918 when he found that only four of his fellow officers were still with the battalion.

In March 1918 the Germans launched Operation MICHAEL, using forces withdrawn from the eastern front in an effort to defeat the Allies before large numbers of American soldiers could join the Allied armies in France. British forces were forced to withdraw and move back to new positions from which they began the preparations that would lead to the final Allied offensive to destroy the German armies. Those preparations included training of American personnel; fifteen US Army officers and eighty-five NCOs joined 3rd Grenadiers near Ransart and proved to be 'quite a curious mixture, being of Polish, Italian and German origin'. However, they proved enthusiastic and were keen to learn. On 8 August the offensive began and, within four days, 'the Allies had advanced twelve miles, captured 22,000 prisoners and over 400 guns'. Haig's great assault with fifty-nine divisions was underway.

On 21 August 3rd Grenadiers took part in the battle of Moyenneville. Almost as soon as the guardsmen left their trenches a fog descended on the battlefield and there was much confusion until the fog burned away to leave a fine, sunny day. Assisted by a tank that had also lost its way in the fog, Adair's company took its objective against stiff German resistance. A German counter-attack next morning was broken up by artillery fire and Guards Division then launched a further attack before dawn on the following morning.

> The attack was a tremendous success although our companies by now were very weak. Fortunately the Germans were taken quite by surprise and surrendered in vast numbers.

At the end of September the Guards attacked the Hindenburg line where, although not heavily engaged, 3rd Grenadiers captured almost two-dozen machine guns. The Allied advance continued and, on 2 November, the eve of Adair's twenty-first birthday, 3rd Grenadiers moved to Capelle in readiness for a divisional assault on the villages between Capelle and Maubeuge. The battalion advanced under heavy fire and, some 200 yards short of the objective, Adair, now commanding his company, felt 'a terrific bang' on the top of his head and fell into a shell hole. However, it was his knee that had been injured rather than his head. He continued to lead his company on to its objective and remained with them for the rest of the day before he was sent back to hospital. Although he did not know it then, his war was over. From the hospital he was sent to England and arrived in London at 11.00am on 11 November, Armistice Day.

Allan Adair ended the war as a company commander with the Military Cross. In the inter-war period he carried out the usual round of regimental duties that were the responsibility of the Brigade of Guards. Promotion was slow, even in the Guards, and he noted that twenty years 'after commanding a company in 1918, I was still commanding one'. However, he chose not to take the Staff College entrance examination, as he did not consider the Army to be a permanent career. Nonetheless, he remained a soldier and in November 1933 sailed for Egypt with his battalion, which was to form part of the Cairo Brigade. Infantry training in Egypt was 'really excellent' although 'there was insufficient attempt to exercise different arms together', in spite of the presence of cavalry regiments, a tank battalion, gunners and engineers. Nor was there any attempt to exercise with the RAF which had two squadrons in Egypt, including one designated as an army co-operation squadron.

By the time 3rd Grenadiers returned to Britain, in April 1936, the threat posed by Adolf Hitler to Europe's peace was becoming ever more clear. Hitler had already obtained parity in the air with the RAF and introduced conscription while, a month earlier, he had re-occupied the Rhineland in contravention of the Treaties of Versailles and Locarno. Nonetheless, the British political establishment seemed not to be concerned and Adair's battalion returned to the round of public duties in and around London. Not until 1938 did the level of training increase and 3rd Grenadiers received the first of their ten Bren-gun carriers. By the time war was declared, Allan Adair was second-in-command of 3rd Grenadiers, now part of 1 Guards Brigade in Major-General Harold Alexander's 1st Division. At the end of September 1939 the division was in France with the BEF.

Adair left the battalion to command 161 OCTU at Sandhurst but, on 10 May, when Germany invaded the Low Countries, he was ordered back to France to command 3rd Grenadiers. Quickly he made his way to France and then to the front, at one time as a passenger in a taxi driven by a former wrestling champion of France. He took over command of his battalion in Belgium and one of his first tasks was to help cover the withdrawal of 3 Brigade from the river Dyle before 1st Division withdrew to the Escaut. In the desperate fighting that followed, the Guards maintained their traditional discipline and proved a doughty foe to the advancing Germans. One of Adair's soldiers, Lance-Corporal Harry Nicholls, became the first British soldier to earn the Victoria Cross in the Second World War. For a time, 1 Guards Brigade was under command of Major-General Harold Franklyn's 5th Division and 3rd Grenadiers mounted a counter-attack that ensured the integrity of the British line. Of the battalion, Franklyn, later wrote:

> I give this example of the highest form of discipline. Last May, when my Division was being hard pressed on the Ypres–Comines Canal I was given a Battalion of the Grenadier Guards as a reserve. After marching well over twenty miles on a very hot day they arrived at my Headquarters at 7.30 p.m. An hour later they were put into a vital counter-attack in the half light, over unknown ground. They advanced as efficiently as if on a field day at Pirbright – and their efforts were completely successful.

Alexander, now commanding I Corps, witnessed another example of Grenadier discipline when Major Allan Adair's battalion marched past him at Dunkirk. One eyewitness described their bearing as 'outstanding'.

Following evacuation to Britain, 3rd Grenadier Guards took their place in Home Forces ready to defend the United Kingdom against a German invasion. The summer and early autumn of 1940 proved a hectic time for the battalion which then bade farewell to Allan Adair in October when he was promoted to command 30 Guards Brigade, which had the role of defending London's eastern approaches as well as helping the police in case of civil disorder or heavy bombing in the East End. The brigade included four battalions: 4th Grenadier, 4th Coldstream, 3rd Scots and 2nd Welsh Guards. In very little time the brigade was trained up to a very high standard and was ready to meet any possible enemy attack in the Thames estuary.

In May 1941 a decision was taken to form more armoured divisions for the defence of Britain. One of these was to be formed from the Brigade of Guards and thus Guards Armoured Division was created on 17 June. Its first commander was Major-General Sir Oliver Leese, who was later to command Eighth Army in Italy. When

Leese moved on to become a corps commander in North Africa, Brigadier Allan Adair was appointed as temporary GOC. This appointment was confirmed only nine days later, on 21 September 1942, when he was promoted major-general. Leese wrote that he 'could not have handed over to a better or more efficient leader' than Adair.

High standards were set and achieved in Guards Armoured Division. Officers had to master the various trades of an armoured unit as well as the tactics of armoured warfare. Training was intensive, at first on Covenanter tanks and then on Crusaders. Exercise followed exercise and particular attention was paid to the standards of gunnery in the division. In 1943 the Crusaders, no match for any German tank, were replaced by American Shermans, which had already proved their worth in North Africa. Even so, the Sherman was not in the same league as the later German tanks and suffered from several main drawbacks. Chief among these was the propensity of petrol-engined Shermans to burst into flame when hit. Sherman crews referred to their mounts as 'Ronsons' from the advertising slogan. 'lights first time', of the eponymous cigarette-lighter company. The tank was also under-gunned and only a British conversion, known as Firefly, that mounted a 17-pounder gun could take on most German tanks. Only one Sherman in four was a Firefly.

By January 1944, when he first learned of the outline plans for the invasion of France, Adair was confident that his division would perform well in battle.

> We had now been going for two and a half years and I doubt if any other Division had ever trained so intensively over so long a period, yet the dash and enthusiasm of everyone was quite outstanding. I had never felt more confident in the future of the Division than now. Our team-work was so excellent; we were such a happy family; all that we needed was battle experience. But for me this was also a most difficult time. Outsiders would come along and suggest that our whole training was too reminiscent of the barrack square, that the discipline of the Brigade of Guards and the dash required of armour would not combine in battle, but those above us expressed full confidence and we could only await results.

Guards Armoured Division was not found wanting when it was introduced to battle. The formation was not included in the attacking waves on D-Day but landed in France at the end of June. Its first major action was Operation GOODWOOD, Montgomery's attempt to break through German defences in the Caen sector using a mass of armour. For this attack Richard O'Connor's VIII Corps was to deploy three armoured divisions, Guards, 7th and 11th, with some 800 tanks. But the plan for GOODWOOD, made by Dempsey and approved by Montgomery, was flawed deeply. It relied on obtaining maximum surprise by holding the armour well back from the front before H-Hour, which meant that the tanks had to travel a considerable distance before reaching the start line. That was bad enough but there were few roads and so all three divisions would have to use routes which were being shelled regularly by the Germans, crossing the Orne river and canal between Ranville and the sea over three double bridges. Since they could not attack as a solid corps but had to follow each other across the bridges the armoured brigades preceded the infantry brigades into battle. O'Connor's suggestion that the infantry be made more mobile, and better protected, by improvising armoured personnel carriers from SPGs was over-ruled by Dempsey; the offensive suffered as a result. Artillery support would also suffer; most guns had to be kept west of the Orne until the advance had begun and, as the tanks moved forward, the guns' effectiveness would be reduced until they, too, could cross the Orne. And

> the attack was to be made not where the enemy was weak but where he had prepared his strongest defence, in country which gave him almost everywhere the advantage of ground observation and fields of fire.

The first problem that the armoured divisions met was that of congestion in the approach march which knocked the timetable out of kilter. That was exacerbated by the fact that the infantry brigades were following the armour rather than advancing with them. Montgomery and Dempsey both seem to have believed that armour could operate without close infantry support. Not surprisingly, there were heavy casualties in the face of well-designed and well-sited German defences. Guards Armoured Division suffered 330 casualties, of whom seventy-nine were killed. One battalion lost two commanding officers on successive nights but the division took its objective, the village of Cagny. Adair resolved to eliminate one problem in the future by re-organizing his division so that the infantry was always 'right up with' the armour.

> I therefore regrouped within the Division our armour and infantry. Instead of confining almost all the armour to one brigade and the motorised infantry to the other, I grouped together in 32nd Guards Brigade, 1st (Motorised) Battalion and 2nd (Armoured) Battalion of the Grenadiers, while 1st Armoured Coldstream went with 3rd Battalion Irish Guards, leaving in 5th Guards Brigade, 5th Coldstream with the 2nd (Armoured) Irish Guards. The Welsh Guards battalion remained ungrouped for the time being.*

This regrouping would be refined further by marrying Irish and Coldstream armoured and motorized battalions into regimental battlegroups similar to that already created with the two Grenadier battalions. Such was the success of the new system that it remained in place until the end of the war; similar battlegroups were created across Second Army.

GOODWOOD was called off when heavy rain turned the ground into a morass. Guards Armoured Division deployed to the Caumont sector at the end of July at the beginning of two weeks of hard fighting that began on the 31st when the Grenadiers

---

* The Welsh Guards provided the reconnaissance battalion of Guards Armoured Division and were equipped with the British Cromwell tank rather than the American Sherman.

forced river crossings at Catheolles near St Charles de Percy and obtained a bridge-head on the high ground on the far bank. A battle ensued that lasted until 6 August with the Guards' opponents, soldiers from the SS, putting up a determined and ferocious resistance. In spite of SS counter-attacks, the Guardsmen prevailed and the battlegroup of 5th Coldstream and 2nd Irish Guards advanced to Le Busq on the night of 6–7 August. Although this loosened up the front, there was still stern opposition and 3rd Irish Guards lost heavily at Sourdeval on 11 August during a divisional attack designed to cut the main Vassy–Vire road, which was one of the few west–east escape routes still available to the Germans in Normandy. Gradually, the pressure told on the Germans and Guards Armoured took Chénédolle on 11 August. As the American advance was now developing rapidly the Germans began a general withdrawal a few days later and Guards Armoured was withdrawn into reserve.

Adair's men had fought their last battle in Normandy and had acquitted themselves well. On 28 August the division was transferred to XXX Corps, now under the command of Brian Horrocks. The Seine had been crossed and Horrocks was keen to push on towards the Somme and Guards Armoured was assigned the task of seizing crossings over the Somme at Corbie.

> These orders were most exciting. For the first time we would be carrying out the mobile operations for which we had been training for the last three years. With the arrival of the Household Cavalry Regiment* I could change the grouping so that each Brigade could control an equal proportion of infantry and armour; the Welsh Guards were no longer needed for specific reconnaissance.

On 30 August the division was assembled on the Seine's north bank and, led by 2nd Household Cavalry Regiment, advanced through Beauvais. The Household Cavalry seized intact a bridge over the Somme and the way was clear for the division to push on. In two days 200 miles were covered and over a thousand prisoners taken. Douai fell to the Irish Guards and, with the division concentrated there on 2 September, Horrocks gave his orders for the next phase: the Guards were to liberate Brussels the following day.

This may have seemed an overly ambitious order but the division, moving in regimental groups on two routes with the Household Cavalry screening their advance, swept away enemy opposition en route and reached Brussels on the evening of the 3rd to be greeted by the jubilant citizenry of the Belgian capital.

> Tank guns were stuffed with plums and pears, and most tanks had at least one girl in the turret shouting '*Vive Les Anglais*' over the wireless. As darkness fell the rejoicing Capital was lit by the full moon and by the flames of the burning Palais de Justice, which the Germans had set on fire before they left.

---

* This regiment, with its armoured cars, had just been assigned to the division as a reconnaissance regiment.

On 4 September Allan Adair 'officially handed back to the Burgomaster his beautiful city'. By now XXX Corps had covered 250 miles in six days and was to continue to lead Second Army's advance. Guards Armoured was to lead the corps.

Over the next week the division continued its steady advance, liberating towns and villages, often against stiff opposition. Then the Household Cavalry discovered an unmapped road that ran to De Groote Barrier on the Escaut canal and a plan was formulated quickly to seize the bridge over the canal. This was carried out by Irish Guards under Colonel Joe Vandeleur; as a result the bridge was dubbed 'Joe's Bridge'.

Montgomery now planned to seize bridges over the Maas, or Meuse, Waal and Lower Rhine rivers to outflank the Siegfried line and, hopefully, end the war by Christmas. The operation involved dropping Allied airborne soldiers at bridges over the rivers to hold those bridges until the ground forces of Second Army could relieve them and consolidate and exploit their gains. This was Operation MARKET GARDEN. Second Army's element – GARDEN – was to be led by XXX Corps with Guards Armoured in the van. Montgomery believed that the armour could reach the furthermost bridge – at Arnhem – in two days and assured Lieutenant-General Browning, commanding the Airborne Corps, that this was so. As Adair wrote: 'We now know that even eight were insufficient.'

On 17 September Guards Armoured, led by the Irish Guards Group,* began their advance. Opposition was strong and even with the support of considerable artillery and the tactical air forces, the advance was thirty-six hours behind schedule at 6.00am on the 19th. At Nijmegen 82nd US Airborne Division had dropped too far away and a joint British-American assault had to be organized to reach the bridge. The Grenadier Group was assigned to the operation with 505th US Airborne Regiment. In spite of the tremendous courage shown by both Grenadiers and US paratroopers the attack was unsuccessful and a second operation had to be laid on. The Grenadiers would renew their assault on the bridge with 504th Regiment crossing the river in assault boats after 2nd (Armoured) Irish Guards and 502nd US Airborne Regiment had cleared the western outskirts of Nijmegen. One Irish Guards officer described the US paratroopers who paddled across the Waal under heavy fire as the 'bravest soldiers he had ever seen'. At last the Nijmegen bridges fell into Allied hands in what was later described as a 'brilliantly co-ordinated and executed [operation] by the Guards Armoured Division and the US 82nd Airborne Division'. General James Gavin, commander of 82nd Airborne, later said that he had 'never met such courage and gallantry and co-operation on the part of Allied troops as the Guards Armoured Division' had displayed at Nijmegen.

But the delay at Nijmegen proved fatal for 1st British Airborne Division at Arnhem. Under assault from strong German forces that had been refitting nearby the division held out for a week before being forced to surrender, although more than 2,000 men managed to escape across the Rhine. The country between Nijmegen and

---

* Both Irish Guards battalions had been linked to form this group; the Coldstream battalions were linked in similar fashion.

Arnhem was unsuitable for armour, being low, criss-crossed by dykes and water-logged. Horrocks ordered 43rd (Wessex) Division to take over the lead; but the Wyverns were blocked behind the Guards on the single road to Arnhem. Montgomery's gamble, which was totally out of character for him, had failed.

Not until November did Guards Armoured Division return to action and then it was in a defensive role in the Maastricht area with tank crews acting as infantry soldiers; the division was responsible for some 20,000 yards of front line. It was unpleasant and the weather did not help as December rains brought floods that threatened to wash away bridges. When the Germans launched their offensive in the Ardennes, the division was moved to positions near Brussels to cover the city against a possible German breakthrough. However, 2nd Household Cavalry had a more active role, providing information of enemy progress while the offensive lasted.

In February 1945 Guards Armoured took part in Operation VERITABLE, the battles to clear the Germans from the area between the Meuse and the Rhine. These were hard slogging battles with little scope to deploy armour to real effect. Nonetheless the division captured the Bonninghardt feature overlooking the river Wesel and 2nd Scots Guards seized a crossing over the Romer on 7 March. Thereafter a further advance by the Coldstream Group reached the main road to Xanten and broke the resistance of the paratroopers covering the bridge, forcing them to withdraw.

Almost as soon as these battles ended planning was underway for the next phase of operations, the Rhine crossings. Operation PLUNDER opened on the night of 23 March and Guards Armoured Division was soon across the river, crossing by a Bailey bridge at Rees. Over the next seventeen days the division fought its way forward, earning two Victoria Crosses as it did so, to Captain Ian Liddell of the Coldstream and Guardsman Edward Charlton, Irish Guards. Both were posthumous awards; Charlton was wounded fatally while Liddell was killed by a stray bullet just over two weeks after the deed that earned him his country's highest award for gallantry. As the war drew to its close Guards Armoured were advancing on Bremen and liberated the prisoner-of-war camp at Westertimke on the day that Bremen fell. Adair and Horrocks visited the Sandbostel camp, which had housed inmates from Buchenwald. Horrocks ordered the local burgomasters to provide parties of German civilians to clean the camp and look after the prisoners, many of whom were dying of typhus. Finally, on 5 May, Major-General Allan Adair took the surrender of a German corps commander, General Golztach, at Cuxhaven. The war was over and Guards Armoured Division could look forward to peace and a return to civilian life for those who were wartime volunteers or conscripts. Behind them they left 956 of their number dead, another 3,946 wounded and 545 missing. It was a high price to pay but it might have been higher had they not had such a competent and caring divisional commander. He had also lost his son, Desmond, a captain in the Grenadiers, who was killed at Monte Camino in Italy. Since his only other son, Robin, had died in infancy, the baronetcy which Allan inherited from his father would die with him.

But Allan Adair's military career was not over. He was ordered to form 13th Infantry Division in England and take it to Greece in December 1945 to carry out what would now be termed peacekeeping duties in a country riven by civil war. Assistance was also given to training the Greek army as well as providing security for elections. In November 1946 his division was broken up and soon afterwards Allan Adair left Greece and the Army for civilian life.

Adair's retirement was a busy one. He inherited his father's baronetcy in 1949 to become Sir Allan and became an officer of the Yeomen of the Guard and a governor of Harrow School as well as being a busy farmer. He also inherited a house near Strabane in County Tyrone, which he kept until 1984. Perhaps he was most pleased by his appointment as Colonel of the Grenadier Guards in 1960. Since the formation of the regiment, some three centuries before, he was only the second Colonel who had not been a duke or an earl and only the third since 1770 who had not been a member of the Royal family. He held the appointment for fifteen years and was succeeded by Prince Philip, Duke of Edinburgh. During his tenure he visited battalions of the Grenadiers in the many locations in which they were serving across the globe. He also maintained his links with Ireland, being a deputy lieutenant for County Antrim, a governor of Ballymena Academy as well as keeping some of the land at Ballymena that had been in his family since 1610. He remained active almost until his death at the age of ninety in 1988.

~ 12 ~

Gore, Dawnay and Vandeleur

On 14 May 1900 Adrian Clements Gore was born, a scion of an old Donegal family. At first he was thought to have been stillborn and was put to one side but when a nurse later looked at him she realized that he was alive and he was cared for immediately. Thus the life of an outstanding soldier began with his first crisis. A happy childhood and teenage years were blighted when Adrian's father, Robert, was killed in action while commanding a battalion of Argyll and Sutherland Highlanders in April 1918.

The young Gore's early life was spent in Kildare where, he later recalled, he 'smoked with the butler, played bicycle polo with the groom and gardener, and was taught to shoot by the 'keeper'. Educated at Eton he then entered Sandhurst from which he was commissioned into the Rifle Brigade in 1920, the same year in which he represented the Combined Services against Australia at cricket. (Remarkably, while still at Eton, he was selected as one of Wisden's five cricketers of the year in 1919.) Gore's battalion served in Ireland in 1921 before being sent to Chanak the following year when hostilities with Turkey appeared imminent. However the crisis soon passed and the battalion returned to Britain.

Over the next few years Adrian Gore's reputation as a sportsman increased and his skills were not limited to cricket; he also played golf, was one of the winning pair in the Army Racquets Doubles Championship and 'distinguished himself in point-to-points'. However, it was as a cricketer that he excelled, representing the Gentlemen, Kent and the Army. He was also a first-class shot and a notable angler, catching a 36lb salmon in the Blackwater in 1929. Regimental duties took him to Malta in 1933 where he was a member of the Army team that beat the Royal Navy at polo; he also went to sea on destroyers during exercises.

On his return to Britain, he was appointed training officer for The Rifle Brigade and posted to the regimental depot at Winchester; shared with The King's Royal Rifle Corps, this was known as The Rifle Depot. Thus he did not go with the 2nd Battalion to France where most of the battalion were killed or captured at Calais. When the Green Jackets Officer Cadet Training Unit (OCTU) was established in 1941, as part of the larger Royal Armoured Corps OCTU at Perham Down, Adrian Gore was chosen to be its first commander by Jock Burnett-Stuart, Colonel Commandant of The Rifle Brigade. Since the two Green Jacket regiments – The King's Royal Rifle

Corps and The Rifle Brigade – provided the motor battalions for the armoured divisions, this meant that Gore had the responsibility for training the platoon commanders who would serve with those divisions.* These had to be trained to the traditional Rifles' standards, emphasizing speed of movement and the ability to exercise initiative – Sir John Moore's 'thinking fighting man'. Gore was not found wanting.

> Adrian approached his task with typical pragmatism and common sense; the fact that platoon commanders in both The Rifle Brigade and the 60th[†] proved so outstandingly good throughout the war was due in great measure to the excellent training given them at this key stage of their development.

The motor battalions were mounted in light vehicles, both wheeled and tracked, capable of travelling across country with the armoured brigades. Since each armoured brigade deployed three regiments, the structure of a motor battalion reflected this, with one motor company assigned to each regiment. (A motor company deployed a headquarters, a scout platoon with ten carriers – often referred to as Bren-gun carriers – and three motor platoons, each with a headquarters and three sections, each carried in a 15-hundredweight truck.)

Such was Adrian Gore's success with the Green Jackets OCTU that he was given command of 10th Battalion The Rifle Brigade in 1942.

> Adrian was fortunate that in 10 RB he was able, to a considerable extent, to choose his own team. He also inherited the most marvellous collection of riflemen who merely needed the right leadership to set them alight. Adrian had particularly good Company Commanders, especially Dick Fyffe and Bobby Selby. I enjoyed enormously working for him as his Adjutant. He told you what he wanted and left you alone to get on with it.

Tenth Rifle Brigade was the motor battalion of 26 Armoured Brigade,[††] part of 6th Armoured Division, which was training for active operations. The feeling within the division was that it would not be sent to Egypt and Eighth Army but would deploy elsewhere on operations. Thus, in November 1942, Adrian Gore arrived in Tunisia with his battalion. Sixth Armoured Division was part of First Army which provided the British element of the Operation TORCH landings. Eighth Army had defeated Rommel's Panzer Armee at El Alamein and the Desert Fox was retreating in a long withdrawal that would eventually take him into Tunisia. The Allied landings in that

---

* The first Greenjacket battalion to convert to the motor battalion role was 1st Rifle Brigade in 1937.
† The King's Royal Rifle Corps preferred to use its pre-1881 title of 60th Rifles.
†† The armoured regiments of the brigade were 16th/5th Lancers, 17th/21st Lancers and 2nd Lothians and Border Horse. The lorried infantry brigade of 6th Armoured Division at this time was the Irish Brigade, commanded by Nelson Russell.

country were intended to trap the Axis forces in a pincer operation and bring the North African campaign to a speedy conclusion.

However, Hitler had other ideas and ordered the deployment of German forces into Tunisia. No ground was to be given up to the Allies and First Army's drive for Tunis was stopped in early-December. Foul weather came to the aid of the Axis with Allied aircraft unable to operate over the front lines since their temporary airfields had become quagmires. In contrast, the Luftwaffe had all-weather bases closer to Tunis and was soon able to dominate the battlefields. For those British soldiers who had served in France in 1940 there was an element of déjà vu. Not only did the enemy have command of the air but they 'outmatched us in the quality and training of their armour'.

Adrian Gore was undaunted by this situation. One of his officers described him as having been 'in his element' and never allowed any of his soldiers to get the impression that the enemy was in any way better, although, in the early stages, they were certainly better equipped and more professional in their outlook. In one instance Gore's optimism was misplaced.

> 'When they see the carriers, they'll run', I recall him saying about an early sweep down the Bou Arada valley, an operation which, with hindsight, was far too ambitious and only narrowly avoided disaster. It was not in fact Adrian's plan, and he was merely supporting loyally those in higher places, who were doing their best to make omelettes without breaking too many eggs. Nevertheless Adrian's enthusiasm and total disregard for his own safety were an inspiration at this difficult time, when a lesser commander could easily have taught us all to be unduly cautious and invariably to take counsel of our fears.

The failure of First Army's race for Tunis in December led to a period of almost static warfare in which the Allied forces were stretched severely. Attempts to break the deadlock came to naught and the initiative remained with the Axis forces. Gore's battalion had made an unsuccessful attempt to take the feature known as Two Tree Hill from the German paratroopers who defended it. The battalion had made some inroads into the forward enemy positions but suffered many casualties and was relieved by 6th Royal Inniskilling Fusiliers, from the Irish Brigade. In turn, the Skins' attack on Two Tree Hill was also repulsed. A company of 10th Rifle Brigade, with a company of 1st Royal Irish Fusiliers, covered the withdrawal of the Inniskillings.

During this period, Adrian Gore demonstrated the two main characteristics that impressed themselves on his officers and soldiers: 'his eternal optimism and confidence in success and his readiness to lead from the front'. These were inspirational qualities although they could, occasionally, cause problems.

> when we were at Bou Arada he was driven out on his own to [Jebel] Argoub 4 miles down the road to Pont du Fahs where the Germans were thought to

be to recce the ground ahead. While [he was] on the hill top a German armoured car drove up and bagged his scout car and driver. I doubt if the 4 mile walk back improved his temper.

In February the Germans launched operations that were intended to break First Army and its American and French Allies. Both elements of Army Group Africa, General Jürgen von Arnim's Fifth Panzer Army and Panzer Armee Afrika, renamed First Italian Army on 23 February, attacked, with Rommel throwing his forces against the American II Corps' front across southern Tunisia. The Desert Fox aimed to take advantage of the fact that the Americans were spread too thinly to punch his way through their lines and roll up First Army. His objectives were Thala and Tebessa, the fall of which would threaten First Army's logistical infrastructure. When Axis forces smashed through the Americans at Kasserine pass the threat to First Army increased as its southern flank was now exposed. To counter that threat, 6th Armoured Division was rushed to Sbiba and Thala to close the gap. Adrian Gore was given command of a battlegroup including two companies of 10th Rifle Brigade, a squadron of twelve Valentine tanks from 2nd Lothians and Border Horse and an anti-tank battery, with support from a battery of 12th Regiment, Royal Horse Artillery. Dubbed Gore Force, this small group was to cover the main force of 6th Armoured as it occupied the Thala position.

As ever, Adrian Gore faced this daunting task with an 'infectious calm and confidence', in spite of being outnumbered greatly by the foe. However, he came close to being captured before battle was even joined when he decided to make a personal reconnaissance of the ground ahead.

> After stopping us three miles short of the [Kasserine] pass, he went on alone to contact the Americans, unaware they had already allowed some Germans to infiltrate behind them. Luckily an ambulance was ahead of him, and when that was ambushed his driver just had time to spin round and return to us.

Gore Force could do nothing but withdraw in the teeth of such overwhelming opposition but it made a masterly withdrawal, pulling back slowly from ridge to ridge and allowing 6th Armoured Division more time to establish its positions. Colonel Gore showed outstanding leadership and his inspiration contributed to the tenacity of the defence against 10th Panzer Division. Such was the determination shown by Gore Force that the Germans believed they were facing a much stronger force. Steadily, Gore Force pulled back, the tanks of the Lothians' squadron being equally steadily knocked out one by one. Rommel later criticized 10th Panzer for the slowness of their exploitation but this cannot detract from the resolution shown by Adrian Gore and his men, who forced 10th Panzer's command to tread more carefully than the Desert Fox would have wished.

> This difficult action showed Adrian at his best; he had outstanding tactical flair at the regimental level and without his skilful withdrawal 26 Armoured

Brigade would never have been able to occupy its defensive position as, fortunately, it was able to do.

Gore Force achieved its objectives and 6th Armoured Division was able to stabilize First Army's southern flank. For his part in the operation Adrian Gore was awarded the Distinguished Service Order. He had come close to losing his life when the 15-cwt truck that was both his sleeping quarters and his office was struck and destroyed by shellfire less than a minute after he had left it to walk forward to a point where he could observe the battlefield.

Gore continued to command 10th Rifle Brigade throughout the rest of the Tunisian campaign. The battalion played its part in the Allied advance through the mountains to Tunis as First Army gained the advantage over its opponents. By the time the campaign ended, on 12 May 1943, Adrian Gore had become recognized as one of the most effective battalion commanders in the Rifle Brigade. Although there had been no further opportunities on the scale of Gore Force to demonstrate his qualities, he had shown his mettle in many ways and his reputation had spread beyond the confines of his own regiment. Following the Axis surrender the Allied armies began preparations for the next phase of operations in the Mediterranean theatre. However, 10th Rifle Brigade were not involved in the invasion of Sicily in July 1943, nor in the early phases of the invasion of Italy, which began on 3 September. The battalion remained in Tunisia and Algeria where a training programme was implemented to maintain and hone the soldiers' fighting skills. As men waited to be told what their next task might be there was an understandable air of frustration and Gore did well to keep morale and enthusiasm high within the battalion. No doubt his own behaviour helped in promoting morale: he adopted a rabbit and a hedgehog, both of which he kept in his tent.

Gore was not to lead 10th Rifle Brigade in any more actions. In February 1944 he left the battalion on promotion to brigadier and took command of 2 Brigade in 1st Division on the 23rd. At that stage the brigade was in the Anzio bridgehead and Adrian Gore was immediately immersed in the turmoil of that fiercely disputed area of ground. The Anzio operation had been launched on 22 January in an effort to break the deadlock of the Gustav line but, due to the timidity of the commander in the bridgehead, the initial surprise gained by the attackers had been lost. The Germans had made determined counter-attacks on the Allied forces, which had suffered heavy casualties. Morale had suffered in the Allied formations and 2 Brigade was no exception. Morale in the brigade 'had become understandably depressed'. Adrian Gore was an excellent choice to turn around that situation and he soon had his brigade's conceit of itself back to its former high levels. He was involved in the Anzio battles until the final breakout as Fifth and Eighth Armies pushed the Germans back towards and beyond Rome.

On 25 May Gore relinquished command of 2 Brigade to take over a newly formed brigade. This was M Brigade, which included three battalions of his own regiment: 2nd, 7th and 10th Rifle Brigade. M Brigade had been formed on 21 May under

Lieutenant-Colonel Darling. Four days after Gore assumed command the brigade was redesignated 61 Infantry Brigade, although the preferred title was 61 (Rifle) Brigade, to emphasize the fact that it was an entirely Green Jacket formation. This was the only brigade composed entirely of Rifle Brigade battalions and it was thus unique. However, commanding the formation was not as straightforward as it might appear. Motor battalions were more accustomed to serving with the armoured brigades of armoured divisions and working together as a highly mobile infantry brigade was a novel experience; the brigade continued to serve under 6th Armoured Division although only 10th Rifle Brigade remained as a motor battalion. The appointment of Adrian Gore to command 61 Brigade proved inspirational: with 'much tact and his invariable commonsense' he was able to weld the three battalions together as a fighting formation and to get the best out of his brigade. He was also blessed with a good chief of staff in Major Hugo Baring.

In the days that followed the fall of Rome, the Germans were retreating rapidly with Allied forces in equally rapid pursuit. For a time it seemed as if the Italian campaign might come to an early conclusion. But this was not to be. Enemy resistance hardened as the Allies met the first outposts of a new German defensive line; this was the Albert line, which was intended to delay the Allies so that the Germans could complete the fortification of the Gothic line, intended to hold the Allied armies during the winter of 1944–5. This was hard fighting in difficult country but Adrian Gore's 61 Brigade adapted to it quickly. 'In a succession of difficult battles, notably round Perugia in June, his Brigade achieved admirable results with fewer casualties than a more orthodox commander might have induced.' The brigade was serving with 6th Armoured Division, which became part of Richard McCreery's X Corps on 9 June. Sixth Armoured's objective was the hilltop city of Perugia, some ten miles east of Lake Trasimene. First they had to cross the Nera river at Narni, fifty miles south of Perugia and this was achieved, against very little opposition, with sappers erecting a Bailey bridge across the gorge through which the Nera flows. As the division closed on Perugia the countryside became more hilly and rain began to fall. Some five miles from Perugia enemy shells also began to fall.

It was at this stage that Adrian Gore's skill came into play. On the night of 18 June, 10th Rifle Brigade was launched on a daring thrust against Monte Lacugnano, three miles west of Perugia. This was a typical Gore stroke and it achieved success, bypassing many groups of defenders and leading to some confused fighting on the following day. On the night of the 19th Gore ordered 61 Brigade forward even farther; 7th Rifle Brigade advanced three miles in heavy rain and what seemed to be absolute darkness to capture the Monte Malbe feature, northwest of Monte Lacugnano and higher than that point. On the 20th Grenadier Guards from 1 Guards Brigade entered Perugia to find that the Germans had abandoned the ancient city.

Gore's command methods owed nothing to the teachings of the Staff College, which he had never attended. Instead he based his command style on common sense, taking account of his own experience and listening to advice from others whom he trusted. Each situation was tackled as it arose and 61 Brigade's efforts generally met with success. The exception was at Tossignano in December 1944 where Brigadier Gore's judgement 'may, for once, have been at fault' and heavy casualties were taken by 2nd Rifle Brigade in an action that had little chance of success. As a result 10th Rifle Brigade was later renamed 2nd Rifle Brigade while 1st King's Royal Rifle Corps joined 61 Brigade.* However, both XIII Corps' and Eighth Army's commanders were also mistaken in their appreciation of the situation; these were Major-General John Harding and Lieutenant-General Sir Richard McCreery, both outstanding commanders.

In early 1945 a scheme for home leave came into effect and Adrian Gore was able to have a short spell at home before returning to 61 Brigade for the final phase of operations in Italy. This was fluid, mobile battle for which 61 Brigade was suited ideally and in which the brigade commander's drive and enthusiasm, refreshed by that spell of leave, ensured that his command functioned at its best. Sir James Wilson notes that he 'was especially successful after the crossing of the River Po when he used his three motor battalions to exploit the German weaknesses after their defeat south of the river.' As the Germans retreated, 61 Brigade was part of the relentless pursuit and, following the German surrender in Italy, the brigade crossed into Austria to become part of the British Army of Occupation, faced with the many problems that beset that conquered land.

Adrian Gore was awarded a Bar to his DSO for his leadership in the final defeat of the German armies in Italy. He applied himself to the problems of post-war Austria with the same level of enthusiasm and commonsense that he had applied in war. And he was also keenly aware of the welfare needs of his soldiers. One officer wrote that

> I found him to be a wonderful person to work for. He was so very kind and approachable to a person new to his job like me at that time ... He was a great man who will be loved and remembered.

That assessment would not have been unique. His concern was appreciated by his soldiers and also by their families as he endeavoured to ensure that families were able to join their menfolk in Austria.

Returning to England, Brigadier Gore took command of the lorried infantry brigade of 56th (London) Infantry Division in the Territorial Army, which was re-formed in 1947. This was his last appointment as brigade command was 'his absolute limit', a fact that he recognized. He retired to a long and active civilian life in which he maintained his interests in sport, became a farmer and played an active part in the life of his adopted Kent. He died in 1990 at the age of ninety. His obituary in the *Royal Green Jackets' Chronicle* concluded:

---

* In the summer of 1945 the Green Jacket battalions were replaced by ordinary line battalions.

Those who served with Adrian will always remember his courage and lightness of touch. He was a truly Riflemanlike leader, and we were lucky to have served with and under him.

Sir James Wilson summarizes him as

an exceptional and versatile soldier with whom it was a delight to serve and who provided exactly the right kind of leadership for most of the tasks he was called upon to undertake. Perhaps he had his share of luck but I, for one, never complained about this factor when serving under him. Perhaps, too, he remained an 'amateur' soldier but this was no disadvantage with so many talented territorials and wartime soldiers around. I am very proud of having served him and enjoyed doing so enormously – he was a superb leader at the battalion/brigade level.

* * *

David Dawnay was born at Whitfield Court, County Waterford into an old Waterford family in 1903. His father, Major the Hon. Hugh Dawnay DSO, 2nd Life Guards,* was killed in action near Ypres on 6 November 1914. From school, David Dawnay entered Sandhurst from where he was commissioned into the Rifle Brigade in December 1923. However, he soon realized that he would be more suited to a cavalry regiment and transferred into 10th Royal Hussars (Prince of Wales's Own), the regiment of which his grandfather, Viscount Downe, was then Colonel. He served with his regiment in England, Egypt and India and gained a tremendous reputation as a sportsman, excelling in cricket and tennis but especially at polo. He was selected to captain the British polo team in the 1936 Olympics in Berlin; the team finished in the silver medal position, losing to Argentina in the final.

Returning to Britain, 10th Hussars gave up their horses to become a mechanized regiment and David Dawnay undertook a Driving and Maintenance (D and M) course at Bovington in 1937. That he passed this course convinced him that the staff of the Royal Tank Corps Centre, who conducted the course, must have had a sense of humour.

When war was declared in September 1939 David Dawnay was a major commanding C Squadron of his regiment and he led the squadron through the 1940 campaign in France as of the British Expeditionary Force. Soon after his return to Britain he was transferred to the North Irish Horse as second-in-command and joined that regiment at Enniskillen, County Fermanagh.

The North Irish Horse had been raised in 1902, as the North of Ireland Imperial Yeomanry, and served during the Great War but it had been 'disembodied' after the

---

* Until 1922 there were two regiments of Life Guards.

war and had existed only on paper until it was re-raised in the Supplementary Reserve in 1939. At one stage the regiment's entry in the Army List included only one combatant officer, giving rise to the soubriquet 'the one man regiment'. Recruiting for the Horse had begun in autumn 1939 and when David Dawnay arrived in Enniskillen at the end of June 1940 the regiment was still undergoing training. At this stage it was an armoured car regiment, although equipped with vintage Rolls Royce cars, and it continued to train for the armoured car role, which was essentially that of reconnaissance. In early 1941 the War Office announced that the Horse would convert to armour but a shortage of Cruiser tanks meant that it was issued with Valentine I-tanks. These were infantry support tanks and their arrival presaged the role that the regiment would subsequently play.

Although the North Irish Horse may have appeared very different from a regular cavalry regiment, David Dawnay was almost the ideal man to post to the regiment. An Irishman himself, he was married to Lady Katherine Beresford, daughter of the marquis of Waterford who had raised the South of Ireland Imperial Yeomanry, the sister regiment of the North Irish Horse. He developed an enthusiasm for his new regiment and was disappointed to leave it on promotion to command 2nd Battalion, Reconnaissance Corps. However, in November 1941, Lieutenant-Colonel J.A.L. Powell, commanding officer of the Horse, was posted to take command of 2 Recce and David Dawnay was appointed to command the North Irish Horse.

On his return to the regiment, Dawnay demonstrated his concern for morale in a most effective manner. The Horse's highly popular padre, the Reverend Elwyn Hughes, had been posted to 53rd (Welsh) Divisional Battle School, much to the chagrin of everyone in the regiment. Dawnay applied for Padre Hughes' return but was refused. Undaunted by this he then applied direct to the corps commander but was admonished for improper procedure and refused again. But his persistence paid off when, in mid-January, Padre Hughes was posted back to the North Irish Horse with whom he would serve for the rest of the war. David Dawnay's commitment to the regiment was to become legendary. Within the Horse he was known simply as 'D. D.'.

David Dawnay led his regiment though the remainder of its training and preparation for active service, which included a further conversion, this time to the Churchill I-tank with which the regiment would go into battle. In January 1943 the North Irish Horse, as part of 25 Tank Brigade,* sailed from Britain for North Africa. Landing at Algiers the regiment then moved to Phillippeville, in readiness for deployment in Tunisia. It was not the most propitious time for a regiment to arrive in an active service area. German offensives had hit the Allies hard with Rommel striking through the Kasserine Pass. A small force was created to defend Le Kef and this included tanks from 51st Royal Tanks and the North Irish Horse, commanded by Brigadier R.H. Maxwell of 25 Tank Brigade. David Dawnay was given command of

---

* The British Army maintained a distinction between cruiser tanks and I-tanks with the former deployed in armoured brigades and the latter in army tank brigades; these became tank brigades in June 1942.

an improvised infantry force that included North Irish Horse headquarters personnel. This defensive arrangement lasted until 24 February, by which time the Germans had been driven back and the regiment was able to re-assemble. But there was to be no respite as von Arnim launched an attack at dawn on the 26th and the North Irish Horse was to move immediately to help counter the threat.

The fighting that followed was bitter and confused with elements of the regiment being rushed to a series of locations to strengthen defences. Much gallantry was shown by its soldiers and several gallantry awards were gained; but a number of personnel were killed. At one point some Churchills were left to hold part of the line overnight without infantry support, an uncomfortable experience for the tanks' crews. By the evening of 7 March the Germans were withdrawing their armour although their infantry still held the high ground from which they would not evicted until First Army launched its offensive in April. North Irish Horse tanks were still in action and the regiment did not even have the opportunity to celebrate St Patrick's Day as they provided support for various infantry formations and units in a series of operations intended to drive back the Germans. During this phase of the fighting Major John Rew, commanding B Squadron, was killed and David Dawnay paid tribute to his courage and leadership. Not until 14 April was the regiment able to concentrate in one location for the first time since it had sailed for Africa.

As the Allies moved over to the offensive a series of attacks was made on some of the heights held by the Germans. Squadrons and troops of the Horse deployed in support of these attacks. In one case, No. 1 Troop, C Squadron was to support the Irish Brigade as it advanced from Jebel el Mahdi to capture Jebel Guernat. At the same time the remainder of the regiment, less C Squadron, would engage any enemy tanks found in the valley. A Squadron advanced cautiously onto Point 361, which was clear; B Squadron then advanced northwest to Point 391. Realizing that the Irish Brigade advance could be helped, Dawnay ordered both squadrons to advance to Jebel Rmel. A Squadron was delayed by a minefield while B moved forward and forced the Germans off the Djebel Rmel feature; having by-passed the minefield, A Squadron then moved southeast of Der Rmel farm.

The actions of the two squadrons were a positive contribution to the Irish Brigade attack, which was completely successful. Nelson Russell, commanding the Irish Brigade, described how No. 1 Troop, C Squadron, under Lieutenant Mann, 'sailed up the Djebel Guernat as if it was the last furlong at the Maze'. He also noted that Irish Brigade soldiers were both amused and pleased to be supported by a Churchill emblazoned with the name 'Lily from Portaferry'. Co-operation between Irish infantry and Irish armour was first-class and the Irish Brigade would continue to hold the North Irish Horse in high esteem.

As First Army's offensive operations continued the North Irish Horse was called upon to support 78th Infantry Division, now the parent formation of the Irish Brigade, as it assaulted German positions on Longstop Hill. In carrying out this task the Horse supported both 36 Brigade and the Irish Brigade; once again, the partnership with the latter proved successful. No. 1 Troop of A Squadron was to assist the

Irish Brigade in clearing Heidous and Jebel Tanngoucha while the remainder of the regiment would support 8th Argylls and the Surreys in assaulting Jebel Ahmera, the westernmost feature of Longstop. John Horsfall, who was then commanding D Company, 1st Royal Irish Fusiliers, described the arrival of the tanks.

> Our cavalry regiment, The North Irish Horse, was free of inhibitions sometimes found in the traditionally minded units. They did not consider that all hunting should be over flat country, and they did not mind about their machines. Yes, they might lose a tank or two up the three thousand feet over Djebel Ang, and if they couldn't get them down again they would, no doubt, be given others. So they set off to prove it, with seventy mules behind them loaded with petrol. Two days later they had done it. Three of them, and they were the only power-driven vehicles ever to get over Ang. It was scarcely mule country. I do not think that anyone can appreciate the achievement of The North Irish Horse tank crews unless they had carried out that climb themselves, preferably in charge of a mule column. Nothing in Italy, or elsewhere in my experience, was comparable to those trackless and precipitous mountain wastes, fit only for Berber goats and shunned even by them.

Nelson Russell was equally enthusiastic in his praise of the Horse, as was Brigadier Speedy Howlett of 36 Brigade when the regiment supported 5th Buffs in the capture of Jebel Rhar.

> It is impossible to speak too highly of the support given by the North Irish Horse, or of the steady advance of the Buffs, under heavy shell fire, two factors which made the capture of Djebel Rhar possible.

German officers had not believed that tanks could operate in such country and had not implemented any anti-tank defence measures. Their soldiers received a severe shock on seeing British infantry supported by tanks advancing on their positions. Such was the part played by the regiment in the capture of Longstop that it received special mention in General Sir William Jackson's book on the North African campaign. The regiment continued to play its vital role as First Army closed on Tunis and received a rapturous welcome in the city before pressing on to carry out further operations in the final days of the campaign.

Recognition of the outstanding service of the regiment came with the award of the DSO to David Dawnay for 'devotion to duty and outstanding leadership' between 5 and 26 April 1943.

> During this period Lieutenant-Colonel Dawnay's 'Churchills' accomplished feats in support of the infantry which were previously considered impossible. Owing to his skilful manoeuvring, outstanding leadership and determination

to give the maximum support to the infantry he was very largely responsible for the capture of at least three important objectives, including 'Longstop' with comparatively light casualties to personnel and tanks.

During battle Lieutenant-Colonel Dawnay keeps the closest control over his sub-units and by his firm command combined with encouragement invariably gets the very best out of his officers and men. His own action in battle is an inspiration to his [regiment].

As with Adrian Gore, Dawnay was then faced with the task of maintaining the morale of his regiment while the war moved on. The North Irish Horse remained in Tunisia and Algeria while Allied forces invaded Sicily and Italy. It would be May 1944 before the regiment again went into action but its skills were honed by a training programme that ensured that boredom did not set in. For a short time, between 26 May and 7 July, David Dawnay commanded 25 Tank Brigade; Brigadier Maxwell had been wounded and it was several weeks before his successor arrived. There were also sports and social activities. The latter included a celebration of the 'Twelfth', the anniversary of the battle of the Boyne, in which both Protestant and Catholic soldiers of the regiment engaged with considerable enthusiasm. One 'Orange' banner even carried the title 'Strickland's Chosen Few', a reference to one of the regiment's most popular officers, Major Eugene Strickland, a Kerryman and a Catholic.

The North Irish Horse wintered at Ain Mokra in Algeria where the standard order to add anti-freeze to the radiators of the tanks was issued. Checking the paperwork, Dawnay noticed that the Recce Troop did not appear to have conformed with this order and sent for the troop leader, to whom he gave a dressing down. Only then did 'D.D.' discover that the Recce Troop's Stuart, or Honey, tanks had air-cooled engines. He must have reflected with a chuckle on that pass in the D and M Course at Bovington six years before.

In April 1944 the regiment arrived in Italy without David Dawnay who had been promoted to Colonel and appointed deputy commander of 23 Armoured Brigade. Lieutenant-Colonel The Lord O'Neill was the new commanding officer but was in hospital when the Horse went into battle for the first time in Italy and Eugene Strickland took his place. This was the battle for the Hitler line in which the regiment suffered its heaviest ever casualties for a single day in the two world wars. As his regiment was fighting its way through the Hitler line, David Dawnay was taking over command of 21 Tank Brigade; he would remain as brigade commander until the end of the war. In December 1944, as part of a re-organization of armoured forces in Eighth Army, the North Irish Horse became part of 21 Tank Brigade and once again found themselves under the steady hand of D.D.

On 22 May 1944 David Dawnay took over command of 21 Tank Brigade, which included two Royal Tank Regiment battalions, 12th and 48th, and one RAC regiment, 145th, formerly 8th Bn, The Duke of Wellington's Regiment.* The latter would be disbanded in northern Italy and replaced in 21 Tank Brigade by the North Irish Horse. For 21 Tank Brigade's units their first action since Tunisia came in August 1944 with Operation OLIVE, the assault on the German Gothic line in northern Italy. For this operation the Churchills of Dawnay's brigade were assigned to support the infantry of 1st Canadian Division under General Vokes. In turn Vokes' division formed part of I Canadian Corps, one of the three with which Eighth Army's commander, Sir Oliver Leese, hoped to break through the Gothic line; the others were General Anders' II Polish Corps and the British V Corps. Leese was so optimistic about his plans that he believed that Eighth Army could be in Vienna by Christmas.

D-Day for Operation OLIVE was 26 August and the initial assaults met with success, inspiring enthusiasm in Allied headquarters, especially when the assaulting brigades from the British, Canadian and Polish divisions reported that they had advanced some two miles against little opposition by dawn on the 26th. Steady progress continued during the first two days of the operation with the Canadians advancing eight miles beyond the Metauro river. With support from Dawnay's tanks the Loyal Edmontons were ready to assault the hilltop town of Monteciccardo. The Edmontons entered the town at one o'clock in the morning of the 28th but met such tough opposition from German paratroopers, with one tank in support, that they were forced to withdraw. But they regained the town following a day of skirmish and heat; the nearby monastery was also taken. However, enemy opposition was hardening, especially in the Canadian sector where a parachute division was holding the German line.

Eighth Army's advance continued with Leese still hoping that he could bounce the Gothic line rather than having to mount a major setpiece battle to break through it. Air support was called in with planes of the Desert Air Force carrying out bombing raids to ease the passage of the attacking formations by destroying enemy minefields. On 1 September Vokes' division thrust towards the coast, cutting across the front of the Poles; Monte Luro fell to the Edmontons, supported by 12th Royal Tanks, while the neighbouring Monte Peloso fell to Princess Louise's Dragoon Guards, a Canadian cavalry regiment lately converted to infantry.

Dawnay then took over the pursuit from Monte Luro, 'with Canadian infantry in support of his Churchill tanks' while 5th Canadian Armoured Division thrust out on the left flank, smashing a German counter-attack as it did so. I Canadian Corps had forced the German paras out of the Gothic line before they could man properly their positions and the Canadian divisions, with 21 Tank Brigade, went on to reach the Conca river on 2 September. By dawn on the 3rd, the fifth anniversary of the outbreak of war, they had crossed the Conca. Rimini was now in their sights. 'It was a great triumph and it raised great hopes.'

However, the advance stalled. Once again it seemed that Eighth Army could

---

* Almost three dozen infantry battalions were converted to armour as numbered regiments of the Royal Armoured Corps.

launch a successful assault but did not have the strength in depth to follow through, especially against such skilled defenders as they now met. Leese had failed to have 1st Armoured Division far enough forward to exploit the achievements of the assault formations and push through the enemy line. Thus V Corps was stalled before the Coriano ridge, ten miles southeast of Rimini and the last such feature before open country. German reinforcements were rushed to the sector and a major operation had to be mounted to push them off. Leese had planned that Eighth Army would leap for Ravenna, thirty-five miles away, but the army was no longer fit enough to leap. A series of bloody battles of attrition followed in which 21 Tank Brigade supported Canadian troops. Battalions of 1st Canadian Division went forward to battle on the night of 17–18 September, each supported by tanks of Dawnay's brigade. The result was catastrophic.

> The Canadians met disaster and spent the 18th writhing amid ditches and vineyards on the flats below San Fortunato, with shells pelting upon them, together with bombs from Allied aircraft, and with black smoke billowing from Churchills of the hard-fought 21st Tank Brigade.

In the battles that followed the Canadians were able to make some progress, although 1st Armoured Division suffered heavily. With 4th British Division under command, the Canadian Corps pushed forward and the Churchills of 21 and 15 Tank Brigades provided invaluable support for the Canadian infantry. However, Eighth Army's painfully slow advance, which had reached the Romagna plain, was soon to bog down as another Italian winter approached. As the campaign bogged down, Leese was promoted to command 11 Army Group in the Far East and Sir Richard McCreery succeeded him as Eighth Army commander.

McCreery used the winter to prepare Eighth Army for its spring offensive. Armoured units were sent into the line as infantry and to carry out other duties that would allow infantry to rest, re-organize and train for the final phase of the campaign. Part of McCreery's preparation was the creation of a specialized engineer assault brigade, which was achieved by converting 25 Tank Brigade to the new role. From that brigade, the North Irish Horse was transferred to Dawnay's command, replacing 145 RAC. The regiments of 21 Tank Brigade performed defensive tasks along the line, supporting infantry battalions, and took part in some minor operations before Operation BUCKLAND was launched on 9 April.

Dawnay's regiments were assigned to the support of 8th Indian Division and were quickly across the Senio river, on bridges erected by Royal Engineers, to fight alongside the battalions of 8th Indian. The tanks performed well and many decorations were earned by 21 Tank Brigade's soldiers in one of the finest examples of armour support for infantry of the war. Liaison between tanks and infantry was first rate and it was a troop of Churchills from 21 Tank Brigade – No. 3 Troop of C Squadron, North Irish Horse, that was the first element of Eighth Army to reach the river Po, cutting off the German retreat from Ferrara. Elements of the brigade crossed the Po and raced for the Adige river, where the enemy were expected to make a stand. But the speed of Eighth Army's advance had taken the Germans off-balance and by 30 April the brigade was ordered to stand down. Four days later the war in Italy was over as the Germans surrendered to Field Marshal Alexander.

David Dawnay was awarded a Bar to his DSO for his service in the Italian campaign. He remained in the Army after the war and was promoted major-general, becoming the commandant of the Royal Military Academy, Sandhurst and then commander of 56th (London) Division, a TA formation. He then retired from the Army to be appointed Clerk of the Course at Ascot and secretary to the Ascot Authority, duties he discharged with distinction until retirement in 1969. He was also appointed Honorary Colonel of the North Irish Horse, in 1947, and Colonel of 10th Hussars in 1962. In 1967 the latter appointment was extended for a further five years and it was David Dawnay who saw the regiment though the 1969 amalgamation with 11th Hussars to form The Royal Hussars (Prince of Wales's Own).* However, he remained Honorary Colonel of the North Irish Horse until his death in 1971. One of his lasting legacies to the Horse was to ensure that the regiment was awarded the battle honours it deserved from the Tunisian and Italian campaigns.

David Dawnay was buried in his native Waterford and his funeral was attended by four serving officers of the North Irish Horse. A memorial service was also held in the Royal Memorial Chapel at Sandhurst, which was attended by a large number of his friends from the Army and the world of sport.

* * *

John Ormsby Evelyn Vandeleur was always better known by the name formed by his initials, Joe. Born in Nowshera, on India's North-West Frontier, Joe Vandeleur was the son of a soldier, Lieutenant-Colonel C.B. Vandeleur, who was serving in 1st Cameronians. His mother was also Irish, being the daughter of General Thomas O'Leary. The Vandeleurs had been settled in Ireland, principally in County Clare, since 1600 and had produced many soldiers, so that Joe's decision to enter Sandhurst from school at Cheltenham was not surprising. One of his ancestors was Sir John Vandeleur, a Waterloo veteran and the cavalry officer who decided to introduce Polish-style lancers into the British Army. Although he had planned to join a Highland regiment, family ties, sealed in blood, made him opt for the Irish Guards; five of his cousins had been killed serving in the regiment, one in the Boer War and the others in the Great War. Joe therefore passed out of Sandhurst to become a 'Mick' in 1924.

Four years later he was seconded to the Sudan Defence Force, commanding the Camel Company and the Motor Machine-Gun Battery and becoming so fond of the

---

* In 1992 The Royal Hussars amalgamated with 14th/20th King's Hussars to form The King's Royal Hussars.

Sudan that he made several unsuccessful efforts to obtain another posting there following his return to Britain in 1931. That year saw him appointed adjutant to 1st Irish Guards before becoming an instructor at the machine-gun wing of the Small Arms School at Netheravon in Wiltshire from 1933 to 1936. (As a new officer he had undertaken a machine-gun course at the school shortly after joining the Irish Guards.) This was followed by another spell as a machine-gun instructor, this time with the Royal Egyptian Army before he rejoined 1st Irish Guards; the battalion had just returned to Britain from Palestine.

Following a period as a company commander in the 2nd Battalion, which was being re-formed for the war, Vandeleur was appointed to the Training Battalion at Lingfield and assumed responsibility for training officers, working 'them like demons from dawn to dusk'. His next appointment was as second-in-command of the 1st Battalion, which had seen active service in the Norwegian campaign. This battalion would serve in Tunisia and Italy while 2nd Irish Guards would become the armoured battalion of the Micks; but Vandeleur had meanwhile moved on to command another new battalion, 3rd Irish Guards. The new battalion was born 'by the most rudimentary form of reproduction' in February. When the prospect of invasion receded with the onset of winter in November 1941, the Irish Guards Training Battalion was ordered to Northwood to relieve the 1st Battalion. Command and administration were split and the companies that moved to Northwood became known as the 'Holding Companies', commanded by Major Joe Vandeleur. With the addition of new recruits the 'Holding Companies' increased in numbers until in February they were constituted formally as 3rd Battalion, Irish Guards with Joe Vandeleur as their commanding officer. This was the unit that he would take to war in 1944 and he played a major part in its training and preparation for war. The battalion was by then part of 32 Brigade in Guards Armoured Division.

The battalion assembled in an orchard outside Bayeux on 25 June and sat there for two days 'without a sign of the war' as Vandeleur commented. On the 28th the battalion moved with 32 Brigade into the left corner of the British salient west of Carpiquet, close to Caen. However, there was still no action and Vandeleur's 'Micks' were spectators as Second Army pressed in on and took Caen. Their turn was to come with Operation GOODWOOD, which opened on 18 July. This was the operation in which General Dempsey, commanding Second Army, planned to push a corps of three armoured divisions through the crust of the German defences. We have already seen that this operation failed to achieve its objectives although many soldiers lost their lives in the fighting. Joe Vandeleur's battalion went into action near the village of Cagny and was then ordered to advance to Frénouville under cover of darkness. This was a confused action in which the battalion suffered casualties, having run into German defensive positions, before being ordered to take up a defensive stance. Over the next four days, 3rd Irish Guards remained on the defensive, suffering thirteen dead and almost forty wounded or missing. Vandeleur noted that the lesson from Cagny was 'the old one of the futility of a night advance over unreconnoitred ground.'

On 28 July Guards Armoured Division rejoined VIII Corps in readiness for another offensive, this time in the Caumont sector with the attack thrusting into the difficult bocage country where movement by tanks was restricted because of the many small fields surrounded by high banks and sunken roads. In many cases tanks could not even travel along those roads, since they were too narrow. For this offensive Guards Armoured had adopted what was at first known as the Bocage Battlegroup system in which an armoured battalion and an infantry battalion operated in close harmony. But, due to the haste with which the system was adopted, the two Irish Guards battalions in the division were not linked; 2nd (Armoured) Battalion operated with 5th Coldstream while 3rd Irish Guards worked with 1st (Armoured) Coldstream. In each 'marriage' the senior of the commanding officers became the group commander. The re-organization had been carried out in ninety minutes on the road and was based on 'immediate convenience'; the Coldstream/Irish groups occurred because battalions happened to be in adjacent fields.

The 5th Coldstream/3rd Irish Guards Battlegroup went into action near St Martin des Besaces on a hot and 'unbelievably dusty' day, with 3rd Irish Guards taking part in a well-supported and completely successful attack against defiant Germans. With the Micks established on their new positions, a small group was sent forward, consisting of King's Company, 1st (Motor) Grenadier Guards and Lieutenant Patrick McCorkell's tank troop of Irish Guards to seize the bridge at Le Tourneur. The bridge was defended too strongly for this force to take it and 5 Brigade headquarters, in the absence of the Brigadier, issued an order to Colonel Finlay of 2nd Irish Guards to find Colonel Vandeleur of 3rd Irish Guards and 'persuade him to capture the bridge by three o'clock in the morning at the latest'. Since his forward companies had already despatched patrols to the river and knew the ground, Joe Vandeleur agreed to carry out this 'extraordinary order'. Two companies advanced at 2 o'clock in the morning and, an hour later, reported back that they had captured the bridge, which was still intact.

Vandeleur's battalion remained active throughout August, fighting at Maisoncelles and Sourdeval. At the latter heavy casualties were sustained as the battalion, supported by the Coldstream tanks, advanced towards La Jarriere. Two companies lost thirty-three killed and seventy-two wounded and were cut off in the positions that they had fought so hard to take. Joe Vandeleur was determined to collect the many wounded and withdraw Nos. 2 and 4 Companies. Both were achieved under cover of smoke. The following day, 12 August, was quiet and the bodies of the dead were sought and buried. On the 13th the battalion moved to Le Busq and then, via Montilly, to Vernon where they crossed the Seine on the morning of 30 August. The battle for Normandy was over.

The Germans were falling back quickly across France, making no effort to establish a defensive line along the Seine, or elsewhere in the country. Veterans recall those days as the 'great swan' when 21 Army Group raced across France towards the Belgian frontier. As Guards Armoured Division prepared to move up the road to Brussels the battlegroups were reformed to produce regimental groups. The forced marriages of July were annulled and 2nd Irish married with 3rd Irish to produce the Irish Guards Battlegroup; across the division Grenadiers, Coldstream, Irish and Welsh were wedded, armoured battalion with infantry battalion. From that day until the war ended, Guards Armoured Division fought on the basis of the regimental battlegroup.

> The Irish Group was born at six o'clock on the evening of 2nd September. Few unions can have had such a splendid result; the two battalions worked in perfect accord and mutual trust. Each knew that it could depend absolutely on the other, and that either would take any risk to help the other. The tedious theoretical volumes preaching 'Infantry and Tank Co-operation' reduced themselves to the practical fact that 'the Micks muck in'.

Joe Vandeleur, as the senior commanding officer, became group commander. His first order from Sir Allan Adair's headquarters was the succinct 'The Division will capture Brussels'. In turn, Vandeleur issued an order that was to become legendary in the Irish Guards: 'Enemy information – one word, Chaos. Our intentions: The Irish Guards will dine in Brussels tomorrow night'.

Vandeleur's order was complied with and, following rapturous scenes of liberation, the Irish Guards Group did dine in Brussels, in the Flemish suburb of Auderghem where they were also to be prepared to meet any attempt by the Germans to retake Brussels. One such attack, a rather pathetic effort by hundreds of clerks, cooks and other corps troops, urged forward at pistol point by Nazi officers, met a calamitous end from the machine guns of the Micks' Shermans. After two days in Brussels the Group was directed on the Escaut canal, which marked the Belgo-Dutch border. En route the division fought its way through the mining town of Beeringen and then, some twenty miles from the canal, the Irish Guards took the lead.

There followed another action that was to become part of the Micks' history and, as Sir John Gorman describes it, 'a typical Vandeleur action'. Learning of a road that was not marked on the pre-war maps issued to Second Army, Vandeleur assembled a small force of an Irish Guards tank troop, an Irish Guards infantry platoon and a team of Royal Engineers to make its way along the new road and seize the bridge before the enemy could demolish it. The force reached the bridge before dark but remained in hiding until Colonel Joe decided the time was right for an assault. Once the order was given the tank troop, 'closely supported by the Irish Guards foot-soldiers, broke cover, raced through the little village and turned right towards the bridge'. Although some of the defending 88mm guns got some shots off the Shermans were quickly over the bridge and on the far side, while the Engineers worked to defuse the demolition charges. A counter-attack was launched but the rest of the Group was on its way to the bridge and the original group held on grimly.

> At last it became clear that this daring exploit had succeeded. The delight at the capture of this precious bridge, which was to be the key to the Arnhem

operation, was being conveyed to the Irish Guards from Montgomery downwards.

The bridge, the only surviving bridge over the Escaut, was dubbed 'Joe's Bridge' in tribute to Joe Vandeleur; although a new bridge has been built nearby the old bridge continues to bear the name 'Joe's Bridge'.

Joe Vandeleur was very modest about this achievement, writing in 1967 that

> I am not at all clear in my mind as to whether we had been ordered to capture the Escaut Bridge. Vaguely I remember knowing that the bridge was a vital objective. I feel that some of the matter which has been written about the Escaut affair is an 'afterthought', but I may be wrong. To the best of my recollection, I acted on impulse.

There followed the expansion of the bridgehead provided by the capture of the Escaut bridge and then Guards Armoured Division learned of their role in the next operation, the attempt to seize bridges over the Lower Rhine, Waal and Maas rivers at Grave, Nijmegen and Arnhem. 'Airborne carpets' were to be laid by 101st US, 82nd US and 1st British Airborne Divisions while XXX Corps was to race up the road to Arnhem to link the 'carpets' together. XXX Corps' commander, Lieutenant-General Brian Horrocks addressed Guards Armoured Division's officers in a cinema and informed them that the ground operation would be led by the Irish Guards. This caused one young Micks' captain to exclaim 'Oh my God, not again!' After the war Horrocks told John Gorman that he had heard the remark but that he had not been offended by it.*

However, the success of Joe's Bridge was not to be repeated. The story of Arnhem is too well-known to be rehearsed here; the airborne operation, Operation MARKET, was partly successful but 1st Airborne failed to hold the Arnhem bridge; the ground operation, GARDEN, failed to push XXX Corps through to the beleaguered airborne troops at Arnhem and Oosterbeek. Vandeleur's Irish Group had done their best, suffering heavy casualties in their phase of the operation but the restricted front, and the flaws in Montgomery's planning, ensured that Arnhem and its bridge would remain in German hands until 1945.

On 15 November 1944, Joe Vandeleur was promoted to command 129 Brigade, an infantry formation that included three West Country battalions, 4th Somerset Light Infantry and 4th and 5th Wiltshires. The brigade was part of 43rd (Wessex) Division, commanded by Major-General G.I. Thomas. Except for a two-week period in early-1945, Vandeleur commanded 129 Brigade until the end of the war and led it through the ferocious fighting in the Rhineland in February and early-March and the Rhine crossing at the end of March.

---

* In the film 'A Bridge Too Far' the remark is attributed to Joe Vandeleur and, therefore, spoken by Michael Caine who played Vandeleur.

Joe Vandeleur succeeded a highly respected and popular brigade commander, Brigadier Mole, who died of wounds on 14 November. Mole, originally an Ulster Rifles' officer, had been one of the few officers in 43rd Division who would stand up to Thomas, who was known variously as 'Butcher' Thomas or von Thoma due to his uncompromising attitude to battle. As a guardsman, Vandeleur was in strange company but he appreciated the qualities of his staff and, in particular, the commanding officer of his artillery regiment, Lieutenant-Colonel Michael Concannon, who he described as 'the finest gunner I have ever come across'. Concannon commanded 94th Field Regiment.

The first action fought by 43rd Division after Vandeleur joined it was Operation CLIPPER, the battle for Geilenkirchen, a bloody and ferocious engagement in which 129 Brigade was not involved. Thereafter the division held defensive positions through the bitterly cold winter months. Vandeleur, however, emphasized to his soldiers that such positions are only temporary as they awaited the opportunity to go over to the offensive.

> It is therefore vital that all the ground over which they are to attack can be seen in detail. I therefore made plans immediately to capture the schoolhouse at Tripsrath to deny the enemy observation and to gain it ourselves.
>
> Next, I never allowed troops to occupy cellars when in a defensive position. Cellars should be reserved for the wounded and vital communication centres.

When the schoolhouse was captured 'a great number of prisoners' were taken who had been hiding in the cellar, thus driving home Vandeleur's lesson about not occupying these in defence.

In January, the Wessex Division, now part of XII Corps, took part in Operation BLACKCOCK, designed to destroy German formations west of the Siegfried line in the Roer triangle. Three objectives were assigned to 43rd Division; these were code-named Hart, Jug and Kettle and included the capture of several villages. Vandeleur's 129 Brigade was to execute the first part of Hart, the capture of Wetterath. Strong artillery support was to be provided and, on 20 January, 129 Brigade was in action with 4th Somerset taking Schummer Quartier and then Langbroich. Operation JUG began on the 23rd and 4th Somerset and 4th Wiltshire were the battalions involved. The Wiltshires moved forward in Kangaroos – extemporized armoured personnel carriers – clad in white camouflage with Churchills of the Grenadier Guards in support together with Sherman flails to destroy mines, Crocodile flamethrower tanks and self-propelled anti-tank guns. In spite of determined opposition, Waldenrath fell to the Wiltshires for the loss of eight men dead and thirty-two wounded; over 200 enemy soldiers were captured.

It was then the turn of the Somersets who advanced on Scheifendahl where the defenders hastily surrendered, allowing an attack to be made on Erpen, almost a mile away. This was also successful with nearly 200 Germans being captured. A sharp counter-attack on Erpen was beaten off that evening. On the 24th a Somerset company took Schleiden while 5th Wiltshires captured Utterath. As 129 Brigade handed over to 214 Brigade the division was scenting success and when BLACK-COCK came to an end on 28 January that was certainly the case. And the success had been gained with Thomas at the helm; he had been commanding XXX Corps while Horrocks was on leave.

When 129 Brigade next went into action, Vandeleur was on leave but the brigade fought well in a desperate battle in the Reichswald. Joe Vandeleur was back in command on 15 February by which time the brigade was still engaged heavily in the Reichswald battles. He was at the helm when, as Horrocks described

> The turning-point came on 16th February, when the 43rd Wessex Division carried out a brilliant 8,000 yards advance which brought them to the escarpment overlooking the fortified town of Goch, which was subsequently captured by the Jocks of the 51st Highland and 15th Scottish Divisions.

The Reichswald battles came to an end on 10 March when all organized German resistance west of the Rhine ended. It had been a hard battle under 'the most unpleasant conditions imaginable' in which the Germans suffered some 75,000 casualties against 15,634 Allied.

On 9 March, Vandeleur's brigade was ordered to take the village of Xanten which was defended by 'elements of a German parachute regiment and by elements of 16th Panzer Regiment'. The attack was preceded by a 'pepperpot' bombardment of the area, using every artillery piece that was available and drenching it with fire; Xanten was also subjected to attack by aircraft. Even so, the attack met with fierce resistance and the first phase did not go well, causing Vandeleur to put in a second effort that, with the aid of engineers who bridged a crater on the approach road, artillery and flamethrower tanks, wrested the village from the Germans. A number of Tiger tanks had been encountered which knocked out several British tanks 'in pitch darkness at a range of 200 yards'.

> At the end of this battle I told my brigade staff to stand in respectful silence as the battle-weary German prisoners passed us. I personally saluted them. This was not approved of by the Press.

Then followed the Rhine crossing, which 43rd Division accomplished in Buffaloes. They were soon in contact with the enemy and were engaged in intermittent fighting between the river and Bremen where the division fought its last major engagement of the war. The objective assigned to 129 Brigade was the Burgher Park, a stronghold on the eastern side of the city; Vandeleur was also told to capture, if possible, the German army, navy and air commanders of the Bremen garrison.

The attack on the Burgher Park was made under cover of darkness and with the aid of Churchill flamethrower tanks. In the morning the Park was in 129 Brigade's hands and a solider of 4th Wiltshires brought the three German commanders to Vandeleur's headquarters, from where they were transported to captivity by the Brigadier himself. Following the capture of Bremen the division pushed on towards Hanover. Along the way there were some minor engagements and 129 Brigade was the first to cross the Aller river. Shortly after this the brigade came upon Belsen concentration camp. The camp was being guarded by Hungarian soldiers and Vandeleur ordered their commanding officer to disarm his men immediately. He was told that Hungary and Britain were not at war with each 'so to put matters right I declared war on Hungary immediately and instructed the Hungarian colonel to place his men at the disposal of our medical services'. Thus Vandeleur's war came to an end with a ghastly reminder of the price of total war and the outworkings of nationalism.

After the war, Joe Vandeleur was appointed to command 32 Guards Brigade at Lubeck, including four battalions of guards, 1st Royal Fusiliers and 10th Royal Hussars. Among their responsibilities were the 175,000 displaced persons in the brigade area and Vandeleur had to arm the German police to protect themselves from the DPs.

> Soldiering was a very secondary consideration. We spent most of our time visiting the displaced persons' camps.

Twice awarded the DSO as well as a Mention in Despatches during the northwest Europe campaign, Vandeleur returned to Britain to become Regimental Lieutenant-Colonel of the Irish Guards, following which he was appointed to command a TA brigade in Kent and Sussex. Tragically, his wife died at the age of thirty-four and he was 'quite lost and helpless' until he was given command of a TA brigade in London and, with an excellent brigade major, threw himself into the training of that formation, 'the keenest soldiers I have ever had the pleasure to meet'.

On retiring from the Army, Joe Vandeleur became Chief Constable of the War Department Constabulary and later a member of Her Majesty's Bodyguard of the Honourable Corps of Gentlemen-at-Arms. He was also chairman of the London Branch of the Irish Guards Old Comrades' Association, which pleased him particularly. Joe Vandeleur died in 1988. Although he had remarried he outlived his second wife and there were no children from either marriage.

~ 13 ~

Loftus Tottenham, Lentaigne and Dorman-Smith

The Burma campaign is often described by the veterans who served there as 'the forgotten war' but even within that description there are degrees of oblivion. While many who are interested in the history of the Second World War will be able to name Fourteenth Army – the 'forgotten army' – and its redoubtable commander, General Bill Slim, how many are aware that two divisions of West African soldiers served in Burma? And are the names of their commanders remembered? Those two formations were 81st and 82nd (West African) Divisions. The former was commanded by an Irishman during one of the most outstanding operations of the war in Burma: Major-General Frederick Loftus Tottenham led 81st (West African) Division in its campaign in the Kaladan valley in 1944.

Frederick Joseph Loftus Tottenham was born in Naas, County Kildare in 1898. The Loftus Tottenham family made a major contribution to Irish military history in the twentieth century and members of the family were to be found in the British and Indian Armies, the Royal Air Force, the Australian Imperial Force, the Royal Australian Air Force and the women's auxiliary forces. Educated in France and at Bedford School, Frederick then went to the Cadet College at Wellington in India from where he was commissioned into 2nd King Edward's Own Gurkha Rifles (The Sirmoor Rifles)* in 1916. He was then aged seventeen and the Great War was underway.

Lieutenant Frederick Loftus Tottenham was posted to the 1st Battalion Depot before being attached temporarily to 51st Sikhs with whom he served in Mesopotamia. In September 1917 he joined his own regiment's 1st Battalion at Beled Ruz. On 17 July 1918 he was wounded accidentally by a sentry of the Hampshires whilst carrying out a night patrol in search of rifle thieves. He was evacuated to India and rejoined the 1st Battalion Depot on being discharged from hospital. In 1919 he was transferred to the 2nd Battalion, which deployed in India's North-West Frontier province in the Waziristan campaign of the Third Afghan War. During this campaign

---

* During the brief reign of Edward VIII the regiment modified its title to King Edward VII's Own. It also preferred the spelling Goorkhas and thus referred to itself as 2nd Goorkhas.

two posthumous Victoria Crosses were earned, one by a young Irishman, William David Kenny from County Down. Freddie Loftus Tottenham served on the North-West Frontier with his regiment for two years before moving to the Indian Signal Corps to learn more about signalling in modern warfare. He was already demonstrating that he would make a good commander.

His experience in mountain warfare stood him in good stead during an attachment to the French army in the Pyrenees in 1927, following which he was appointed as Envoy Extraordinary to the King of Nepal in Katmandu. Nepal is, of course, the home of the Gurkhas. Returning to 2nd Gurkhas in 1929 he served once again on the unsettled North-West Frontier until 1934 when he assumed command of the Mewar State Forces. Mewar, or Udaipur, was one of the Indian princely states, which continued to be controlled by the traditional, hereditary rulers and were not part of 'British India' although their rulers had entered into treaties with the Crown. These states, in which lived about a quarter of India's population, maintained their own forces but, in the aftermath of the Great War, had agreements with the Crown on training and equipment; units trained and equipped to 'field service' standards would be available to the Crown in the event of war. When Freddie Loftus Tottenham went to Mewar it was to modernize the state forces, which consisted of a cavalry detachment and an infantry battalion. His task complete, he returned to the Gurkhas and was commanding 1st Bn, 2nd (King Edward VII's Own) Gurkha Rifles on the North-West Frontier when war came again in September 1939.

When the decision was taken to raise parachute troops in the British and Indian armies, Loftus Tottenham volunteered to train as a parachutist and then went on to raise and train 153 Gurkha Parachute Battalion, which was formed of volunteers from all the Gurkha regiments except 9th Gurkhas. Since the latter was recruited solely from high-caste men, its soldiers could not have lived and eaten with other Gurkhas. Although he was not to command the battalion in action, Loftus Tottenham gave it 'form and substance, and above all a unique self-confidence and character that would remain with it until disbandment at the end of the war'. In 1942 he was sent on a special reconnaissance mission to eastern Persia, now Iran, before returning to India to take command of 33 Brigade of 7th Indian Division.*

Japanese forces had invaded Burma in early-1942 and advanced as far as the frontier with India where they were held by British and Indian forces. In 1943 a British operation in the Arakan, on the coast of Burma, failed in its intent and Allied attention turned to building up the forces, equipment and supplies necessary for a further offensive. A major re-organization saw the creation of South-East Asia Command (SEAC), with Lord Mountbatten as its supreme commander, at the end of August and Fourteenth Army, under General Bill Slim. Allied intentions for 1944 included re-occupying northern Burma and re-opening land communication with China along the Burma road. Assam was key to this strategy with roads and railways constructed

---

* The brigade included 1st Queen's Royal Regiment, 4/15th Punjab Regiment and 4th Battalion, 1st Gurkhas.

or improved throughout the region and massive supply bases established around Imphal. These required the deployment of a corps to ensure their safety.

However, before the main operations would begin there was a return to battle in the Arakan when two divisions of XV Corps pushed into the region on either side of the Mayu range. On the right was 5th Indian Division and on the left 7th Indian. Their respective objectives were Maungdaw and Buthidaung; between these two points the Japanese had created defensive systems following the first Arakan expedition.

Having secured their objectives the two divisions attempted to push on to Donbaik but suffered repulse and were then threatened when the Japanese 55th Division, under Lieutenant-General Hanaya Tadashi, swung around their left flank, took Taung Bazar and pushed westwards, cutting 5th Division's supply routes in the north and at Ngakyedauk Pass. Operation HAGO was commanded by Lieutenant-General Sakurai Shozo; the attack on 7th Indian Division was led by Major-General Sakurai Tokutaro, known as 'Tokuta' to his fellow officers. Both Indian divisions concentrated into defensive positions at Sinzweya, the 'Admin Box' and a lengthy battle ensued. In these operations Brigadier Freddie Loftus Tottenham 'led his brigade with inspiring energy and determination' during the period from 4 February 1944, when the Japanese attacked, to 29 February, when the enemy were defeated.

> During this time his brigade was holding the central portion of the line from Able to the Kalapanzin River and, in addition, was responsible for the protection of the majority of the division's artillery which was sited in their area. It was against this sector of the front that the Japanese frontal attack was launched.
>
> In spite of his most difficult task he held all the hard-won positions on the whole front and lost not a single gun. Cool and fearless in action, he instilled in all ranks supreme confidence in their ability to kill and conquer the Jap. His brigade never lost a position in defence and on resuming the counter-offensive never failed in an attack.

This was the first time that British forces had dug in and fought the Japanese to a standstill. Superior logistics helped but the determination of the soldiers on the ground and the leadership of their commanders were critical factors. Nowhere in the 'Admin Box' was anyone safe from Japanese fire and the British advantage in logistics could not, of itself, have won the battle. Courage and leadership were not wanting and Loftus Tottenham was awarded the DSO for his handling of 33 Brigade.

The Japanese then launched their attack on Assam and 7th Indian Division was redeployed by road, rail and air to the northern front where the battles of Kohima and Imphal were underway. On this front 'Loftus Tottenham was involved in some of the toughest fighting, including had-to-hand combat, until the Japanese were routed.' During this fighting Loftus Tottenham demonstrated his feel for battle when he declined to allow his brigade to be used in an attack on the central Japanese position at Kohima. When he reconnoitred the route his soldiers would have to use he realised that they would come under fire from Japanese bunkers on GPT Ridge and he chose to use another route. It was several days before the Japanese were driven out of these positions and they inflicted heavy casualties on their attackers in the meantime. Loftus Tottenham gave one last chance to take the Naga village to 4th/1st Gurkhas, whose commanding officer used infiltration tactics to achieve success. Following the victory at Kohima and Imphal, Fourteenth Army was able to move to the offensive and the long march through Burma began.

Loftus Tottenham had proven himself to be an excellent jungle commander and when, in August 1944, Major-General Woolner, commander of 81st (West African) Division, was relieved of his command by XV Corps' commander, Lieutenant-General Christison, the Irishman was a logical choice to replace him. Woolner and Christison had had an uneasy relationship and the latter showed little confidence in the African soldiers. In spite of their achievements in 1943, he decided that they had somehow failed and his subsequent account of the campaign makes this point. Woolner is also said to have had some strange ideas on fighting in the bush, one of which was 'that his soldiers should not dig in at any time, but stay upright and fight their enemy like men'. In practice, however, his soldiers proved adept at jungle warfare and were good at digging in when necessary. Loftus Tottenham, therefore, came to a division that was not certain why its commander had been relieved. The historian of 81st (West African) Division notes that although, as a Gurkha officer, Loftus Tottenham had no experience with West African soldiers

> he was quick to appreciate their potential – not only their strength and stamina, but also their intelligence, for he realised that men who had acquired a thorough working knowledge of modern arms and equipment, learning in a foreign language, were not stupid. He had every confidence in the Division's future success; he had seen the Japanese defeated twice, in the 'Box' battle and at Kohima. He had spent some years with the Indian Corps of Signals, experience which was very valuable to a commander whose troops were so totally dependent on their signallers as they waged their very private war.

The soldiers of 81st (West African) Division were drawn from the British colonies of The Gold Coast, The Gambia, Sierra Leone and Nigeria. Each country was represented in the division by infantry battalions from the Royal West African Frontier Force (RWAFF): 3 West African Brigade included 6th, 7th and 12th Battalions of the Nigeria Regiment; 5 West African Brigade included 5th, 7th and 8th Battalions, Gold Coast Regiment; 6 West African Brigade included 4th Nigeria Regiment, 1st Gambia Regiment and 1st Sierra Leone Regiment. When Loftus Tottenham took command the division deployed only 5 and 6 Brigades, 3 Brigade having been detached to 3rd Indian Division (Special Force), better known as the Chindits. There was also a reconnaissance unit, 81st (West African) Reconnaissance Regiment, which earlier had been detached to XV Corps and to 5th Indian Division with which it had earned distinction. The division's soldiers inspired fear in their Japanese opponents, who believed that the Africans practised cannibalism on their enemies. This belief was reinforced when the Japanese learned that many African soldiers filed their teeth into sharp points. Japanese sensibilities were outraged by this, since they could not 'conceivably go to join their ancestors through the bowels of black men'.

Although the RWAFF had been raised as security forces for Britain's West African colonies they proved excellent jungle fighters, although not all came from bush country; the colonies had as many different people as Europe and land that varied from desert to bush and pastureland. West Africans had already served with distinction in the East African campaign but the two divisions were lightly armed and not equipped for conventional mobile warfare. However, this was to prove an advantage in the Arakan and Loftus Tottenham would demonstrate just how good his soldiers were. The Japanese were on the retreat, having lost some 50,000 dead in battle; another 20,000 would die of sickness on the withdrawal to the Chindwin river. Loftus Tottenham's division had withdrawn to the hills where rise the Kaladan river. The country there is so wild that myth has it that an entire British regiment was lost without trace in the region during the Burma war of 1824. In this country the West Africans saw out part of the monsoon season and waited for the order to move forward. That order finally came in September, before the monsoon had ended: 81st (West African) Division was to advance down the line of the Kaladan river to turn the Japanese right flank before moving to Paletwa where it would hold a line until relieved by 82nd (West African) Division in December.

Operations began in early October and, as the main body of 81st Division moved down the Kaladan valley, C Squadron, 81st Reconnaissance Regiment struck east out of Taung Bazar deep into the Arakan Yomas to obtain information on enemy dispositions in the division's line of advance and to find tracks that 82nd Division could use for a secret move from the Kalapanzin area to Paletwa. However, events moved so quickly that much of these plans became redundant. Given the tasks of clearing the Upper Kaladan, securing the Arakan flank and driving the last Japanese troops out of India, by playing 'Jackson in the Valley',* Loftus Tottenham was then to place his division in the rear of the Japanese forces in the Lower Kaladan valley and, by threatening enemy communications with their base at Akyab, force the Japanese to weaken their Akyab garrison to deal with the West Africans.

Instead of handing over as planned to 82nd Division at Paletwa in December, 81st Division took part in another forward move that saw its soldiers advance to Kyingri where 81 Recce deployed to hold the airstrip, which was vital to the division for casualty evacuation and re-supply. Meanwhile, the division moved into the hills to the east. XV Corps was now about to launch another attack on the Japanese and 81st Division's objective was Myohaung. Loftus Tottenham decided to use 81 Recce in a diversionary role, deploying the regiment to the Kanzauk area where it was to simu-

---

* A reference, by the writer of the citation for Loftus Tottenham's Bar to the DSO, to Confederate General Thomas 'Stonewall' Jackson's Shenandoah valley campaign during the American Civil War.

late a much larger force. It would also link up with 25th Indian Division. Buthidaung was taken by 81st Division 'in a rapid descent of the Kalapanzin Valley' and Donbaik fell to 8th Oxford and Buckinghamshire Light Infantry on 23 December. The corps was now about to undertake a major operation to take Akyab island using commandos. This was followed by an assault on Ramree Island. Both were unopposed; the Japanese had abandoned the islands as a direct result of the operations by 81st Division. With their supply lines along the coast severed the Japanese were forced to withdraw from the region and, on 25 January 1945, 81st and 82nd (West African) Divisions took Myohaung in a pincer movement. This marked the end of 81st Division's part in the campaign.

For his leadership, Frederick Loftus Tottenham was awarded a Bar to the DSO he had earned as a brigadier. The citation emphasized the importance of his role in XV Corps' operations.

> This role called for bold action and hard knocks and [Loftus Tottenham] drew two thirds of the garrison out of Akyab in the end.
> The Jap tried to concentrate against him and knock him out as he had done successfully in Mar 1944, but Gen. Loftus-Tottenham maintained his mobility and the Jap failed to pin him down.

One of Fourteenth Army's historians, Michael Hickey, notes that

> Under their new commander, Maj General Loftus-Tottenham, a carefully-chosen former Gurkha, the 81st had justified all the hopes placed in it, and had certainly expunged the unhappier memories of its setbacks in the 1944 campaign, when it had been called upon to perform tasks beyond its capacity at that time.

Hickey's comment about the 'unhappier memories' of the earlier campaign typify the negative comments about the Africans; they had done well in spite of the poor manner in which their operations were managed by Christison. Overall, little has been written about the West Africans and their successful campaign in the Arakan, especially in contrast to the operations of the Chindits. The comparison is valid since the West Africans achieved much more than the Chindits while carrying out similar operations deep in the jungle and depending on air support. That the Japanese paid tribute to the West Africans as the best Allied soldiers in jungle fighting is proof positive of what they achieved, and the leadership of Freddie Loftus Tottenham, who had faith in his soldiers, was a vital ingredient in the success of 81st (West African) Division.

Major-General Loftus Tottenham continued to command 81st (West African) Division until 1946 when he was appointed GOC, Iraq; he had begun to prepare his division for amphibious operations in Malaya when these were made redundant by the atomic bombs on Hiroshima and Nagasaki. After Iraq came an appointment as GOC, 7th Division in Pakistan following the partition of India in 1947. This was far from being a pleasant posting, carrying as it did responsibility for internal security in the new state while the division also had a counter-attack role as the key operational formation in the event of an Indian invasion. One British officer in Pakistan at that time described him as being 'solid and sensible' while 'his common sense gave everyone confidence, while his deliberate tactical approach well complemented Gracey's fiery temperament'.* This was Loftus-Tottenham's last post before retirement in 1949 although he had not finished with soldiering completely; he would later command the Home Guard in Northern Ireland during the four years, 1952–6, in which that body was revived in cadre form.

Loftus Tottenham was a reliable and determined commander, if not a brilliant one. His eye for ground and feel for battle stood both himself and his soldiers in good stead and he had no time for fools. When one officer tried to justify his action on the grounds that he hoped to surprise the enemy, Loftus Tottenham riposted: 'Surprise the enemy? Or merely amaze him?' His war was also marked by personal tragedy. Two of his sons died in action: Ralph Frederick, a lieutenant in 2nd Gurkhas, was killed at Monte Cassino in Italy in February 1944 and John, a lieutenant in 6th Gurkhas, was killed in Burma.

* * *

Walter David Alexander Lentaigne, better known as Joe, was one of the many Irishmen who served in the Indian Army. Commissioned at eighteen into 1st Battalion, 4th Gurkha Rifles in 1918 too late to see active service in the Great War he, nonetheless, saw much action in the mountains of India's North-West Frontier Province. Although the Gurkhas were part of the Indian Army, they were citizens of Nepal and served under the terms of a treaty between Britain and Nepal. All ten Gurkha regiments were rifle regiments, adopting the rifle-green of their British counterparts, and were limited to two battalions each in peacetime, with no more than 100 reservists per regiment. Gurkha soldiers demonstrated a fierce loyalty to their comrades and to their British officers and it was this, rather than allegiance to the Crown, that drove them in battle. Service in the ranks of the Gurkha regiments was hereditary, which increased the sense of loyalty to those regiments.*

---

* Douglas Gracey was the British Commander-in-Chief in Pakistan.
† The ten regiments were: 1st King George V's Own Gurkha Rifles (The Malaun Regiment); 2nd King Edward VII's Own Gurkha Rifles (The Sirmoor Rifles); 3rd Queen Alexandra's Own Gurkha Rifles; 4th Prince of Wales's Own Gurkha Rifles; 5th Royal Gurkha Rifles (Frontier Force); 6th Gurkha Rifles; 7th Gurkha Rifles; 8th Gurkha Rifles; 9th Gurkha Rifles; 10th Gurkha Rifles. During the war additional battalions were raised for each regiment and some new regiments were also raised. With Indian independence in 1947 most of the Gurkha regiments remained with the Indian Army but four regiments – 2nd, 6th, 7th and 10th – transferred to the British Army to become the Brigade of Gurkhas in 1948. Today the latter four form a single regiment, The Royal Gurkha Rifles.

In 1921 Lentaigne was quartermaster of his battalion in the Waziristan campaign, in which he earned a Mention in Despatches, the first of many in his long career. But he also showed an extremely active sense of humour and 'was conspicuous in alleviating the tedium of perimeter camp life by a series of leg-pulls which assumed epidemic proportions at Sarwekai in 1921'. The climax of this series of jokes came with Lentaigne's creation of an Elephant Transport Company.

> Rumour of the impending arrival of this pachydermic figment of a lively imagination became so widespread that it was eventually credited at Column H.Q. in Wana and the A.D.S.T. [Assistant Director, Supply and Transport] misguidedly referred to the C.O. of a Mule Transport Company in Sarwekai for advice on the feeding of elephants. The fun grew fast, but the High-Ups got furious when the gaff was blown by the caustic reply: 'Try buns', and relations with Column H.Q. were further strained by the receipt of an advertisement for 'Staff Howdahs', from Messrs. Hook Line and Sinker.

There followed a dressing down at brigade headquarters by Colonel Commandant Oswald Borrett who, having delivered the edict from General Leslie, murmured to Lentaigne, 'Bad luck, Joe'.

Lentaigne's battalion remained in Waziristan until the fighting at Makin in 1923. In the following year, the regiment was renamed 4th Prince of Wales's Own Gurkha Rifles and Lentaigne transferred to the 2nd Battalion as its Adjutant, remaining with that battalion until 1935 when he went to Britain to attend the Staff College. One comment made about his time as a student was that 'In spite of his almost completely regimental experience he did well'. From Camberley he returned to India to become Deputy Assistant Quartermaster General (DAQMG) at Army Headquarters until he was selected to become an instructor at the Staff College at Quetta.

Joe Lentaigne joined the staff at Quetta in October 1940 and was a successful and inspiring instructor until July 1941 when his wish to return to regimental duty was granted. He was appointed to command 1st Battalion, 4th Gurkhas, which was destined to be one of the first units to meet the Japanese invasion of Burma. He ensured that the battalion's training and readiness for war were at the highest levels and the regimental historian was later to comment:

> That our 1st Battalion fought through the campaign of 1942 with a success that was conspicuous showed not only that its basic training had been better than we had dared to think possible, but that its core was thoroughly sound, and above all that the Battalion was most ably and inspiringly led and commanded.

The retreat through Burma to India was one of the toughest campaigns fought by British armies in the Second World War and many battalions suffered heavily as they struggled to stem the flow of Japanese forces. A series of determined actions was fought to delay the Japanese advance and to allow the frontier defences of India to be strengthened against the expected onslaught. For his courage and leadership Lieutenant-Colonel Lentaigne was awarded the DSO.

He had also gained what was described as 'an almost legendary reputation for bravery'. Another officer of his regiment, Jack Masters, better known as the novelist John Masters, wrote of him:

> In the first Burma campaign, as a lieutenant-colonel in command of the 1st battalion of our regiment, he had done brilliantly, leading the battalion like a tiger, personally heading half a dozen bayonet charges, time and again saving the battalion and damaging the Japanese through that long, painful retreat, by his quick thinking and aggressive actions.

For its stand at Pegu on 6/7 March, the battalion was awarded the battle honour 'Pegu'.

Lentaigne was also rewarded with promotion to brigadier and command of a brigade on the Assam front where preparations were being made not only to rebuff the Japanese efforts to invade India but also to take the offensive against them by liberating Burma. In 1943 Lentaigne was appointed to command the newly raised 111 Indian Infantry Brigade. Jack Masters was appointed, at Lentaigne's request, as brigade major of this new formation, based at Ghatera in the Central Provinces and said to have 'a mysterious and top secret mission, something to do with long-range penetration'. At this time, Orde Wingate's 77 Brigade was operating behind Japanese lines in Burma on what became known as the first Chindit expedition, Wingate having chosen the 'Chinthe', the mythical beast that guards Burmese pagodas, as the badge of the long-range penetration soldiers. Needless to say, the soldiers were responsible for corrupting Chinthe to Chindit. General Wavell, the C-in-C, India, had been so impressed with 77 Brigade that he ordered the formation of a second brigade and appointed Lentaigne to command it. At first, Lentaigne believed that 111 Brigade would carry out a brigade-sized operation following Wingate's expedition. For 111 Brigade he chose 'a snarling leopard's head badge and told Masters: 'That's us, pack of hungry leopards'. However, Lentaigne was to be disappointed as Wingate persuaded Churchill to approve a divisional-strength expedition in 1944. Wingate was promoted to major-general to command the division, known as Special Force, and 111 Brigade became part of his command. Of the brigade commanders in Special Force, Lentaigne was the only one not appointed by Wingate who 'never really approved of him'. According to Shelford Bidwell,

> Lentaigne was a deeply orthodox product of that most professional of corps, the Gurkha Rifles, and the Staff College, who was forced into unorthodoxy against all his instinct and training.

Bidwell's assessment is at variance with that of Masters who saw Lentaigne as committed to the idea of long-range penetration but convinced that his brigade could do better than Wingate. He told Masters that he considered Wingate 'a genius in some ways' but considered that he had made mistakes 'and we've got to do better'. It was Lentaigne's belief that his brigade had to learn to think for themselves as well as learning from Wingate's mistakes and thus he set about the training of 111 Brigade in the Ghatera area.

When permission was given for Wingate's 1944 expedition, Operation THURSDAY, Lentaigne had to resign himself to the fact that he would be operating under Wingate's command. The two men did not see eye to eye, especially as Wingate did not have a high regard for the Indian Army. In January 1944, 111 Brigade entered the war zone in Assam and the final phase of its preparations for action. Wingate had arranged air transport for most of his brigades and 111 Brigade was to be flown in by glider to a jungle clearing codenamed Piccadilly. This was east of the railway and the brigade was to strike out for the area south of Indaw and prevent interference with Fergusson's 16 Brigade.

The Chindit brigades were flown in to their jungle landing areas in an operation that began on the night of 5 March.* Last minute changes were made to the plans for 111 Brigade, which was to be re-routed to the Chowringhee clearing, named for the main street of Calcutta. This was because Piccadilly was blocked by logs. Although this was thought to indicate that the Japanese knew a landing was to take place there, it turned out to be normal seasonal logging operations. Then a further change in plan was imposed on 111 Brigade: its two British battalions were to be flown into Broadway and not Chowringhee. 'Brigadier Lentaigne was pardonably angry when his plans were changed twice, and to make matters worse he had to shift his columns from one airfield to another.' However, by 8 March, before any significant enemy reaction had occurred, 1,200 men, 2,000 mules and all the equipment and ammunition needed for 111 Brigade's expedition had been flown into the jungle.

Lentaigne has come in for considerable criticism in studies of the Chindits. He has been accused of 'lack of leadership and [of a] ... supine attitude' by one historian, a criticism echoing that of Sir Robert Thompson. Certainly there is no evidence that 111 Brigade acted as 'snarling leopards' as Lentaigne had told Masters they would. Many veterans of the brigade had little confidence in either Lentaigne or Masters who succeeded him in command of 111 Brigade.† However, it was not long before Lentaigne parted company with 111 Brigade.

On 24 March Wingate was killed when the aircraft in which he was flying crashed. There was a number of contenders for the succession, including Brigadier 'Mad' Mike Calvert, who shared much of Wingate's philosophy and Major-General Symes, who had earlier commanded the division that had been converted into Special Force. But it was Lentaigne who was plucked from the jungle to succeed Orde Wingate as the commander of the Chindits. His obituary in *The Times* suggests that he was the natural choice as his views 'chimed with those of Wingate and ...

---

* Bernard Fergusson's 16 Brigade marched into the Japanese rear areas through the mountains between India and Burma.
† The brigade was split with Masters commanding the larger portion.

Lentaigne was one of Wingate's most trusted lieutenants'. However, Thompson believes that his appointment was a mistake while David Rooney notes that Wingate 'had had Lentaigne imposed upon him, and never established a good rapport with him'. Shelford Bidwell also notes that 'Far from being the officer most in Wingate's mind and the natural choice to translate his ideas into future action, he despised both Wingate and his theories'. Under his command the Chindit operation continued but did not achieve the success that Wingate had expected, although it is not certain that even with Wingate in control, that it would ever have done so. However, it did cause problems for the Japanese and disrupted their lines of communication; but a much smaller force could have obtained similar results at much less cost in men and effort. Lentaigne lacked Wingate's drive and sense of destiny and the Chindits came under control of the American General 'Vinegar Joe' Stilwell who misused them by maintaining them behind enemy lines when they ought to have been withdrawn. Lentaigne proved unable to stand up to Stilwell.

But it should also be remembered that Lentaigne was suffering from ill-health at this time and he was probably too old, forty-five, to command a brigade in the extreme conditions in which the Chindits were operating. His marriage had also broken down and he and his wife had recently separated. Had he reached his professional limit as a brigade commander?

> In open combat where he could see his enemy he had proved a paladin, but even in the few days he spent in the field he had found the physical and mental strain of Chindit fighting too much for him ... A general may be liked and this may be part of his equipment for leadership, but he must also have an element of steel in his make-up and abrasiveness as well ... Lentaigne's military judgement was excellent and it is probable that he could have commanded an orthodox Indian division with distinction. But the troubles he was to meet in Burma, above all from Stilwell, were to pain him deeply and wear him down until he was ineffective.

That his command of the Chindits was not a success was indicated by the fact that he did not receive a Bar to his DSO. Instead, in 1945, he was appointed CBE for his services. However, his career was far from over.

In 1946 Joe Lentaigne was nominated to attend the Imperial Defence College from which he returned to India to take up the post of Director of Military Operations at GHQ in New Delhi. He was awarded the CB in 1947 as India was on the verge of independence. With independence it seemed that Lentaigne's military career would come to an end but the new Indian government decided to offer him the appointment of Commandant of the new Indian Staff College. Quetta, the location of the original Indian Staff College, was in Pakistan and so India had to create a new college. Lord Louis Mountbatten suggested that it should be an inter-service college, catering for army, naval and air officers, and his suggestion was accepted by the government.

Lentaigne's was one of the names put forward as Commandant and, once again, the government acted on a recommendation from Mountbatten who considered that Lentaigne was the best choice for the appointment.

India's new Staff College was established in the south of the country, at Wellington, and it was there that Joe Lentaigne had to start from scratch to build up a college that soon gained a worldwide reputation for excellence. This was no easy assignment but it was one for which his many attributes made him eminently suitable for it required initiative, adaptability and an original mind. Before the three years of his tenure of command had ended, the Government pressed him to continue for a further two years and subsequently its reluctance to lose him led to more requests that he should remain at his post. Each time, heedless of his health and faithful to the interests of the Indian Army, he agreed to extend his service until finally, after seven years' command of the Staff College, he decided that the time had come when he must retire.

Many tributes were paid to Joe Lentaigne on his retirement. These included one from Lieutenant-General Kalwant Singh, an old friend, who wrote that, with Lentaigne's departure, 'the Indian Army has lost one of its most distinguished and versatile officers' while another friend, David Davidson, wrote: 'India owes him, and indeed most sincerely acknowledges, a very deep debt of gratitude'.

In 1950 Joe Lentaigne had been appointed Colonel of 4th Gurkha Rifles, which lost its royal title when India became a republic, and remained in that post until his departure from India in 1955 when he handed over to Brigadier Moti Sagar. He had also been promoted to the honorary rank of Lieutenant-General in the Indian Army and, as he boarded ship at Bombay, a guard of honour, mounted by order of the Indian government, gave him his final salute on Indian soil.

Joe Lentaigne died on 24 June 1955 and his passing was marked by many tributes to his service. Among those who paid him tribute was Lord Louis Mountbatten, the last Viceroy of India, Major-General P S Gyani, his successor as commandant of the Staff College, Brigadier Moti Sagar, and many fellow Gurkhas. Perhaps the finest tribute came from Major-General Gyani who wrote that

> He provided a fine example for [his staff and students] to follow, for the qualities which stood out above all others were his deep love of his fellow-men and his enduring affection and respect for the Gorkha soldier.*

And he finished by quoting from Wordsworth's 'Happy Warrior':

> This is the happy warrior; this is he
> Whom every man in arms should wish to be.

* * *

* This is an alternative, and older, spelling of Gurkha; the spelling Goorkha is also used.

Eric Dorman-Smith, Chink to his military compatriots, was born in County Cavan in July 1895, the son of a Catholic father and a Protestant mother. He was baptized in the Catholic tradition but his two younger brothers, Victor and Reginald, followed their mother's faith and were baptized in the Church of Ireland. One of Eric's most vivid memories of his childhood years was the tolling of the bells of Cavan's Anglican churches to mark Queen Victoria's death in January 1901. At that time, Eric's father, Edward, was serving in the Leinster Regiment, having volunteered to fight in the South African, or Boer, War.

Initial education was at home, isolating young Eric from most of the local children, although he did have one companion, a boy of his own age whose mother had died not long after his birth and who would later become archbishop of Dublin: John Charles McQuaid. Eric later went to preparatory school in England and then to Uppingham School, in Rutlandshire, where an exact contemporary was Brian Horrocks. Both entered the school on the same day and went to Sandhurst together in February 1913. Gentleman Cadet Dorman-Smith devoted himself to his studies and was a diligent cadet, passing out before Horrocks. With a Scottish cadet he had also taken a stand against a group of fellow cadets who had planned a ritual humiliation of another cadet who happened to be Jewish. Dorman-Smith had a lifelong aversion to mobs.

His first choice of regiment had been the Royal Fusiliers (City of London Regiment), raised in the reign of James II and later the 7th Regiment of Foot. However, he was assigned to the Northumberland Fusiliers, which did not please him at first although the regiment was senior to the Royal Fusiliers. The Northumberlands had been the 5th Regiment of Foot and had originated as an Irish regiment in the reign of Charles II.* They were more usually referred to as the Fifth Fusiliers. He soon came to be proud of his regiment, however, and discovered that many of its soldiers were Irishmen. On 11 August 1914 he sailed from Southampton with 1st Northumberland Fusiliers to join the BEF in France.

Dorman-Smith was wounded at Mons on his first day in action and evacuated to England. Rejoining his battalion in November he was shocked to discover that only four of the twenty-five officers with whom he had sailed from Southampton were still with the battalion which had been reduced to 200 men from its original strength of 1,000. He was wounded again, soon after his return to action, and a further period away from the battalion brought even more changes on his return. The battalion was engaged heavily in the St Eloi sector of Ypres in April 1915 where it suffered heavy losses. The action was a disaster but Dorman-Smith, who was wounded for a third time, earned the Military Cross for his courage and leadership; he managed under heavy fire to lead the survivors of his company back to safety. Casualties in the battalion numbered more than two thirds of its strength.

---

* These two regiments, together with the Royal Warwickshire Fusiliers and the Lancashire Fusiliers, were amalgamated in 1968 to form the Royal Regiment of Fusiliers, a four-battalion regiment that has now been reduced to two battalions. In 1935 the Northumberlands had been retitled the Royal Northumberland Fusiliers.

After a spell in London he rejoined his battalion as a company commander with the acting rank of captain. Once more he returned to the trenches but before long his commanding officer recognized that Dorman-Smith was suffering from nervous exhaustion. He was pulled out of the line and sent to London for treatment where he appears to have had a nervous breakdown but he returned to duty as an instructor at his regiment's depot in Newcastle before moving on to the Army School of Trench Warfare. There he remained until, at his own insistence, he was sent back to his battalion in France as a substantive captain in February 1916. He was the sole combatant officer still serving from those who had landed in France in 1914.

In April he was presented with his Military Cross by King George V at Buckingham Palace but, on return to his battalion, his commanding officer again referred him to London for a medical board where he was diagnosed as suffering from nervous disability due to shellshock. The prescribed cure was rest. Once again he asked to be allowed to train recruits and was able to return to France in July where he was stationed at brigade headquarters. Soon he was promoted to major as second-in-command of 10th Northumberlands for a three-week period.

His next move was to the Italian front where he became an instructor at 68 Infantry Brigade School. By now his experiences in the line had convinced him of the need for a much more professional attitude to soldiering than he had seen hitherto. He became absorbed in his role as an instructor; his biographer suggests that he 'had found his métier' although she goes on to comment that 'the men who were the centre of his attention would much rather have been left alone'. He returned to the line, on the Asiago front, with 12th Durham Light Infantry but when the war ended in Italy he was in a convalescent's post, as Commandant, British Troops Milan; this followed a spell in hospital with gastroenteritis.

He remained in Italy for some time, making the acquaintance of the American writer, Ernest Hemingway, who later used Chink as a model for characters. And it was Chink who gave Hemingway his soubriquet of 'Pop', an abbreviation of the name Popplethwaite with which he dubbed the young American. On his return to Britain and regimental duty he became adjutant of 1st Northumberlands and was determined to see the battalion trained to the highest standards. Significantly for the future, he applied for a machine-gun officers' course and earned a distinguished certificate. With the Machine Gun Corps being disbanded, the machine-gun platoons of infantry battalions were to be strengthened to company strength. In 1921 Chink's battalion was posted to Ireland as part of 5th Division, based at the Curragh; the Northumberlands were stationed in Carlow and covered County Kilkenny, which was under martial law. It was an unpleasant episode which no one was sorry to see end; when the Union flag was lowered at Carlow barracks, it was Chink as Adjutant who folded it under his arm.

He continued as adjutant in Germany but, in 1924, applied for an instructor's post at Sandhurst and took up his posting in the autumn. Chink met a number of fellow instructors who excited his imagination, including Richard O'Connor, 'Boy' Browning of the Grenadiers, later to command an airborne corps, and Alec

Gatehouse, an ex-fusilier who had transferred to the new Tank Corps. When the latter was discussing the question of suitable headgear for the Tank Corps, Chink showed him a Basque beret, a souvenir from a holiday with Hemingway in Pamplona. Thus the black beret of the Tank Corps, later Royal Tank Regiment, was born. One of the senior Sandhurst staff at the time was Bernard Montgomery who would later adopt the black beret as his trademark. Had Monty known of Chink's part in the choice of the tankmen's headgear would he ever have chosen the black beret?

Deciding that he would like to attend Staff College, Chink then chose to sit the competitive examination for entrance. Awarded 1,000 marks out of 1,000, an unprecedented score, he was one of the sixty new students admitted that year. Determined to become more professional in his calling, Chink had little time for those he considered amateurs and made several enemies at Camberley; these were to haunt him in the future. The man most offended by Chink was a Royal Signals' officer, Ronald Penney, who, in 1944, would be instrumental in ending the Irishman's career. He also disagreed with Montgomery, although both had the same avowed aim: to improve the Army's professionalism so that the mistakes of the Great War would not be repeated. Chink considered Monty's approach akin to using a sledge-hammer to crack a walnut. When he learned of this comment, the future victor of El Alamein was not impressed. The antagonism between them became obvious. Chink passed out in the top four from his course but 'had failed to understand the most important lesson of all. The part goodwill plays in a career.' Nonetheless his career appeared to be in the ascendant, especially when he was appointed to the staff of the Royal Engineers' equivalent of Staff College at Chatham. He was the first infantry officer to become instructor of tactics there.

In July 1931, as a brevet major, he was appointed Brigade Major to 6 Experimental Brigade at Blackdown in Hampshire. His brigade commander was another Great War veteran, Brigadier Archie Wavell, a man of great intellect and a soldier who never disregarded the unorthodox. Wavell was the type of commander who could bring out the best in Chink. The Wavell–Dorman-Smith team worked well, and the brigade constantly beat other brigades in exercises, generally through unorthodox tactics, mobility and rigorous training. Wavell made men go seventy-two hours without sleep to simulate better the chaos, exhaustion and confusion of war. At the same time Chink was experimenting with more flexible deployment of the Vickers machine gun, which took a team of six to operate; he devised a drill that allowed it to be used by a two-man crew from a lorry as an assault weapon.

Chink had also turned his attention to tanks and to cooperation between armour and infantry. He had written a textbook on tactics that led to the official handbook, *Infantry Section Leaders' Training*. He was also asked to update the *Elementary Tactics* textbook and to comment on Montgomery's *Infantry Training*. Although he felt that tanks had already replaced cavalry on the battlefield he continued to believe that they were not as flexible as mechanized infantry, which he advocated strongly. His thinking was given further impetus when he joined the directorate of Staff Duties in the War Office. Although he made further friends and admired the thinking of a number of his acquaintances, he succeeded in storing up more trouble for his own future by making more enemies. One was the Inspector of Artillery, Alan Brooke, who, Chink felt, did not want to leave the horse behind. Brooke's job had little influence – and he only held it for nine months – and Chink was probably unaware of his reputation as an authority on artillery. Hostility grew between the pair.

From his experience with Wavell and 6 Brigade, Chink believed that the Army should be updated by phasing out horse transport, mechanizing the artillery and providing them with long-range equipments, improving the weapons and equipment of the infantry as well as making them more mobile, replacing the cavalry with tanks and using the RAF to provide support. His ideal re-organization called for heavy tanks for frontal assault, mobile tanks for speedy infiltration and infantry in mechanized carriers to work with the armour under an umbrella of air support. But money was not available to implement such ideas. His thinking on armour, splitting it into two types, presaged the disastrous demarcation between infantry and cruiser tanks that would be employed by both Britain and France. However, his ideas for mechanized infantry, in armoured carriers, were a glimpse into the future. Although his ideal infantry battalion did not come into being, it is significant that, at the beginning of the Second World War, the British Army was the only one in the world with a fully mechanized field army.

From the War Office, Chink went to Camberley as a member of the staff where he fell foul of the commandant, Lord Gort of Limerick vc. His tour of duty was cut short by his appointment to command 1st Royal Northumberland Fusiliers. The battalion was stationed in Egypt and Chink's task was to convert them to a machine-gun battalion. He organized an intensive training programme that included driving as well as machine-gun drills; the battalion would have to be highly mobile in its new role. Desert navigation exercises were carried out and Chink applied his mind to tactics that might be used in desert warfare. His enthusiasm for the battalion's new role ensured that high standards were achieved. Although he may not have been the most popular commanding officer the battalion ever had, there is no doubt that he prepared it well for what lay ahead. Proof positive of his achievement was given by the performance of 1st Royal Northumberlands in Operation CRUSADER in November 1941 when the battalion was involved in the breakout from Tobruk and Captain James Jackman, another Irishman, earned a posthumous Victoria Cross. In addition to Jackman's VC, Z Company of the Northumberlands also earned two Military Crosses, three Distinguished Conduct Medals and six Military Medals.

Chink was then offered, and accepted, the post of Director of Military Training in India and left for Simla where he became responsible for the training of some 500,000 men, including the 55,000 British soldiers in India. Here he made the acquaintance of Claude Auchinleck and earned a reputation as a man whose thinking was 'concentrated and definitive' as well as being more original. He impressed Auchinleck who was later to recall the quality of Chink's thinking and bring him on to his staff. Chink suggested a radical re-organization of the Indian Army and a committee to draft a plan for that re-organization was established under Auchinleck's chairmanship. This pre-empted the Chatfield Committee, which was established by Westminster and on to which Auchinleck was co-opted.

In 1940 Chink decided to apply for the vacant post of Commandant of the new Staff College at Haifa, set up by his old friend Archie Wavell, now C-in-C, Middle East. He was successful and arrived in Haifa where he set about ensuring that the syllabus reflected the demands of modern warfare and not those of the Great War. While he was at Haifa he went on loan to Western Desert Force and joined Richard O'Connor's planning team for the raid that would become Operation COMPASS. The success of this operation has been outlined in Chapter 5, but if Chink believed that his role would secure him an active service role he was to be disappointed as he was sent back to Haifa. O'Connor's subsequent misfortune in being captured may also have deprived Dorman-Smith of an opportunity for further service in the desert although Wavell did bring him on to his staff for a time in 1941. When Auchinleck arrived in Egypt to succeed Wavell as C-in-C, Chink was hopeful that he would soon be leaving Haifa but this was not to be. Although he met the Auk, and suggested that the forces in the desert should become an army command with Sir Alan Cunningham as the army commander,* there was no appointment for him on the C-in-C's staff. Instead, Neil Ritchie, two years younger than Chink, was appointed as Auchinleck's deputy chief of the general staff (DCGS), the appointment he had anticipated.

Eventually, the Auk was able to give Dorman-Smith a job – reporting on Eighth Army, which was now commanded by Ritchie. Then Auchinleck asked him to work out a plan for creating a higher command school, which was eventually established at Sarafand. Finally, in May 1942, Chink was appointed as Auchinleck's DCGS. The appointment came at a critical time in the desert campaign: Rommel was preparing to attack Eighth Army in its positions on the Gazala line while Eighth Army was preparing for an offensive to ease the pressure on Malta. Rommel struck first and Chink was appalled at the way in which Ritchie responded. He urged the Auk to sack Eighth Army's commander and take direct control of the battle as he had done during Operation CRUSADER; but Auchinleck was reluctant to dismiss Ritchie and allowed him to remain in command.

News from the battlefront became increasingly depressing; a brigade of 50th (Northumbrian) Division was lost to the Germans but Ritchie still considered the situation favourable. However, his armour was being savaged and Rommel was trying to outflank his positions to the south. Tobruk, which had held out for much of 1941, was threatened with capture. At home, Churchill demanded that Tobruk be held at all costs, something Auchinleck was not prepared to do. As the battle raged on, Ritchie ordered an Eighth Army withdrawal, with the intention of meeting Panzer Armee Afrika at Mersa Matruh. Tobruk was isolated and, on Auchinleck's

---

* Auchinleck formed Eighth Army in September 1941 with Cunningham as its commander. At the same time he also formed Ninth and Tenth Armies, neither of which was to see any action; these were responsible for the defence of the general area from Palestine to Persia and north to Syria.

birthday, the South African commander of the garrison surrendered to Rommel. Adolf Hitler announced Rommel's promotion to field marshal, the youngest in the German army, and authorized Rommel to continue his pursuit of Eighth Army.

Auchinleck intervened as Ritchie prepared to make his stand at Mersa Matruh. Once again, this would have allowed Rommel to outflank Eighth Army to the south and would have led to the destruction of that army. Flying up to the front, Auchinleck relieved Ritchie and took over Eighth Army himself. Chink was now his de facto chief of staff as he prepared to meet the Panzer Armee not at Matruh but on the line from El Alamein on the coast to the Qattara Depression – a line that could not be outflanked to the south.

The Alamein battles of July 1942 need no rehearsing; they have been outlined in Chapter 2. Throughout those battles Chink was at Auchinleck's right hand and played a major part in his chief's direction of operations; he was also a constant fund of optimism. But it was after the battles had ended that Chink came into his own by producing his 'Appreciation of the Situation in the Western Desert' of 27 July. This document presented a remarkably accurate picture of forthcoming events. Chink's appreciation noted Eighth Army's object as being 'The defence of Egypt by the defeat of the enemy forces in the Western Desert' and included a summary of the current situation, factors affecting operations – comparative manpower and armour strengths, morale and ground, political pressures and the linkage to the Russian front – summaries of courses open to both armies, tactical techniques and future organization. He concluded that, since it lacked the strength to dislodge Rommel from his positions and required re-equipment and training before being fit for offensive operations, Eighth Army was committed temporarily to a defensive battle. With neither side likely to be reinforced strongly on land during August, he argued that no immediate offensive was likely; but an Axis offensive was possible towards the end of August. Provided there was no change in the land and air situation, Eighth Army would receive reinforcements of two armoured and two infantry divisions about mid-September, thus permitting a new Allied offensive in late-September.

This Appreciation gives the lie to Montgomery's assertion that Auchinleck was a defeatist and that there were no plans for an offensive by Eighth Army. Sir Francis de Guingand, whose abilities were identified initially by Auchinleck although his name is more closely connected with Montgomery, wrote:

> ... to put the record straight – for there has been much controversy over this point – a great deal of the Staff's time was taken up in carrying out the studies necessary for producing plans for a future offensive against Rommel.

However, neither the Auk nor Chink would see Eighth Army move over to the offensive in October for both were removed in mid-August. Chink returned to Britain as a brigadier, since his major-general's appointment had been temporary, and command of 160 Brigade, which was preparing for the invasion of France. However, at the end of March 1944 he was appointed to command a brigade in 1st Division, then serving in the Anzio beachhead and commanded by his old adversary from Camberley, Penney. The latter objected to Chink's appointment but was over-ruled. However, he greeted his new brigadier as he landed with the comment that he had not wanted him and still did not want him.

Nonetheless, Chink set about making changes in 3 Brigade. He had communication trenches dug, including one that a jeep could drive along, and demanded higher standards of turnout in his soldiers; litter was banned, as was smoking in certain circumstances while the wearing of white vests in the open was prohibited. But he also sought the support of his three battalion commanders and his brigade staff. He was helped by the fact that, a week after his arrival, Penney was evacuated on sick leave and his place taken, temporarily, by 'Ginger' Hawkesworth, with whom Chink had a good relationship.

The American commander of the Anzio forces, Major-General Lucian Truscott, had been ordered to plan a breakout from the beachhead in the aftermath of the Allied offensive against the Gustav line. This was Operation BUFFALO, scheduled to take place in late May; Truscott's corps was to link up with the advancing Allied armies and complete the destruction of the German forces. As a prelude to BUFFALO, 1st Division was to attack along the west flank of the Anzio positions; 3 Brigade was to lead the advance. The brigade's attack was successful and the village of Pantoni fell to Chink's soldiers, thus helping to divert German attention from Cisterna against which the Americans then moved. As the Anzio force continued its advance, 3 Brigade pushed forward towards Rome and, on 2 June, the brigade was ordered to take the Aquebona ridge next day.

In spite of having little time to plan – that afternoon he had moved his brigade to Velletri – Chink made a thorough plan for the attack that was to pay dividends in success and light casualties. He reconnoitred the ground himself and decided to attack at midday, which he considered to be the time the Germans least expected an assault and when a relief might be taking place. Three Brigade attacked at noon on 3 June after a short artillery bombardment and with the support of tanks. The ridge was in British hands by 4.30pm and another brigade passed through while 3 Brigade dug in. From German prisoners it was learned that a front-line relief had been taking place when the attack occurred. No more than eighteen British troops were either killed or wounded. It had been, as Chink himself noted, a model operation. He recommended two of his commanding officers for Bars to the DSOs they already held and the third for the DSO.

There followed a period of training for the brigade during which Penney returned to 1st Division. But he was relieved that summer as the division continued to await a call to action and, soon afterwards, Chink was amazed to be told that he was also to be relieved. Penney had submitted an adverse report on his handling of 3 Brigade that was, allegedly, based on information from the three battalion commanding officers. However, Chink's biographer, Lavinia Greacen, is confident that the COs did not complain about their brigade commander as Penney asserted. The end result was that Chink lost his active command and returned to the UK, a very embittered man, although he realised that he had made an enemy of Penney many years before.

Command of 3 Brigade was Eric Dorman-Smith's only active command. On his return to Britain he applied to be released from the Army and he entered civilian life in December 1944. There was one final blow: he was to retire as a colonel and not as a brigadier, since he had been an acting brigadier and not amassed sufficient service in that rank to become substantive.

For the rest of his days Chink nursed a grudge against the establishment that he believed had wronged him. After a brief fling at politics he returned to the family home in Monaghan and there established a relationship with local republicans that led to his permitting the IRA to use his grounds for training. He is also believed to have given the organization advice but there is no evidence to support claims that he helped plan the IRA's campaign between 1956 and 1962. As a sign that he had turned his back on his previous life he gaelicized his name to Dorman-O'Gowan. In spite of his feelings he never betrayed the secrets to which he was privy, especially Ultra, information from which had been available to him in his days with Auchinleck. He continued to admire the Auk and defended his position against Montgomery when the latter's *Memoirs* appeared in 1958, suggesting that Auchinleck had intended to retreat from the El Alamein positions. Chink had even threatened legal action against Churchill for comments in his history of the war. Both cases were settled by legal agreements. Those agreements allowed the myth-making indulged in by both Churchill and Montgomery to persist.

While there is no doubt that Eric Dorman-Smith was a man of great ability and intellect, who might have joined the ranks of the great commanders, his attitude to others helped bring about his downfall. Had Chink been more diplomatic he would have risen higher in the Army but his inability to conceal his feelings about those whose intellects did not impress him was a major flaw in an Army officer. Nonetheless, he played a significant role in the desert campaign and his brief command of 3 Brigade proved that he knew his business as a soldier and had the flair to be a great commander.

Conclusion

Examining the lives of the generals we have considered in this book indicates a number of points that they had in common. The two most obvious of all are the facts that they chose military careers and their Irish family connections. In many cases the choice of a military career was probably influenced by family tradition but, in others, there was either no real military tradition or a very weak tradition. For example, Auchinleck's father and uncle had been soldiers but the family had a greater tradition of entering holy orders than martial orders. Montgomery's family boasted some distinguished soldiers in its ancestry but this was too far back to have been a real influence on Bernard whose decision to join the Army class at St Paul's School took his family by surprise. It may have been an act of rebellion against his mother rather than a considered choice. The Alexander family had military tradition that seems to have influenced the future field marshal but the family with the strongest military tradition of all was that of Lord Alanbrooke; the Fermanagh Brookes had centuries of service and sacrifice behind them and that continued into the twentieth century. Families such as the Gores and Vandeleurs also had strong military traditions and the same may be said of the Loftus Tottenham family. David Dawnay and Pat Scott were the sons of eminent soldiers but John Dill's father was a bank manager, an unlikely background for an aspiring Army officer at the end of the nineteenth century. Gerald Templer was also the son of a soldier as was Richard O'Connor – their fathers served in the same regiment, Princess Victoria's (Royal Irish Fusiliers). Allan Adair's father was one of the few Adairs never to have been a soldier but there must have been many tales of military service recounted in the household and many visits from uncles in magnificent uniforms. So it was that in many, but not all, cases the existence of a family military tradition may have inspired the choice of a career in uniform.

All of our generals had Irish family connections but may not have regarded themselves as Irish in a sense that John Redmond might have agreed with and certainly not in a sense with which Patrick Pearse would have agreed. Sir Tim Pile had no difficulty in describing himself as the son of a nationalist lord mayor of Dublin, nor in recounting how some in political life thought that his father had sold the pass by welcoming Queen Victoria on a visit to the city. Some of our subjects would have considered themselves as being English but not in the strictly nationalistic meaning. Rather their definition of being English would have equated more closely with a sense of Britishness; that there was no contradiction in being Irish and British. Some, of course, chose to use identity as it suited them; Montgomery often referred to himself as being English and yet when he met soldiers from 9th (Londonderry) HAA Regiment at Tripoli in 1943 he had no hesitation in describing himself not just as an Irishman but specifically as 'a Derryman'. He had made the same claim to soldiers of D Troop, 6 Light AA Battery when they had provided air defence for Eighth Army's tactical headquarters from El Alamein to Benghazi, reminding these Coleraine men that his home was at Moville, across Lough Foyle from their own county.

Alexander was intensely proud of his Irish identity, which was encapsulated in the ethos of the Irish Guards. When he was ennobled after the war he chose to become not simply Earl of Tunis, recalling his greatest victory, but Earl of Tunis and Errigal, the latter recalling the Donegal mountain in whose shadow he had spent so many happy childhood days. Gerald Templer, likewise, had no doubt that he was an Irishman and abhorred being described as an 'Ulster field marshal' which, he felt, associated him with the narrow-mindedness of the province. Auchinleck made it clear to Dorman-Smith in the summer of 1942 that he regarded himself as Irish in his comment that the English had become too accustomed to being 'good losers' but that he was not English and was not a good loser. And, of course, Dorman-Smith through changing his name to Dorman-O'Gowan and claiming the leadership of his Gaelic clan made it more than clear how he saw himself. But, interestingly, he would have identified more closely with England earlier in his life. Those who served in Irish regiments – Alexander, Dill, Templer, Pat Scott, Nelson Russell and Joe Vandeleur – had no ambiguities about their identities; they were proud Irishmen and Irish soldiers. When Michael Caine played Joe Vandeleur in the film 'A Bridge too Far' he did so with a clipped accent that gave the impression that Vandeleur was English but he wore a green scarf as Vandeleur had done to assert his Irishness. Alan Brooke had a greater problem than most with the concept of being Irish. In the post-war era he objected to the creation of either a Regular or a TA Irish Brigade and thus the three Irish infantry regiments were brigaded in the North Irish Brigade and the TA had an Ulster Brigade. David Dawnay may have served most of his Army career in 10th Royal Hussars but his birthplace in County Waterford and his wartime command of the North Irish Horse were badges of being Irish. Both Joe Lentaigne and Freddie Loftus Tottenham were remembered by contemporaries as Irishmen, which suggests that they were emphatic about that fact. The historian of 81st (West African) Division, which the latter commanded, referred to how General Fred's 'Irish temper showed more often in volcanic explosions' when the division was '[s]tuck in the baking heat of the southern India plains, in temperatures up to 117°F'. However, those whose service was in regiments other than Irish – such as O'Connor and Gore – seem to have lost their Irish identity in the eyes of many of their contemporaries; some even believe that O'Connor was a Scot since he chose to serve in the Cameronians. Those who came from families with Irish connections appear to have been proud of the fact; both Adair and Horrocks in their memoirs demonstrate pride in their Irish ancestry while Richard McCreery was in no doubt that he came of Irish stock.

But to suggest that the combination of being Irish and choosing a military career were all that was required to become a great commander would be naïve. Indeed, most of those studied in this book would not have considered the description 'great commander' as applying to them. Perhaps only Montgomery would have been conceited enough to do so. Certainly neither Alexander nor Auchinleck would have sought such acclamation; they, together with Dill, Templer, Pile and others would have considered that they had simply done their duty as best they could. And therein, I believe, lies the one factor that is common to all the men whose stories we have looked at: a sense of duty.

That sense of duty was something that would have been inculcated in each of these men from infancy. Their family backgrounds and their education would have emphasized the importance of duty: to their fellow men, to their monarch and country, and to God. In many respects the military career had parallels with that of a priest since it involved a dedication to duty and a loyalty to the crown that matched that of the priest. The idea of putting oneself before others would have been alien to each of these men, with the notable exception of Montgomery who developed an egotism that was out of kilter with most of his contemporaries. In the wake of El Alamein, Montgomery acquired a taste for publicity that none of the other subjects of this book evinced. To them the idea of seeking publicity would have been anathema; it was believed that a gentleman's name should appear in the newspapers only on the occasions of his birth, marriage and death. By this definition Montgomery was no gentleman.

It was this same sense of duty that allowed men such as Dill and Brooke to soldier on in the service of the crown in spite of Churchill's many demands. They knew that they were serving something much greater than Churchill and they also knew that Churchill would have shared that view. In the aftermath of the war, few of these generals sought acclamation; Montgomery was the most notable exception and, of course, Dill was dead. Montgomery's *Memoirs* caused offence that prompted Dorman-Smith to initiate legal action, as he also did over Churchill's *History of the Second World War* but his sense of duty gave him pause and he did not follow through as he might have done in either case. Alexander must have been offended grievously by much of what was written about him in the post-war era, yet he never sought to defend himself. Auchinleck chose not to write his version of events, opting to allow history to be the true judge of what had happened and, as the decades pass, his choice is vindicated more and more. Neither O'Connor nor McCreery rushed into print and the latter has suffered from not having had a full biography to demonstrate his great ability, especially as an army commander. Although Pile did write an auto-biography this was much more a vindication of the work of Anti-Aircraft Command, which he believed had not received the credit it deserved for its achievements during the war.

Most of our subjects were born in the late Victorian era or in the early years of Edward VII. Duty was something that was instilled into Victorian and Edwardian gentlemen and our subjects were no exceptions. Irrespective of where in the United

Kingdom, or the Empire, they were born and raised, the common factor that is to be found in each of them is a belief in duty to their fellow men, the crown and God. The choice of a military career would only have emphasized that sense of duty as they learned of the traditions and honours of their regiments and developed a sense of duty to those regiments and to the Army.

Each of our subjects belonged to a group in Irish society that has all but vanished. For many years they would have been denied by Ireland as west Britons or Anglo-Irish and, therefore, less than Irish. They would have been seen as part of a system of repression rather than as Irishmen deserving of admiration. Only in Northern Ireland would they have been acknowledged and then with a certain political agenda. Not for nothing did Gerald Templer object to being called an 'Ulster Field Marshal'. However, several have been commemorated in Northern Ireland with streets in Belfast and Castlereagh named for them.

Ireland today is accepting the full scope of its history and acknowledging the contribution that Irishmen made to history on a much broader landscape. That includes the service of Irishmen and women to the British crown, a service that has endured for centuries and which produced many notable soldiers and leaders. The achievements of Ireland's generals in the Second World War are, arguably, the apotheosis of that service and deserve to be remembered in Ireland as well as elsewhere.

Notes

Much information in these chapters has been gleaned from a range of published and unpublished materials. In each case the principal sources are indicated under each chapter heading; specific notes refer to information from other sources.

PROLOGUE

PAGE 13: **was a bounder** This description was used by the widow of an Irish general when discussing Montgomery with the author in 1993
PAGE 15: **from Ireland** Murphy, *Ireland and the Crimean War*, p. 22. **by the end of the war** Ibid. **to soldiers or seamen** Doherty & Truesdale, *Irish Winners of the Victoria Cross*, passim. **St Patrick's Day** Army Orders 74 and 77 of 1900

CHAPTER 1: MONTGOMERY

Barnett, *The Desert Generals*
Hamilton, *Monty* (2 volumes)
Keegan, *Churchill's Generals*
Montgomery, Brian, *A Field Marshal in the Family*
Montgomery of Alamein, *Memoirs*

PAGE 18: **at Tripoli in Libya** A number of veterans of 9th (Londonderry) HAA Regiment recalled Montgomery making this comment
PAGE 21: **difficult and peculiar character** De Guingand, *Operation Victory*, p. 168
PAGE 22: **come to the same conclusion** Horrocks, *A Full Life*, p. 86. **owed much to Montgomery** NA, Kew, WO106/1741, Bartholomew Committee Report
PAGE 23: **was in good spirits** NA, Kew, WO201/2856, Alexander's Despatch
PAGE 24: **is a moot question** Greacen, *Chink*, p. 95
PAGE 27: **reasonably be made to do'** Fraser, *And We Shall Shock Them*, pp. 243–4. **those of the enemy** Fitzgerald, *Irish Guards*, p. 427
PAGE 31: **had his way** Jackson & Bramall, *The Chiefs*, pp. 273–5. **threatening legal action** Greacen, op. cit., p. 329

CHAPTER 2: AUCHINLECK

Barnett, *The Desert Generals*
Connell, *Auchinleck, A Critical Biography*
Greenwood, *Field Marshal Auchinleck*
Keegan, *Churchill's Generals*
Liddell-Hart, *The Rommel Papers*
Parkinson, *The Auk – Auchinleck, Victor at El Alamein*
Pitt, *The Crucible of War. Vol. II: Auchinleck's Command*
Warner, *Auchinleck, The Lonely Soldier*

PAGE 33: **he had done** Liddell Hart, *The Rommel Papers*, p. 260
PAGE 39: **a very short time** De Guingand, *Operation Victory*, p. 90
PAGE 40: **sure of stopping it** Hogg, *British and American Artillery of World War 2*, p. 73
PAGE 43: **active command** Tedder, *With Prejudice*, p. 304
PAGE 44: **panic and rout** Von Mellenthin, *Panzer Battles*, p. 127. **make one weep** Liddell Hart, op. cit., p. 257. **attack was resumed** Young, *Rommel the Desert Fox*, pp. 188–9
PAGE 46: **I intend to win** Greacen, op. cit., p. 209

CHAPTER 3: ALEXANDER

Alexander, *Memoirs, 1940–45*
Blaxland, *Alexander's Generals – The Italian Campaign, 1944–1945*
Clarke, *With Alex at War*
Keegan, *Churchill's Generals*
Kipling, *The Irish Guards in the Great War – The First Battalion*
Kipling, *The Irish Guards in the Great War – The Second Battalion*
Nicolson, *Alex*

PAGE 48: **above my standard** Slim, *Defeat into Victory*, pp. 55–6
PAGE 52: **Brooke, Commander Home Forces** Brooke, pp. 186–7. Although the criticisms made on these pages are general and relate to all the senior commanders, Brooke expresses his dislike of Alex in many occasions throughout his diaries.
PAGE 54: **therefore implemented it** Strawson, *McCreery*, p. 48; De Guingand, op. cit., p. 206
PAGE 60: **in Eighth Army** Doherty, *A Noble Crusade*, p. 225

CHAPTER 4: DILL

Danchev, *Very Special Relationship*
Danchev, *Establishing the Anglo-American Alliance*
Jackson and Bramall, *The Chiefs – The Story of the United Kingdom Chiefs of Staff*
Keegan, *Churchill's Generals*

PAGE 63: **entering Sandhurst** Information from Methodist College, Belfast
PAGE 65: **a first-class brain** Horrocks, op. cit., p. 70

CHAPTER 5: O'CONNOR

Barnett, *The Desert Generals*
Baynes, *The Forgotten Victor – General Sir Richard O'Connor*
Forty, *The First Victory – General O'Connor's Desert Triumph, Dec. 1940–Feb. 1941*
Keegan, *Churchill's Generals*
Latimer, *Operation Compass 1940. Wavell's whirlwind offensive*
Pitt, *The Crucible of War. Vol. I: Wavell's Command*
Destruction of an Army. The first campaign in Libya Sept. 1940–Feb. 1941

PAGE 81: **of an offensive** Churchill, *The Second World War*, vol. iv, p. 261
PAGE 86: **fell on deaf ears** D'Este, *Decision in Normandy*, p. 389
PAGE 87: **in the campaign** Roberts, *From the Desert to the Baltic*, p. 220. **with Eisenhower** Ibid.

CHAPTER 6: PILE

Dobinson, *AA Command. Britain's anti-aircraft defences of the Second World War*
Haining, *The Flying Bomb War*
Hogg, *British and American Artillery of World War II*
Ministry of Information, The, *Roof Over Britain. The official story of the A.A. Defences, 1939–42*
Pile, *Ack-Ack – Britain's Defence Against Air Attack during the Second World War*
Routledge, *Anti-Aircraft Artillery, 1914–55*

PAGE 91: Hamilton, *Monty: The making of a general, 1887–1942*, pp. 227–31. **AA Command of Great Britain** De Guingand, op. cit., p. 168
PAGE 98: **wall of steel** Squadron Leader Douglas Cooper DFC; Doherty, *Wall of Steel*, p. 112
PAGE 102: **the Victoria Cross** *London Gazette*, 3 Sept. 1940

CHAPTER 7: BROOKE

Bryant, *The Turn of the Tide*
Danchev and Todman, *War Diaries, 1939–1945. Field Marshal Lord Alanbrooke*
    Fraser, David, *Alanbrooke*
Fraser, *Alanbrooke*
Jackson and Bramall, *The Chiefs – The Story of the United Kingdom Chiefs of Staff*
Keegan, *Churchill's Generals*
Marrinan, *Churchill and the Irish Marshals*

PAGE 114: **in the last war** See also Montgomery's comments on Brooke's influence on his own career in *Memoirs*, pp. 534–5

CHAPTER 8: TEMPLER

Blaxland, *Alexander's Generals – The Italian Campaign, 1944–1945*
Cloake, *Templer – Tiger of Malaya*
Cunliffe, *The Royal Irish Fusiliers, 1793–1968*
Hinsley, *British Intelligence in the Second World War*
Jackson and Bramall, *The Chiefs – The Story of the United Kingdom Chiefs of Staff*

PAGE 118: **history and traditions** Colonel K.G.F. Chavasse
PAGE 119: **secured Montanaro** Military historian James Lucas served under Templer's command at this time and told the author of the great respect that the soldiers had for their commander.
PAGE 120: **nerves, they said** Trevelyan, *Rome, 1944*, p. 154
PAGE 127: **officers and men** Col. K.G.F. Chavasse

CHAPTER 9: RUSSELL

Blaxland, *Alexander's Generals – The Italian Campaign, 1944–1945*
Cunliffe, *The Royal Irish Fusiliers, 1793–1968*
Doherty, *Clear the Way! A history of the 38th (Irish) Infantry Brigade, 1941–1947*
Doherty, *A Noble Crusade. The History of Eighth Army, 1941–45*
Ford, *Battleaxe Division. From Africa to Italy with the 78th Division, 1942–45*
Gunner, *Front of the Line*
Horsfall, *The Wild Geese are Flighting*
Horsfall, *Fling Our Banner to the Wind*
Ray, *Algiers to Austria. The history of 78th Division 1942–46*

PAGE 139: **of greatest use** Col. A.D. Woods to the author

CHAPTER 10: SCOTT

Blaxland, *Alexander's Generals – The Italian Campaign, 1944–1945*
Cunliffe, *The Royal Irish Fusiliers, 1793–1968*
Doherty, *Clear the Way! A history of the 38th (Irish) Infantry Brigade, 1941–1947*
Doherty, *A Noble Crusade. The History of Eighth Army 1941–45*
Ford, *Battleaxe Division. From Africa to Italy with the 78th Division, 1942–45*
Gunner, *Front of the Line*
Horsfall, *The Wild Geese are Flighting*
Horsfall, *Fling Our Banner to the Wind*
Ray, *Algiers to Austria. The history of 78th Division, 1942–46*

PAGE 140: **Church of Ireland** This information was supplied to the author by Mrs Biddy Scott, widow of Pat Scott.

PAGE 141: **the German invasion** Alabaster Force, the occupation force in Iceland, was formed from 49th Division.

PAGE 142: **a sure hand** Nelson Russell, *Account of the Irish Brigade in North Africa*

PAGE 143: **just like Monty** Jim Hamilton, interview with author

PAGE 144: **language: German** Lt-Col. Brian Clark to author. **in the book** Lucas, letter to author

PAGE 150: **further than discussion** Mrs Biddy Scott

CHAPTER 11: MCCREERY, HORROCKS AND ADAIR

Carver, *El Alamein*
D'Este, *Decision in Normandy*
De Guingand, *Operation Victory*
Doherty, *A Noble Crusade. The History of Eighth Army, 1941–45*
Doherty, *The Sound of History. El Alamein, 1942*
Doherty, *Normandy 1944. The Road to Victory*
Graham and Bidwell, *Tug of War. The battle for Italy: 1943–45*
Horrocks, *A Full Life* (London 1960)
Lindsay, *A Guards' General. The Memoirs of Major-General Sir Allan Adair*
Strawson, *General Sir Richard McCreery. A portrait*

PAGE 154: **under Dick McCreery** Brooke, op. cit., p. 142

PAGE 155: **existing northern corridor** Alexander, *Memoirs*, p. 28. **change his mind** Hamilton, *Monty: The making of a General*, p. 828

PAGE 156: **with the left** Montgomery, *Memoirs*, p. 132. **Montgomery change his mind** Carver, *El Alamein*, pp. 141–2. **running his corps** Brooke, op. cit., p. 501

PAGE 157: **chances of survival** Doherty, *Noble Crusade*, p. 276. **higher commander** Strawson, *The Italian Campaign*, pp. 183–4. **professional army commanders** Graham & Bidwell, *Tug of War*, p. 390

PAGE 164: **spirited divisional commander** Keegan, *Churchill's Generals*, p. 233

PAGE 166: **west of Nijmegen** Ibid., p. 238

PAGE 167: **drama personified** Gorman, *The Times of My Life*, p. 53

PAGE 169: **Second World War** *London Gazette*, 30 July 1940

PAGE 174: **Irish Guards** Ibid., 7 June 1945 & 2 May 1945

CHAPTER 12: GORE, DAWNAY AND VANDELEUR

Blaxland, *The Plain Cook and the Great Showman*
D'Este, *Decision in Normandy*
Doherty, *The North Irish Horse. A Hundred Years of Service*
Fitzgerald, *History of the Irish Guards in the Second World War*
Gorman, *The Times of My Life*

Horrocks, *A Full Life*

Lindsay, *A Guards' General. The Memoirs of Major-General Sir Allan Adair*

Rolf, *The Bloody Road to Tunis. Destruction of the Axis forces in North Africa, November 1942–May 1943*

Vandeleur, *A Soldier's Story*

Wilson, *Unusual Undertakings. A Military Memoir*

PAGE 177: **get on with it** Sir James Wilson, notes to author

PAGE 178: **of our fears** Obituary, *The Rifle Brigade Chronicle*

PAGE 179: **improved his temper** Tony Pawson, notes to author. **return to us** Ibid.

PAGE 180: **able to do it** Sir James Wilson, notes to author. **kept in his tent** Obituary, *Daily Telegraph*, 16 June 1990

PAGE 181: **Green Jacket formation** Joslen, *Orders of Battle*, p. 297

PAGE 182: **loved and remembered** Tony Pawson

PAGE 183: **battalion/brigade level** Sir James Wilson

PAGE 185: **'Lily from Portaferry'** Russell, *Account of the Irish Brigade in North Africa.*

PAGE 186: **even by them** Horsfall, *The Wild Geese are Flighting*, p. 161

PAGE 187: *London Gazette*, 21 Sept. 1943

PAGE 188: **Churchill tanks'** Blaxland, *Alexander's Generals*, p. 176. **raised great hopes** ibid.

PAGE 189: **21st Tank Brigade** Ibid., p. 197

PAGE 193: **Micks' Shermans** Gorman, op. cit., p. 49

PAGE 194: **affended by it** Ibid., p. 54

PAGE 196: **15th Scottish Divisions** Horrocks, op. cit., pp. 253–4. **15,634 Allied** Ibid., pp. 254–5

CHAPTER 13: LOFTUS TOTTENHAM, LENTAIGNE AND DORMAN-SMITH

Allen, *Burma. The Longest War, 1941–45*

Bidwell, *The Chindit War. The campaign in Burma 1944*

Forty, *The First Victory – General O'Connor's Desert Triumph, Dec. 1940–Feb. 1941*

Greacen, *Chink – A Biography*

Hamilton, *War Bush: 81 (West African) Division in Burma, 1943–1945*

Hickey, *The Unforgettable Army. Slim's XIVth Army in Burma*

Lewin, Ronald, *Montgomery as Military Commander*

Masters, *The Road Past Mandalay*

Parkinson, *The Auk – Auchinleck, Victor at El Alamein*

Rooney, *Burma Victory. Imphal, Kohima and the Chindit issue, March 1944 to May 1945*

Rooney, *Wingate and the Chindits. Redressing the Balance*

Slim, *Defeat into Victory*
Warner, *Auchinleck, The Lonely Soldier*
Destruction of an Army. The first campaign in Libya, Sept. 1940–Feb. 1941

PAGE 199: **with other Gurkhas** Gaylor, *Sons of John Company*, p. 202. **end of the war** Seaman, *The Battle of Sangshak*, p. 16

PAGE 200: **failed in an attack** *Volunteers from Éire who have won distinctions serving with the British Forces. Supplement*, p. 5

PAGE 206: **and aggressive actions** Thompson, *Make for the Hills*, p. 54

PAGE 213: **six Military Medals** Doherty, *Irish Volunteers in the Second World War*, p. 16

Bibliography

Alexander, Field Marshal the Earl Alexander of Tunis (ed. John North), *Memoirs, 1940–45* (London 1962)

Allen, Louis, *Burma. The Longest War, 1941–45* (London 1984)

Ascoli, David, *A Companion to the British Army, 1660–1983* (London 1983)

Barnett, Correlli, *The Desert Generals* (London 1960)

Bates, Peter, *Dance of War. The Story of the Battle of Egypt* (London 1992)

Baynes, John, *The Forgotten Victor – General Sir Richard O'Connor* (London 1989)

Bidwell, Shelford, *The Chindit War. The campaign in Burma, 1944* (London 1979)

Blaxland, Gregory, *The Plain Cook and the Great Showman* (London 1977)

——, *Alexander's Generals. The Italian Campaign, 1944–1945* (London 1979)

Blumenson, Martin, *Mark Clark* (London 1985)

Brookes, Stephen (ed.), *Montgomery and the Eighth Army* (London 1991)

Bryant, Arthur, *The Turn of the Tide* (London 1957)

Carver, Michael, *El Alamein* (London 1962)

——, *The Apostles of Mobility* (London 1979)

——, *Dilemmas of the Desert War* (London 1986, Staplehurst 2002)

——, *Out of Step. The Memoirs of Field Marshal Lord Carver* (London 1989)

Chandler, David & Beckett, Ian (eds), *The Oxford Illustrated History of the British Army* (Oxford 1994)

Clarke, Rupert, *With Alex at War* (Barnsley 2000)

Cloake, John, *Templer – Tiger of Malaya* (London 1985)

Connell, John, *Auchinleck, A Critical Biography* (London 1959)

Cunliffe, Marcus, *The Royal Irish Fusiliers, 1793–1968* (Oxford 1970)

Danchev, Alex, *Very Special Relationship* (London 1986)

——, *Establishing the Anglo-American Alliance* (London 1990)

    & Todman, Daniel (eds), *War Diaries, 1939–1945. Field Marshal Lord Alanbrooke* (London 2001)

D'Este, Carlo, *Decision in Normandy* (London 1994)

——, *Eisenhower: Allied Supreme Commander* (London 2002)

De Guingand, Major-General Sir Francis, *Operation Victory* (London 1947)

Dobinson, Colin, *AA Command. Britain's anti-aircraft defences of the Second World War* (London 2001)

Doherty, Richard, *Wall of Steel. The history of the 9th (Londonderry) Heavy Anti-Aircraft Regiment Royal Artillery (SR)*, (Limavady 1988)

——, *Clear the Way! A history of the 38th (Irish) Infantry Brigade, 1941–1947* (Dublin 1993)

——, *A Noble Crusade. The History of Eighth Army, 1941–45* (Staplehurst 1999)

——, *The Sound of History. El Alamein 1942* (Staplehurst 2002)

——, *The North Irish Horse. A Hundred Years of Service* (Staplehurst 2003)

——, *Normandy 1944. The Road to Victory* (Staplehurst 2004)

Fitzgerald MC, Major D.J.L., *History of the Irish Guards in the Second World War* (Aldershot 1949)

Ford, Ken, *Battleaxe Division. From Africa to Italy with the 78th Division, 1942–45* (Stroud 1999)

Forty, George, *The First Victory – General O'Connor's Desert Triumph, Dec. 1940–Feb. 1941* (Tunbridge Wells 1990)

Fraser, David, *Alanbrooke* (London 1982)

——, *And We Shall Shock Them. The British Army in the Second World War* (London 1983)

——, *Knight's Cross – A Life of Field Marshal Erwin Rommel* (London 1993)

Frederick, J.B.M., *Lineage Book of British Land Forces, 1660–1978* (Wakefield 1984)

French, David, *Raising Churchill's Army. The British Army and the War against Germany, 1919–1945* (Oxford 2000)

Gaylor, John, *Sons of John Company. The Indian and Pakistan Armies, 1903–1991* (Tunbridge Wells 1992)

Girvin, Brian & Roberts, Geoffrey, *Ireland and the Second World War. Politics, Society and Remembrance* (Dublin 2000)

Gorman, Sir John, *The Times of My Life* (Barnsley 2002)

Graham, Dominick, and Bidwell, Shelford, *Tug of War. The battle for Italy: 1943–45* (London 1986)

Greacen, Lavinia, *Chink – A Biography* (London 1989)

Greenwood, Alexander, *Field Marshal Auchinleck* (Brockerscliffe 1991)

Gunner, Colin, *Front of the Line* (Antrim 1992)

Haining, Peter, *The Flying Bomb War* (London 2002)

Hamilton, John A.L., *War Bush: 81 (West African) Division in Burma, 1943–1945* (Wilby 2001)

Hamilton, Nigel, *Monty, The Making of a General, 1887–1942* (London 1981)

——, *Monty, Master of the Battlefield, 1942–1944* (London 1983)

——, *Monty, The Field Marshal, 1944–1976* (London 1986)

——, *The Full Monty. Montgomery of Alamein, 1887–1942* (London 2001)

Hickey, Colonel Michael, *The Unforgettable Army. Slim's XIVth Army in Burma* (Tunbridge Wells 1992)

Hinsley, F.H., *British Intelligence in the Second World War* (London 1993)

Hogg, Ian V., *British and American Artillery of World War II* (London 1978)

——, and Weeks, John, *The Illustrated Encyclopedia of Military Vehicles* (London 1980)

Horrocks, Brian, *A Full Life* (London 1960)

Horsfall, John *The Wild Geese are Flighting* (Kineton 1976)

——, *Fling Our Banner to the Wind* (Kineton 1978)

Humble, Richard, *Crusader – Eighth Army's Forgotten Victory, November 1941–January 1942* (London 1987)

Jackson, Bill and Bramall, Dwin, *The Chiefs – The Story of the United Kingdom Chiefs of Staff* (London 1992)

Joslen, H.F., *Orders of Battle, Second World War, 1939–1945* (London 1960 & 1990)

Keegan, John (ed.), *Churchill's Generals* (London 1991)

Kipling, Rudyard, *The Irish Guards in the Great War – The First Battalion* (Staplehurst 1997)

——, *The Irish Guards in the Great War – The Second Battalion* (Staplehurst 1997)

Kippenberger, Howard, *Infantry Brigadier* (London 1949)

Latimer, Jon, *Operation Compass 1940. Wavell's whirlwind offensive* (Oxford 2000)

Lewin, Ronald, *Montgomery as Military Commander* (London 1971)

——, *The Chief. Field Marshal Lord Wavell, Commander-in-Chief and Viceroy, 1939–1947* (London 1980)

Liddell-Hart, B.H. (ed.), *The Rommel Papers* (London 1953)

Lindsay, Oliver (ed.), *A Guards' General. The Memoirs of Major-General Sir Allan Adair* (London 1986)

Lucas, James, *Panzer Army Africa* (London 1977)

Makepeace-Warne, Antony, *Brassey's Companion to the British Army* (London 1995)

Marrinan, Patrick, *Churchill and the Irish Marshals* (Belfast 1986)

Masters, John, *The Road Past Mandalay* (London 1961)

von Mellenthin, Major-General F.W., *Panzer Battles* (London 1955)

Messenger, Charles, *For Love of Regiment. A history of British infantry, Volume One 1660–1914* (London 1994)

——, *For Love of Regiment. A history of British infantry, Volume Two 1915–1994* (London 1996)

Ministry of Information, The, *Roof Over Britain. The official story of the A. A. Defences, 1939–42* (London 1943)

Montgomery, Brian, *A Field Marshal in the Family* (London 1973)

Montgomery, Field Marshal the Viscount, *Memoirs* (London 1958)

Murphy, David, *Ireland and the Crimean War* (Dublin 2002)

Myatt, Frederick, *The British Infantry, 1660–1945: the evolution of a fighting force* (Poole 1983)

Nicolson, Nigel, *Alex* (London 1972)

Parkinson, Roger, *The Auk – Auchinleck, Victor at El Alamein* (London 1977)

Pile, Sir Frederick, *Ack-Ack – Britain's Defence Against Air Attack during the Second World War* (London 1949)

Pitt, Barrie, *The Crucible of War. Vol. I: Wavell's Command* (London 2001)

——, *The Crucible of War. Vol. II: Auchinleck's Command* (London 2001)

——, *The Crucible of War. Vol. III: Montgomery and Alamein* (London 2001)

Powell, Geoffrey, *The Devil's Birthday. The Bridges to Arnhem 1944* (London 1982)

Ray, Cyril, *Algiers to Austria. The history of 78th Division, 1942–46* (London 1952)

Reckitt, B.N., *Diary of Anti-Aircraft Defence, 1938–1944* (Ilfracombe 1990)

Roberts, G.P.B., *From the Desert to the Baltic* (London 1987)

Rolf, David, *The Bloody Road to Tunis. Destruction of the Axis forces in North Africa, November 1942–May 1943* (London 2001)

Rooney, David, *Burma Victory. Imphal, Kohima and the Chindit issue, March 1944 to May 1945* (London 1992)

——, *Wingate and the Chindits. Redressing the Balance* (London 1994)

Routledge, Brigadier N.W., *Anti-Aircraft Artillery, 1914–55* (London 1994)

Seaman, Harry, *The Battle at Sangshak* (London 1989)

Schmidt, Heinz Werner, *With Rommel in the Desert* (London 1951)

Slim, Field Marshal the Viscount, *Defeat into Victory* (London 1956)

Strawson, John, *General Sir Richard McCreery. A portrait* (privately published 1973)
——, *The Italian Campaign* (London 1987)
Tedder, Lord, *With Prejudice*, (London 1966)
Trevelyan, Raleigh, *Rome '44. The battle for the Eternal City* (London 1981)
Truesdale, David, *Brotherhood of the Cauldron. Irishmen in the 1st Airborne Division from North Africa to Arnhem* (Newtownards 2003)
Vandeleur, J.O.E., *A Soldier's Story* (Aldershot 1967)
Warner, Phillip, *Auchinleck. The Lonely Soldier* (London 1981)
Wilson, Lieutenant-General Sir James, *Unusual Undertakings. A Military Memoir* (Barnsley 2002)
Young, Desmond, *Rommel. The Desert Fox* (London 1950)
Destruction of an Army. The first campaign in Libya, Sept. 1940–Feb. 1941 (London 1941)

UNPUBLISHED

Various files in the National Archives, Kew (formerly the Public Record Office) were also consulted. These included formation war diaries and other documents, among them reports and despatches written by some of the individuals discussed in the book. Also consulted were documents from the CAB44 series, the official history of the Second World War, and others concerned with the higher command, both military and political, of the war.

For the service of the Irish Brigade, and its two commanders on active service, I had access to accounts of that service written by both men for the Colonel of The Royal Irish Fusiliers. Edited versions of these have been published in the journals of the regiments represented in the Brigade: *The Sprig of Shillelagh* (Royal Inniskilling Fusiliers) *Quis Separabit* (Royal Ulster Rifles/London Irish Rifles) and *The Faugh A Ballagh Gazette* (Royal Irish Fusiliers).

NEWSPAPERS

The Times
The Belfast Telegraph
The Irish Times
The Manchester Guardian

The Daily Telegraph
The Irish Independent
The Anglo-Celt

REGIMENTAL JOURNALS/NEWSLETTERS

The Royal Hussars (PWO) Journal
The Journal of the Royal Artillery
The Gunner, The Magazine of the Royal Artillery
HAC Journal
St George's Gazette, Journal of the Royal Northumberland Fusiliers
4th Gurkha Regimental Association Newsletter
The Sprig of Shillelagh, Journal of the Royal Inniskilling Fusiliers
Faugh a Ballagh Gazette, Journal of the Royal Irish Fusiliers
The Blackthorn, Journal of the Royal Irish Rangers

Acknowledgements

This book is my second study of Irish generals in the Second World War, the first, in 1993, having been based on a BBC Radio Ulster series and covering ten generals, nine of whom had featured in the radio series. However, there were many other generals in Britain's armies during that conflict who had strong family connections with Ireland and I felt that, after the passage of a further decade, there was a need for an expanded and revised version of the study. I am most grateful to Four Courts Press of Dublin for agreeing to publish this new study and I would like to thank Michael Adams and his team for their support, encouragement and understanding.

My thanks are also due to all those who helped with the additional research required to include material on another nine generals: Sir Michael and Lady McCorkell; Major-General John Strawson; Colonel James T. Eaton; Mr Bob McCreery; Mr Alexander Meynell; Mrs Amanda Moreno, Curator, The Royal Irish Fusiliers Museum, Armagh; Major Jack Dunlop, Curator, The Inniskillings Museum, Enniskillen; Major (Retd) G.L. Davis, Curator, and Mr Gavin Edgerley-Harris, Assistant Curator and Archivist, The Gurkha Museum, Winchester; Colonel I.H. McCausland, The Royal Green Jackets Museum, Winchester; Captain Dave Horn, Curator, The Guards Museum, London; Major P.J.C. Beresford, The Royal Hussars Museum, Winchester; Colonel Oliver Lindsay, Editor, The Guards Magazine; Lieutenant-Colonel R.J.S. Bullock-Webster OBE and WO II (RQMS) P.A. Geraghty, Regimental Headquarters, The Irish Guards; the staff of the Reading Room at the National Army Museum, Chelsea, London; the staff of the Reading Room at the National Archives, Kew, Surrey; the staff of the Departments of Books and Documents and of the Photographic Archive at the Imperial War Museum, Lambeth, London; the Linenhall Library, Belfast for their invaluable assistance in tracking down many out-of-print books; and the Central Library, Foyle Street, Londonderry.

Lieutenant-General Sir James Wilson KBE MC DL and Mr Tony Pawson OBE provided much interesting information on Brigadier Adrian Gore for which I am indebted to them. Both served with Adrian Gore and their contributions highlight the importance of being able to draw on the personal experiences of those who served with the men who are the subjects of this book. Many of those to whom I have spoken over the years about some of these generals are now dead but I remain in their debt and I must make special mention of Colonel Kendal Chavasse DSO and Bar, to whom this book is dedicated, Lieutenant-Colonel Brian Clark MC GM, Lieutenant-Colonel Desmond Woods MC and Bar, Mrs Biddy Scott, Mr Jim Hamilton MM and Mr George Doherty.

I would like to thank all those who provided photographs for the book; their names are included in the captions to the illustrations as are those of copyright holders where these may differ. Likewise, my thanks are due to those whose work I have studied in the preparation of this book: the notes and bibliography will give the reader some idea of my indebtedness.

Every effort has been made to ensure that there are no breaches of copyright in this book but it has not proved possible to trace every copyright holder. However, the author and publishers would be pleased to make arrangements to rectify this at the earliest opportunity.

I owe a special word of thanks to Major-General The O'Morchoe, who has provided the foreword for this book. As he notes in that foreword, General David was the last commanding officer of the Royal Irish Fusiliers and knew many of the personalities discussed in the book. He is also a Trustee of the Royal Irish Fusiliers' Museum, a director of the Military Heritage of Ireland Trust and President of the Irish Regiments Historical Society. No one could be better suited to write a foreword to a book on many of his fellow Irish generals.

Finally, I must record my gratitude to my wife, Carol, my children, Joanne, James and Catríona, and my grandson, Ciarán, for their patience and support, without which this book might never have been completed.

May 2004

Index